AF905057

Competition Law in the Slovak Republic

Competition Law in the Slovak Republic

Second Edition

Andrea Oršulová
David Raus

This book was originally published as a monograph in the International Encyclopaedia of Laws/Competition Law.

Founding Editor: Roger Blanpain
General Editor: Frank Hendrickx
Volume Editors: Francesco Denozza & Alberto Toffoletto

Wolters Kluwer

Published by:
Kluwer Law International B.V.
PO Box 316
2400 AH Alphen aan den Rijn
The Netherlands
Website: www.wolterskluwerlr.com

Sold and distributed in North, Central and South America by:
Wolters Kluwer Legal & Regulatory U.S.
7201 McKinney Circle
Frederick, MD 21704
United States of America
Email: customer.service@wolterskluwer.com

Sold and distributed in all other countries by:
Quadrant
Rockwood House
Haywards Heath
West Sussex
RH16 3DH
United Kingdom
Email: international-customerservice@wolterskluwer.com

DISCLAIMER: The material in this volume is in the nature of general comment only. It is not offered as advice on any particular matter and should not be taken as such. The editor and the contributing authors expressly disclaim all liability to any person with regard to anything done or omitted to be done, and with respect to the consequences of anything done or omitted to be done wholly or partly in reliance upon the whole or any part of the contents of this volume. No reader should act or refrain from acting on the basis of any matter contained in this volume without first obtaining professional advice regarding the particular facts and circumstances at issue. Any and all opinions expressed herein are those of the particular author and are not necessarily those of the editor or publisher of this volume.

Printed on acid-free paper

ISBN 978-90-411-9214-1

e-Book: ISBN 978-90-411-9243-1
web-PDF: ISBN 978-90-411-9277-6

This title is available on www.kluwerlawonline.com

© 2017, Kluwer Law International BV, The Netherlands

All rights reserved. No part of this publication may be reproduced, stored in a retrieval system, or transmitted in any form or by any means, electronic, mechanical, photocopying, recording, or otherwise, without the prior written permission of the publisher.

Permission to use this content must be obtained from the copyright owner. Please apply to: Permissions Department, Wolters Kluwer Legal & Regulatory U.S., 76 Ninth Avenue, 7th Floor, New York, NY 10011-5201, USA. Website: www.wolterskluwerlr.com

Printed and Bound by CPI Group (UK) Ltd, Croydon, CR0 4YY.

The Authors

JUDr. Andrea Oršulová, Ph.D. graduated in law from the Faculty of Law of the Comenius University in Bratislava, where she was awarded the 'Mgr.' title (Master of Laws) in 1999. In 2001, she was awarded the 'JUDr.' title. In 2015, she was awarded the 'Ph.D.'. Andrea Oršulová is a member of the Slovak Bar Association and an advocate in Bratislava. Previously, she has worked, for several years, with the Antimonopoly Office of the Slovak Republic, where she has been, *inter alia*, the Director of the Department for Second-Instance Proceedings. During her operation in the Slovak Competition Office, she has actively participated in the preparation of legislation in the area of economic competition protection law. Later, she has worked, for several years, as a specialized legal advisor in the areas of telecommunications, economic competition, and legal relations with sector regulators in the private sector. As an advocate, she still operates in the area of public law, while focusing on economic competition and law of regulated industries. She is co-author of a professional publication on cartel agreements and author, co-author of the commentary on the Czech competition act and author of number of articles in the area of economic competition.

The Authors

JUDr. David Raus, Ph.D. graduated in law from the Faculty of Law of the Masaryk University in Brno, where he gained the titles, 'Mgr.' (1997), 'JUDr.' (1999), and 'Ph.D.' (2002). Formerly, he has worked in a law office specializing in commercial law, thereafter in the Czech Economic Competition Protection Office, where he has been the Director of the Legal Department and Chairman of the remonstrance committee – advisory authority of the Chairman of the Economic Competition Protection Office; subsequently, he has been an assistant judge of the Supreme Administrative Court of the Czech Republic; currently, he is a judge of the Regional Court in Brno and specializes in disputes in the area of economic competition protection and assignment of public orders. He has for a long time participated in the preparation of legislation in the said areas of law; he is an external teacher in several universities (*inter alia* Masaryk University in Brno), co-author of several commentaries on Acts from the areas of economic competition protection and assignment of public orders, co-author of several professional publications and author of tens of articles in the professional press.

Table of Contents

The Authors 3

List of Abbreviations 11

General Introduction 13

§1. General Background of the Country 13

§2. Economic System 15

§3. Legal System 15

§4. Historical Background of Antitrust Law 18

Part I. The Structure of Antitrust Law and Its Enforcement 23

Chapter 1. Sources of Antitrust Law 23

§1. National Sources 23

§2. International Sources 24

§3. Secondary Sources 26

I. Regulations 26
II. Guidelines 26

§4. Sources' Relation and Hierarchy 28

§5. Role and Authority of Precedents 30

Chapter 2. Scope of Application 32

§1. Territorial Reach 32

§2. Special Sectors 32

§3. State-Owned Enterprises and Public Utilities 33

§4. Sensible Effect and De Minimis 34

Chapter 3. Overview of Substantive Provisions 37

§1. Restrictive Agreements 37

§2. Dominant Undertakings 40

§3. Concentrations 41

§4. Other Prohibitions 44

§5. Test of Illegality 45

I. Per se Prohibitions and Naked Restraints 45
II. Balancing Test 46
III. Merger Test 47

Chapter 4. Overview of Main Notions 49

§1. Undertaking 49

§2. Relevant Market 52

§3. Market Power/Dominant Position 53

§4. Agreements and Concerted Practices 56

§5. Restriction of Competition 58

§6. Monopolization and Abuse of Dominance 58

§7. Concentrations 60

§8. Joint Ventures 60

Chapter 5. Consequences of Violations and Enforcement Institutions 62

§1. Administrative Enforcement 62

I. The Antitrust Authorities 62
A. Formation, Composition 63
B. Investigating Powers 65
C. Adjudicating Powers (Ascertaining and Sanctioning) 67

D. Other Institutional Tasks (Consultancy to Parliament/ Government) 70
II. Government Direct Enforcement Activities 70
III. Other Administrative Agencies Applying Antitrust Rules 71
IV. Administrative Fines 76
V. Administrative Injunctions and Other Restrictive Orders 84
VI. Interim Measures 84

§2. Civil Enforcement 84

I. Competent Civil Courts 87
II. Sanctions 87
A. Nullity 87
B. Damages 87
C. Interim Measures 87

§3. Criminal Enforcement 88

I. Criminal Sanctions for Antitrust Violations 88
II. Other Application of Criminal Law to Relevant Conducts 89
III. Role of Prosecutors 90
IV. Competent Criminal Courts 91

Part II. The Application of the Prohibitions 93

Chapter 1. Restrictive Agreements 93

§1. Horizontal Agreements 93

I. Cartels 94
A. Price Fixing 94
B. Market/Client Allocation 97
C. Production/Innovation Limitation 100
D. Group Boycott 101
E. Collusion on Other Objects 101
II. Information Exchange Practices 105
III. Cooperation Agreements 107
A. Research and Development 108
B. Specialization 109
C. Standardization 110
D. Joint Production 110
E. Joint Purchasing 110
F. Joint Selling 111

§2. Vertical Agreements 111

I. Distribution 112
A. Exclusive Distributorship 114
B. Exclusive Dealing 114
C. Selective Distribution 115
D. Franchising 116
II. Technology Licensing 116
A. Patent Licensing 117
B. Trademark Licensing 117
C. Know-How Licensing 117

Chapter 2. Dominant Undertakings' Prohibited Practices 118

§1. Exploitative Practices 119

I. Excessive/Unfair Pricing 119
II. Discrimination 122

§2. Exclusionary Practices 126

I. Predation 126
II. Tying 127
III. Rebates 129
IV. Refusal to Deal 130
V. Price Squeeze 133

Chapter 3. Concentrations 136

§1. Horizontal Mergers 138

§2. Vertical Mergers 142

§3. Market/Product Extension Mergers 144

§4. Pure Conglomerate Mergers 145

§5. Joint Ventures 145

Part III. Administrative Procedure 149

Chapter 1. Administrative Investigation Before the Antitrust Authority 149

§1. Initiative 150

I. General Sector Inquiries 150
II. Ex officio Investigations 151

III. Complaints 152

§2. Powers 154

I. Request for Information 155
II. Investigating and Search Powers 157
III. Cooperation with Other State Institutions 164

§3. Right of Defence 165

I. Content and Notification of Opening Decisions 165
II. The Proceedings: Hearings, Access to Files, Briefs 165
III. Statement of Objections 168
IV. Final Hearing and Decision 170
A. The Decision on the Merits 170
B. Procedural Decisions by Which the Administrative Proceeding is Stopped 171
C. Procedural Decisions by Which the Administrative Proceeding Is Suspended 172
D. Interim Measures 173

Chapter 2. Voluntary Notifications and Clearance Decision 177

Chapter 3. Merger Control 179

§1. Preliminary Filing Obligations 179

I. Criteria and Thresholds 179
II. Turnover Calculation 181
III. Market-Share Calculation 182
IV. Other Relevant Notions 182

§2. Structure of Proceedings 182

I. Preliminary Assessment and Full Investigation 182
II. Time Framework 186
III. Right of Defence 187

§3. Clearance and Conditional Clearance 187

I. Conditions and Undertakings 188
A. Content 188
B. Timing 191

§4. Relations with Other Merger Control Authorities 192

I. Other Authorities Within the Local Jurisdiction 192
II. International Coordination 192

Chapter 4. Challenging of the Administrative Decisions 194

§1. Competent Courts 194

§2. Time Limits and Judicial Review 195

I. Judicial Review of Valid Decisions by Administrative Judiciary 195
II. The Constitutional Court's Review 198

§3. Scope of Judicial Review 199

Selected Bibliography 201

Index 203

List of Abbreviations

AMO	Antimonopoly Office of the Slovak Republic
APC	Administrative Procedure Code
AVC	Average Variable Costs
BTS	Bulk Transshipment Slovakia
CA	Competition Act
CC	Commercial Code
CFR	Collections of Findings and Rulings of the Constitutional Court of the Slovak Republic
CJEU	European Union Court of Justice
Coll.	Collection of Laws of the Slovak Republic
CPAC	Code on Judicial Proceedings in Administrative Cases
CPC	Criminal Procedure Code
CrC	Criminal Code
CSA	Company Czech Airlines
CvC	Civil Code
CvPC	Civil Contentious Procedure Code
EC	European Commision
ECA	Electronic Communications Act
ECJ	European Court of Justice
HHI	Herfindahl-Hirschmann's index
HN	Hosporárske noviny
HORECA	Hotel/Restaurant/Café
IPR	intellectual property rights
LRIC	Long Run Incremental Costs
NATO	North Atlantic Treaty Organization
NIO SR	Network Industries Office of the Slovak Republic
NIRA	Network Industries Regulation Act
OECD	Organisation for Economic Co-operation and Development
OJ	Official Journal

R&D	Research and Development
RPM	Resale Price Maintenance
SAS	Slovak Air Services
SBA	Slovak Bar Association
SIEC	Significant Impediment of Effective Competition
SME	Small and Medium Enterprises
TA	Telecommunication Act
TFEU	Treaty on the Functioning of the European Union
TO SR	Regulatory Authority for Electronic Communications and Postal Services of the Slovak Republic

General Introduction

§1. General Background of the Country

1. The official name of the country is the Slovak Republic (in Slovak: '*Slovenská republika*'), in short: Slovakia (in Slovak: '*Slovensko*'). Slovak Republic after World War I, formed a part of the first Czechoslovak Republic (1918–1938), which was a parliamentary democracy. The territory of Czechoslovakia included Czech lands (Bohemia and Moravia), a part of Silesia, Slovak Republic, and Carpatho-Ukraine. Disintegration of the first Czechoslovakia began after September 1938 (conclusion of the so-called Munich Agreement), when Czechoslovakia was forced to cede Sudetenland to Germany. Subsequently, in November 1938 (after the First Vienna Award), Czechoslovakia was forced to cede Southern Slovak Republic to Hungary. The disintegration was completed after declaration of the independent Slovak Republic on 14 March 1939. The independence was limited by the control of Nazi Germany. Jozef Tiso became the first Slovak president. Consequently, the rest of Czechoslovakia – Bohemia, Moravia, and Silesia became the Protectorate of Bohemia and Moravia. Czechoslovakia was restored after World War II. After the elections held in 1946 and the victory of the Czechoslovak Communist Party, it became a 'satellite state' of the Soviet Union and came under strict communist control. This control was interrupted only for a limited period in 1968 after Alexander Dubček became the First Secretary of the Central Committee of the Communist Party of Czechoslovakia. On 21 August 1968, Soviet, Hungarian, Bulgarian, East German, and Polish troops began occupation of the state. The following political era is known as 'normalization'. Within the period from 1945 to 1990, the common state had the following official names: the Czechoslovak Republic (1945–1960) and the Czechoslovak Socialist Republic (1960–1990). After the 'Velvet Revolution' on 17 November 1989 and the elections in June 1990, Slovak Republic formed a part of the Czech and Slovak Federal Republic (1990–1992). The independent Slovak Republic (the second one in the history) was established on 1 January 2003 after a peaceful split of the former federation.[1]

2. Slovak Republic is a parliamentary democracy with a multi-party system. The last elections were held in March 2016. The head of the state is the President of the Slovak Republic; the National Council of the Slovak Republic as a representative of legislative power, has 150 members; and the supreme executive authority is represented by the Government of the Slovak Republic (more details in §3 below).

1. 'History of Slovak Republic' at: <http://en.wikipedia.org/wiki/History_of_Slovakia>.

The capital city of Slovak Republic is the City of Bratislava,[2] which is currently the largest city with the population of 422,932.[3]

The territory of Slovak Republic is subdivided into eight administrative regions (in Slovak: *kraj*), the so-called Upper-Tier Territorial Units (in Slovak: *Vyšší územný celok*), which possess a certain degree of autonomy. Each region has its principal city, according to which the respective region is named (e.g., the Bratislava Region (in Slovak: *Bratislavský kraj*) with the capital City of Bratislava or the Košice Region (in Slovak: *Košický kraj*) with the capital city of Košice). The regions are further subdivided into several districts (in Slovak: *okres*); the Slovak Republic currently has seventy-nine districts.[4]

Slovak Republic is a landlocked country situated in the middle of Europe, which borders the Czech Republic and Austria to the west, Poland to the north, Ukraine to the east, and Hungary to the south. Its area covers about 49,035 km.^{2} Slovak Republic is a mountainous region with the highest point in Slovak Republic laying in the High Tatras mountains (in Slovak: *Vysoké Tatry*) – the Gerlachovský štít (2,655 metres). The climate lies between the temperate and continental climate zones, as the summers are relatively warm and winters are cold and humid.

The population of Slovak Republic is above 5,400,000[5] inhabitants with the following ethnic representation: Slovak (85.8%), Hungarian (9.7%), Romany (1.7%), Czech (0.8%) and Rusyn, Ukrainian, Russian, German, Polish and others (2%).[6] Roman Catholicism is the dominant religion (68.9%).[7]

The official language is Slovak[8] appurtenant to the West Slavic languages. The widely spoken language in the southern regions is Hungarian. From September 2009, the Czech language can be used in an official communication with state authorities, public administration authorities, and local self-administration authorities.[9]

Slovak Republic became a Member State of the European Union on 1 May 2004 and as of 1 January 2009, its official currency is the Euro. It is a member of international organizations such as North Atlantic Treaty Organization (NATO), United Nations (UN), Organisation for Economic Co-operation and Development (OECD) as well as other international organizations.

2. Article 10(1) of the Constitution of the Slovak Republic.
3. At <http://www.government.gov.sk>.
4. The Act No. 221/1999 Coll. on Territorial and Administrative Organization of the Slovak Republic.
5. The Statistical Office of the Slovak Republic, <http://www.statistics.sk>.
6. At <http://www.government.gov.sk>.
7. At <http://www.government.gov.sk>.
8. Article 6(1) of the Constitution of the Slovak Republic; s. 1(1) of Act No. 357/2009 Coll. on the Full Wording of Act on the State Language No. 270/1995 Coll.
9. Section 3(5) of Act No. 357/2009 Coll. on the Full Wording of Act on the State Language No. 270/1995 Coll.

§2. Economic System

3. The Constitutional Act No. 460/1992 Coll. the Constitution of the Slovak Republic (the Slovak Constitution, in Slovak: *Ústava Slovenskej republiky*), states[10,11] that 'The economy in the Slovak Republic shall be based on the principles of a socially and ecologically oriented market economy.'

Already from the establishment of independent Slovak Republic in 1993, the country has worked to transfer its economy from a centrally planned economy to a market oriented economy.

Slovak Republic has become the country with the most dynamic economics among Central and Eastern European Countries which became members of the European Union in 2004. Major economic reforms were conducted mainly during the Mikuláš Dzurinda's government era (1997–2006). The reforms concerned privatization of enterprises and banks, tax decrease, and application of the flat income tax, health care system, and extensive reform of the pension system (introduction of a mandatory, funded pension pillar). These reforms, mainly the flat rate income tax, in combination with cheap and skilled labour, a liberal labour code and good geographic location, were the main reasons for foreign investors to start businesses in Slovak Republic, even 'green field'. Major investors were Deutsche Telekom (Germany), MOL (Hungary), and ENEL (Italy).

The key industries are automobiles (represented by the car manufactures, PSA Peugeot Citroën, Kia Motors, Volkswagen), electronics (companies such as Sam-sung Electronics or Sony), metallurgy (US Steel), and the refinery industry (Slovnaft). Presently, the main foreign trade partners are Germany, the Czech Republic, Hungary and Russia. Slovak Republic became a signatory of the Schengen Agreement in December 2007, and from 1 January 2009, its official currency is the Euro.

§3. Legal System

4. The Slovak legal system follows from the European legal systems and its basis is laid down by the Slovak Constitution, adopted in 1992 by constitutional Act No. 460/1992 Coll., which is the 'supreme' law of the country dividing state powers into the legislative power, executive power and judicial power.

Pursuant to Article 1(1) of the Slovak Constitution, Slovak Republic is a sovereign, democratic state governed by the rule of law, not bound to any ideology or religion.

Slovak Republic is a parliamentary democracy. The legislative power is entrusted with the National Council of the Slovak Republic (the 'Parliament'), which consists of the 150 Members of the Parliament elected for a four-year term. The elections of the Members of the Parliament are (i) universal, which means that any citizen who has the right to vote, can participate in the elections, (ii) equal – meaning that votes of electors are treated equally, (iii) direct as each elector exercises its voting right *suo*

10. *See* <http://www.economy.gov.sk>; <http://ec.europa.eu/economy_finance/een/007/article_5628_en.htm>; <http://www.statemaster.com/encyclopedia/Economy-of-Slovakia>.
11. Article 55(1) of the Constitution of the Slovak Republic.

nomine (in his own name) and its will has a direct legal effect on the result of elections, and the ballot is secret.[12]

5. The Legislative powers of the Parliament include the adoption of the Constitution, constitutional laws and laws whereby draft laws can be submitted by the Parliament's Committees, Members of the Parliament, and the Slovak Government.[13]

The powers of the Parliament further include the following: primarily, approval of treaties on the union of the Slovak Republic with other states, decisions on proposals for declaration of referendum, approval of international treaties on human rights and freedoms before ratification, establishment of ministries and other governmental bodies, approval of the state budget, approval of the presence of foreign military forces in Slovak Republic, and provision of the consent for dispatching military forces outside Slovak Republic.

A Member of Parliament may even interpellate the Slovak Government or any of the Government members in matters coming under its competence; response to the interpellation must be provided within thirty days and take the form of a debate in the Parliament. The interpellation is followed by a vote of confidence.[14]

6. The executive power is represented by the President of the Slovak Republic as well as by the Slovak Government, which is the supreme executive body.[15]

The President is the Head of the Slovak Republic and represents the state externally and internally and is the Commander-in-Chief of the armed forces. The President is elected in direct elections by a secret ballot for a five-year term. He mainly negotiates and ratifies international treaties; receives, appoints and recalls heads of diplomatic missions; signs laws, appoints and recalls the Prime Minister and other members of the Slovak Government, remits and mitigates sentences imposed by criminal courts in criminal proceedings, grants amnesty, etc. He is the only authority, who can declare war on the basis of the Parliament's decision, and may, upon a proposition of the Slovak Government, order a mobilization of military forces, declare a state of war or an exceptional state and appoint and recall judges of the Constitutional Court of the Slovak Republic and judges of courts.[16]

7. The Slovak Government,[17] as the supreme executive body, comprises of the Prime Minister, the Deputy Prime Minister and other Ministers. The Prime Minister is appointed and recalled by the President, and the other members of the Government are appointed by the President upon the Prime Minister's proposal. The Government is responsible to the Parliament in relation to its policy and administration. The Government is empowered to define state policy mainly on matters of national economy and social security administrations, and it executes implementation of the Government programme objectives as well as decides on other fundamental issues of internal and foreign policies. Furthermore, the Government decides on draft laws, submits the state budget and the final state budgetary account to the Parliament, decides on dispatching

12. J. Drgonec, *Ústava Slovenskej republiky, Komentár*, 2nd edn (Šamorin, Slovak Republic: Heuréka, 2007), 651–652.
13. Article 86 of the Constitution of the Slovak Republic.
14. Article 80 of the Constitution of the Slovak Republic.
15. Article 108 of the Constitution of the Slovak Republic.
16. Article 102 of the Constitution of the Slovak Republic.
17. Articles 108–123 of the Constitution of the Slovak Republic.

military forces outside Slovak Republic for the purpose of humanitarian aid or peace-keeping missions. The Government is empowered to issue regulations implementing law only within the limits laid down by the law. The Government is responsible for its activities to the Parliament, and the Parliament may take a vote of non-confidence in the Government.[18]

The executive powers are further administrated by the central state administration bodies and local administration bodies. Ministries and stated administration bodies are empowered under the law to adopt generally binding legal regulations.

8. The Slovak Constitution divides the judicial power between the Constitutional Court of the Slovak Republic (the Constitutional Court) and the general courts, which are deemed to be two individuals and mutually independent systems for the execution of the judiciary. Each of the mentioned systems has its own function and individual power to take decisions.[19]

The Constitutional Court thus represents an independent judicial authority composed of thirteen judges appointed by the President of the Slovak Republic for a twelve-year term. The proposal is submitted by the Parliament and the judge must be a Slovak citizen.[20] The Constitutional Court is empowered particularly to act and to decide on the conformity of national legal sources with the Slovak Constitution, on the conformity of government regulations and generally binding legal regulations of Ministries and other central state administration bodies with the Slovak Constitution and laws and decide on whether the subject of a referendum is in conformity with the Slovak Constitution or constitutional law.[21]

The Constitutional Court plays an important role also in relation to the protection of fundamental rights and freedoms of natural and legal persons as it decides on complaints submitted by these persons if they claim an infringement of their fundamental rights or freedoms, or human rights and fundamental freedoms resulting from an international treaty ratified by the Slovak Republic and promulgated in the manner laid down by a law[22] (*see* Part III, Chapter 4 below).

Furthermore, the Constitutional Court decides on complaints of territorial self-administrative bodies against unconstitutional or unlawful decisions, or actions into the matters of self-administration.[23]

The most severe decisions of the Constitutional Court relate to the interpretation of the Constitution or constitutional law.[24] Only the Constitutional Court provides an interpretation of the Slovak Constitution or constitutional law, if a matter is disputable.

18. Article 114(1) of the Constitution of the Slovak Republic.
19. Ruling of the Constitutional Court of the Slovak Republic No. II.ÚS 1/95, 10 Jan. 1995, CFR, 1995, 269; for more details in, J. Drgonec, *Ústava Slovenskej republiky, Komentár*, 2nd edn (Šamorin, Slovak Republic: Heuréka, 2007).
20. Article 134 of the Constitution of the Slovak Republic.
21. Article 125 of the Constitution of the Slovak Republic.
22. Article 127 of the Constitution of the Slovak Republic, details in, J. Drgonec, *Ústava Slovenskej republiky, Komentár*, 2nd edn (Šamorin, Slovak Republic: Heuréka, 2007).
23. Article 127a of the Constitution of the Slovak Republic.
24. Article 128 of the Constitution of the Slovak Republic.

The interpretation is *ex constitutione* generally binding from the date of the promulgation thereof.[25]

9. The general judiciary is administrated by independent and impartial courts.[26] The judicial system is composed of the Supreme Court of the Slovak Republic and other courts.[27]

The Slovak Constitution established the Judiciary Council of the Slovak Republic (in Slovak: *Súdna rada Slovenskej republiky*);[28] however, the Constitution does not provide any definition of this authority. The Constitutional Court in its ruling stated that the Judiciary Council was a public authority and a constitutional authority, which insured an independent position of the judicatory in relation to other state authorities.[29] The Judiciary Council of the Slovak Republic *inter alia* submits, to the President of the Slovak Republic, proposals of candidates for judges including proposals for the Chief Judge of the Supreme Court and Deputy Chief Judge of the Supreme Court; it decides on the assignment and transfer of judges.[30]

The general courts rule on civil and criminal matters and also review the legitimacy of decisions made by public administrative bodies and the legality of decisions, measures or other actions of public authorities.[31] The courts decide in panels, save for cases where the law provides that the matter shall be decided by a single judge.[32]

10. The Slovak Constitution has further established the Public prosecution[33] as an independent body for protection of rights and interests of natural and legal persons protected by law and headed by the Attorney General. Moreover, by the Slovak Constitution, the public defender of rights[34] has been created as an independent body, which participates in the protection of fundamental rights and freedoms of natural and legal persons.

§4. Historical Background of Antitrust Law

11. The history of competition law in Slovak Republic is deeply linked to the first Czechoslovak Republic, whose legal system has followed from the Austro-Hungarian monarchy. The first Act governing relations in economic competition was Act No. 111/1927 Coll., on the Protection against Unfair Competition. Under the broad formulation of the general clause of this Act, cartel law cases were also assessed. The individual legal regulation concerning cartel law was adopted by Act No. 141/1993

25. *See* J. Drgonec, *Ústava Slovenskej republiky, Komentár*, 2nd edn (Šamorin, Slovak Republic: Heuréka, 2007), 970–981.
26. Article 141(1) of the Constitution of the Slovak Republic.
27. Article 143 of the Constitution of the Slovak Republic.
28. Article 141a of the Constitution of the Slovak Republic.
29. In, Ruling of the Constitutional Court of the Slovak Republic No. III.ÚS 79/04, 21 Oct. 2004, CFR 2004 – second half, 814; *see* J. Drgonec, *Ústava Slovenskej republiky, Komentár*, 2nd edn (Heuréka, 2007), 1051.
30. Article 141a(4) of the Constitution of the Slovak Republic.
31. Article 142(1) of the Constitution of the Slovak Republic.
32. Article 142(2) of the Constitution of the Slovak Republic.
33. Article 149 of the Constitution of the Slovak Republic.
34. Article 151a of the Constitution of the Slovak Republic.

Coll., on Cartels and Private Monopolies (the Cartel Act), which included, in its section 1, an independent definition of a cartel agreement. The cartel agreement was defined as an agreement of individual entrepreneurs, by which the entrepreneurs are obliged to restrict or eliminate mutual competition by regulation of the production, sale, contractual conditions, and prices. The cartel agreements according to Act No. 141/1933 Collection of Laws of the Slovak Republic (Coll.) were basically treated as legal. This Act further governed conditions concerning the conclusion of cartel agreements, content thereof, as well as conditions for leaving the cartel. Moreover, it included supervision and control of an impact of cartel agreements on the market but primarily, it did not treat these agreements as illegal. The administrative intervention was conducted, only if a public interest was threatened by a cartel agreement. This Act became obsolete after 1950, when the system of the planned economy prevailed in Czechoslovakia.[35]

12. A new phase of the antitrust law in the Czech and Slovak Federal Republic began after the adoption of Act No. 63/1991 Coll., on the Protection of Economic Competition. This Act involved provisions concerning cartel agreements, including exemptions from the cartel agreements prohibition. It also adjusted the '*de minimis*' rule, as the cartel agreement was not prohibited if the market-share of the supplier was below 5% of the market of an individual republic or below 30% of the local market. Act No. 63/1991 Coll. adjusted, in a very limited form, also, control of concentrations and abuse of dominant position practices. The dominant position was held by an undertaking with a market-share of at least 30% of the market.

13. In 1994, Act No. 188/1994 Coll., on the Protection of Economic Competition was adopted in Slovak Republic, revoking Act No. 63/1991 Coll. Act No. 188/1994 Coll. adjusted a new definition of the 'agreements restricting competition', whereby three forms of restrictive agreements were included: 'agreement', 'decision of associations' and 'concerted practices'. The agreement was prohibited, only if the subject matter thereof was a restriction of competition or the agreement might lead to a restriction of competition. The definition was similar to the currently applicable definition of the agreement restricting competition. The *de minimis* rule was incorporated in the law and formulated with one single threshold applied both for horizontal and vertical agreements restricting competition. The hard-core cartels were, as it is now (agreements restricting competition by object), excluded from the exception based on *de minimis* rule. Act No. 188/1994 Coll. enabled undertakings to ask for the so-called individual exemption (the same conditions currently apply in the so-called *ex lege* exemption – *see* Part III, Chapter 1) and for a negative attestation (undertakings could ask the Antimonopoly Office of the Slovak Republic (AMO) to issue a decision whether their agreement is an agreement restricting competition; this provision is not included in the currently applicable Competition Act (CA)). Act. No. 188/1994 Coll. in the area of abuse of a dominant position included a rebuttable presumption that dominance on the market concerned an undertaking with a market share of at least 40%. Moreover, this Act also adopted an individually relevant market definition and a wider regulation of concentrations.

---

35. Jindšiška Munková & Pavel Svoboda & Jiří Kindl, *Soutěžní právo, Beckovy mezioborové učebnice* (Prague, Czech Republic: C.H. Beck, 2006), 31–33.

14. The currently applicable CA was adopted by Act. No. 136/ 2001 Coll., effective as of 1 May 2001 and has been several times amended. The substantial amendment of the CA became effective from 1 July 2014. Along with the CA in 2001, the AMO issued two decrees (the Decree of the AMO No. 269/2004 Coll. laying down details of the calculation of turnover, the Decree of the Antimonopoly Office No. 204/ 2004 Coll. laying down details of particulars of notification of concentration). The aim of the adoption of Competition Act No. 136/ 2001 Coll., was to harmonize Slovak competition law with the acquis communitaire. Competition Act No. 136/2001 Coll., adjusted the *de minimis* rule in the area of agreements restricting competition, whereas it increased the respective market-share threshold from 5% to 10%. Furthermore, the demonstrative list of prohibited practices of agreements restricting competition was extended to a new practice – bid-rigging. It adopted the provision, according to which an undertaking could ask the AMO for the standpoint on a draft agreement. The important change in the competition law was the introduction of the Leniency Programme, based on which the AMO was entitled to grant total immunity or decrease the fine by up to 75% of the fine that would otherwise be imposed. In the area of an abuse of a dominant position, Act. No. 136/2001 Coll., extended the demonstrative list of abusive practices to a refusal to deal practice and predatory pricing practice. The major change in the area of abusive practices was represented by an individual incorporation of the practice of refusal to grant access to an essential facility, to the CA. Another major change was the omission of the rebuttable presumption that an undertaking has a dominant position on the market if its market share is at least 40%. In the area of concentrations, the CA specified definitions of individual forms of concentration, brought detailed merger control rules and increased turnover and market-share thresholds for the notification of concentration. Moreover, the CA included the prohibition of exercising rights and obligations arising from the concentration and the possibility of asking for an exemption from the ban. Furthermore, the CA increased the independence of the AMO by the fact that the Chairman was appointed by the President of the Slovak Republic based on the proposal of the government and at the same time, the Council of the Office as an independent collective appellate body was created.

In 2002, individual Act No. 465/2002 Coll., on Block Exemptions from the Prohibition of Agreements Restricting Competition was adopted. By this Act, the European Commision (EC) block exemptions were incorporated into the Slovak legal order. This Act was revoked by Act No. 204/2004 Coll., amending Act No. 136/2001 Coll., and entered into force on 1 May 2004, whereas the EC block exemptions were applicable directly from that moment.

The amendment of the CA by Act No. 204/2004 Coll., should ensure the full compatibility of Slovak competition law with the EC rules. In the area of agreements restricting competition, the possibility of asking for an individual exemption has been abolished and the self-assessment of agreements by undertakings based on the cumulative criteria has been established. The amendment has also empowered the AMO to issue a commitments decision. In the area of merger control, the threshold criteria for the notification have been changed as the market-share threshold has been omitted, and at the same time, *local nexus* was incorporated into the criteria for the notification.

Act No. 68/2005 Coll., amending the Act on Prices, has empowered the AMO to also assess excessive pricing as an abuse of a dominant position practice (the amendment concerns section 8(2) letter a) of the CA (Act No. 136/2001 Coll.)).

The further amendment to the CA of minor importance was made by Act No. 165/2009 Coll. which entered into force on 1 July 2009. It concerns the abolishment of the disputable provision of section 2(6) of the CA only (*see* Part I, Chapter 5, §1, III) and changes related to the Euro currency conversion.

The Act No. 387/2011 Coll. brought substantial changes to the CA in the merger control area. Mainly, the criteria for the obligation to notify a concentration to the AMO was changed (*see* Part III, Chapter 3, §1, I) a short procedure of the merger control was adopted and the merger test was changed as well. The merger test is currently based on significant lessening of competition test whereas the dominance test is still present (*see* Part I, Chapter 3, §5, III).

The substantial amendment to the CA was adopted by Act No. 151/2014 Coll. The amendment incorporated several major substantive as well as procedural changes. At the same time, several By-laws have been adopted to facilitate execution of the CA.

These are: the Decree No. 169/2014 Coll. on laying down thresholds for determination whether the agreement between undertakings, concerted practice of undertakings or decision by associations of undertakings have an inappreciable impact on competition (*De minimis* decree), the Decree No. 170/2014 Coll. on laying down details of particulars of a notification of concentration (Decree on Notification), the Decree No. 171/2014 Coll. on laying down details on Settlement (Decree on Settlement), the Decree No. 172/2014 Coll. on laying down details on Leniency programme (Decree on Leniency) and the Decree No. 173/2014 Coll. on remuneration of the members of the Council of the Office.

The main substantive changes are related to the definition of the appreciable effect on competition concerning agreements restricting competition, exclusion of the predatory pricing from the non-exhaustive list of abuse of a dominance practices. Moreover, the provisions concerning refusal to grant access to the essential facility have been removed from the CA in line with the justification that this abusive practice is already covered by the refusal to deal practices already present in the CA. The amendment brought several changes in the merger control area. The huge changes relate to the specifications concerning calculation of thresholds for notification of the merger. In the merger area, the definition of 'one single entity' has been added to the CA which is used as a general legal definition for the competition law purposes. The new institute concerning cartels detection has been added to the CA, i.e. remuneration for the whistleblower. The main procedural changes are connected to the ending of the administrative proceedings by the Settlement and the Commitments decision. Substantial specifications have been brought in the area of protection of business secrecy and confidential information.

The new Act No. 343/2015 Coll. on Public Procurement effective from 18 April 2016, ensured new powers for the AMO. The AMO is obliged, in every case of agreement restricting competition concluded in a form of bid-rigging, to impose over cartel participants the ban to participate in public tenders during the period of three years from the effectiveness of the AMO's decision (*see* Part I, Chapter 5, §2, II).

The further amendment of the CA was made by Act No. 125/2016 Coll. on certain measures concerning the adoption of Civil Contentious Code, Civil Non-Contentious Code and mainly Code on Judicial Proceedings in Administrative Cases (CPAC) which entered into force on 1 July 2016. The amendment concerns changes regarding the administrative review of the AMO's decision by the administrative court.

The last amendment of the CA has been adopted by the Act No. 350/2016 Coll. on Certain Rules Concerning the Claims for Damages Caused by the Breach of Competition Rules effective from 27 December 2016 (Act on Damages). According to the Act on Damages, the proceedings on damages compensation can be also terminated by the out-of-court settlement or by mediation. The compensation of the damages based on the amicable settlement or mediation will be treated as the mitigating factor when imposing the fine for the breach of antitrust rules by the AMO.

Except several By-laws, the AMO has issued various soft-law documents explaining its approach during the investigation and assessment of anticompetitive behaviour.[36]

36. At <http://www.antimon.gov.sk>.

Part I. The Structure of Antitrust Law and Its Enforcement

Chapter 1. Sources of Antitrust Law

§1. National Sources

15. The basic source of the antitrust law is represented by the Slovak Constitution which in Article 55(2) stipulates that 'The Slovak Republic shall protect and encourage economic competition. A law shall lay down the details.' This means that detailed principles and specifications of rules concerning protection of economic competition are included in the law.

16. Furthermore, it has to be borne in mind that all legally binding acts of the European Communities and the European Union which take, according to Article 7(2) of the Slovak Constitution, precedence over Slovak laws, thus also represent an individual source of antitrust law (*see* §2 below).

17. The Act No. 513/1991 Coll. Commercial Code as further amended (Commercial Code (CC)) is the basic law from which the antitrust rules are derived whereas section 41 of the CC states that:

> Individuals and legal entities involved in economic competition, even if they are not entrepreneurs (hereinafter referred as 'competitors'), shall be entitled both to engage freely in economic competition with the purpose of achieving economic benefits, and to associate with the purpose above. Notwithstanding the above, they shall be obliged to comply with the legally binding rules of economic competition, and shall not be allowed to abuse their involvement in the economic competition.

The CC defines abuse in economic competition as an 'unfair competition' on the one hand and as an 'illegal abuse of economic competition' on the other hand.[37] Unfair competition is defined by the general clause[38] as 'conduct in an economic competition which is contrary to good manners of competition and is eligible to cause damage to other competitors or consumers'. Unfair competition is, according to the CC, prohibited

37. Section 42(1) of the CC.
38. Section 44(1) of the CC.

whereby claims of competitors concerning unfair competition need to be submitted to the court[39] as the only authority empowered to decide on the breach of the law by unfair competition.

The 'illegal abuse of economic competition' is addressed by the CA[40] and consists of an abuse of a dominant position, agreements restricting competition and mergers with negative effects on competition.

The law on unfair competition has a private law dimension and is aimed at protection of private interests of competitors (the term used in the Slovak language in the CC is *súťažiteľ*[41] and it covers all persons participating in economic competition, not only entrepreneurs). On the contrary, protection of economic competition governed by the CA has a public law dimension and the antitrust law primarily protects public interests. The CA applies to all persons which are covered by the definition of the undertaking stipulated in the CA (*see* Part I, Chapter 4, §1).

18. The currently valid CA (the Act No. 136/2001) was adopted in 2001 and further several time amended. Its last amendment has been effective since December 2016.[42] (In detail, *see* General Introduction, §4). According to the several enabling provisions of the CA, the AMO is entitled to issue a generally binding legal regulations (By-laws) as mentioned in §3 below.

19. It needs to be mentioned that there are several other laws in the Slovak legal order whose aim is the protection of competition; for example, the Electronic Communications Act (ECA),[43] the Network Industries Regulation Act (NIRA),[44] the Public Procurement Act[45] and the State Aid Act.[46] Nevertheless, they do not include antitrust rules.

§2. International Sources

20. The Slovak Republic is member of the EU as from 1 May 2004. On the day of effectiveness of the Accession Treaty,[47] the community law became binding. But, as already mentioned above, according to Article 7(2) of the Slovak Constitution, all generally binding legal acts of the European Communities and the European Union take precedence over the national law. This is applicable also in relation to the antitrust

39. Sections 53–55 of the CC.
40. Section 42(2) of the CC.
41. Section 41 of the CC.
42. The Act No. 350/2016 Coll.
43. Section 1(2) of the Act No. 351/2011 Coll. on Electronic Communications as amended.
44. Section 5(1) letter a) of the Act No. 276/2001 Coll. on Regulation of Network Industries and Amendment and Supplement of some acts.
45. The Act No. 342/2015 Coll. on Public Procurement.
46. Section 2(1) of the Act No. 358/2015 Coll. on Regulation of Certain Relations in the Field of State Aid and *De Minimis* Aid (the Act on State Aid).
47. Treaty concerning the Accession of the Czech Republic, the Republic of Estonia, the Republic of Cyprus, the Republic of Latvia, the Republic of Lithuania, the Republic of Hungary, the Republic of Malta, the Republic of Poland, the Republic of Slovenia and the Slovak Republic to the European Union, published at the Collection of Laws of the Slovak Republic under the No. 185/2004 Coll.

law. This means that any national legal act, if it is in contradiction with EU generally binding legal acts, cannot be applied by public authorities and moreover Slovak competition rules cannot approve behaviour which is contrary to Articles 101 and 102 of the Treaty on the Functioning of the European Union (TFEU) (ex Articles 81 and 82 of the EC Treaty).

In line with the above mentioned, the AMO is obliged to follow and respect Regulation 1/2003 which introduces the basic principles of Articles 101 and 102 of TFEU (ex Articles 81 and 82 of the EC Treaty), and the direct application by national competition authorities as well as by national courts. Moreover, the application of EU law and the national law is parallel[48] because if the AMO proceeds against an undertaking according to section 4 of the CA (agreements restricting competition) or section 8 of the CA (abuse of a dominant position), and the reviewed behaviour at the same time affects or may affect a trade between Member States, the AMO is obliged to apply not only national law, but also provisions of TFEU. The AMO has already applied such parallel application in several antitrust cases.[49]

21. The principle of the precedence of the European law as included in Article 7(2) of the Slovak Constitution is accordingly involved in Article 3(2) of the Regulation 1/2003 according to which:

> The application of national competition law may not lead to prohibition of agreements, decisions by associations of undertakings or concerted practices which may affect trade between Member States but which do not restrict competition within the meaning of Article 81(1) of the Treaty, or which fulfil the conditions of Article 81(3) of the Treaty or which are covered by a Regulation for the application of Article 81(3) of the Treaty. Under this Regulation, the Member States shall not be precluded from adopting and applying on their territory stricter national laws which prohibit or sanction unilateral conduct engaged in by undertakings.

Moreover, in line with section 5 of the CA, EU Regulations concerning block exemptions are also applicable to such agreements restricting competition which cannot affect trade between Member States.

22. The national courts are entitled to apply Articles 101 and 102 of TFEU (ex Articles 81 and 82 of the EC Treaty) directly, when it comes to private consequences of the violation of antitrust rules, mainly damages claims and invalidity of contracts.

---

48. Article 3(1) of The Council Regulation (EC) No. 1/2003 of 16 Dec. 2002 on the implementation of the rules on competition laid down in Arts 81 and 82 of the Treaty, OJ L 1, 4 Jan. 2003, 1–25 (Regulation 1/2003).
49. For example, the decision of the Council No. 2009/DZ/R/2/017, 4 Apr. 2009 on the abuse of a dominant position, by the company Slovak Telekom or the decision of the Council No. 2009/KH/R/2/054, 11 Nov. 2009, <http://www.antimon.gov.sk>.

§3. Secondary Sources

I. Regulations

23. The AMO is empowered by the respective enabling provisions of the CA to issue several generally binding legal regulations (By-laws); all other documents issued by the AMO are of a non-binding nature (soft-law).

There are disputes on whether antitrust rules can by specified by By-laws and whether such an approach is not in conflict with Article 55(2) of the Slovak Constitution. There is an opinion that the inconsistency of the enabling provision of the CA with Article 55(2) of the Slovak Constitution can be derived from the legal opinion of the Constitutional Court expressed in its ruling:[50]

> By the provision of Article 55, section 2 of the Constitution, the Slovak Republic accepts the obligation to create equal legal conditions for protection and support of economic competition. By Article 55, section 2 of the Constitution, the determination of these conditions is referred to the Act without the legislative body being allowed by the Constitution to authorize executive bodies to further restrict economic competition.[51]

Nevertheless, the AMO issued until now several decrees (in Slovak: *Vyhláška*) based on the respective enabling provisions of the CA. These are: Decree on Turnover Calculation, Decree on Notifications, *De minimis* decree, Decree on Settlement, Decree on Leniency.[52]

II. Guidelines

24. The AMO issued several 'guidelines' which in general follow the EU regulations, notices, recommendations or guidelines. The aim of these documents is to explain and clarify the application of antitrust rules or to specify individual provisions of the CA, or to describe the process used by the AMO. These documents, not legally binding, are:

(1) Instructions on setting of fines.[53]

---

50. J. Drgonec, *Ústava Slovenskej republiky, Komentár*, 2nd edn (Šamorin, Slovak Republic: Heuréka, 2007), 603.
51. Ruling of the Constitutional Court of the Slovak Republic No. PL. ÚS 7/96, 27 Feb. 1997, CFR 1997, 50, translation by author.
52. In Slovak at: <http://www.antimon.gov.sk/64-sk/legislativa/>.
53. The AMO, 'Metodický pokyn o postupe pri určovaní pokút v prípadoch zneužívania dominantného postavenia a dohôd obmedzujúcich súťaž', <http://www.antimon.gov.sk/data/files/396_metodicky-pokyn-o-postupe-pri-urcovani-pokut-v-pripadoch-zneuzivania-dominantneho-postavenia-a-dohod-obmedzujucich-sutaz.pdf>.

(2) Guideline on powers to conduct inspections.[54]
(3) Commitments and obligations concerning concentrations guideline.[55]
(4) Leniency guideline.[56]
(5) Commitments guideline.[57]
(6) Ancillary restraints guideline.[58]
(7) Guidelines on bid-rigging cartel agreements.[59]
(8) Vertical agreements restricting competition by object guideline.[60]
(9) Parties to the concentration guideline.[61]
(10) Pre-notification guideline.[62]
(11) Guideline on simplified procedure in merger control proceedings.[63]
(12) Turnover calculation guideline.[64]
(13) Guideline on application of the exception from the ban to implement concentration.[65]

---

54. The AMO, 'Usmernenie k právomoci Protimonopolného úradu vykonávať inšpekcie', <http://www.antimon.gov.sk/data/files/489_usmernenie-k-pravomoci-protimonopolneho-uradu-slovenskej-republiky-vykonavat-inspekcie.pdf>.
55. The AMO, 'Ukladanie podmienok a povinností pri koncentráciách', <http://www.antimon.gov.sk/165/ smernice-a-usmernenia.axd>.
56. The AMO, 'Program zhovievavosti podľa § 38d zákona o ochrane hospodárskej súťaže (Leniency Programme)', <http://www.antimon.gov.sk/data/files/388_program-zhovievavosti.pdf>.
57. The AMO, 'Záväzky (úprava postupu Protimonopolného úradu SR podľa §38f zákona)', <http://www.antimon.gov.sk/data/files/397_zavazky-uprava-postupu-protimonopolneho-uradu-sr-podla-§-38f-zakona.pdf>.
58. The AMO, 'Obmedzenia hospodárskej súťaže, ktoré s koncentráciou priamo súvisia a sú nevyhnutné na jej uskutočnenie', <http://www.antimon.gov.sk/165/smernice-a-usmernenia.axd>.
59. The AMO, 'Indície protisúťažného správania podnikateľov v procese verejného obstarávania', <http://www.antimon.gov.sk/data/files/95_indicie-kartel4-1.pdf>; The AMO, 'Kartelové dohody vo verejnom obstarávaní', <http://www.antimon.gov.sk/data/files/96_kartelove-dohody-vo-vo.pdf>.
60. The AMO, 'Cieľové vertikálne dohody', <http://www.antimon.gov.sk/data/files/422_cielove-vertikalne-dohody-pohlad-pmu-sr.pdf>.
61. The AMO, 'Účastníci koncentrácie', <http://www.antimon.gov.sk/165/smernice-a-usmernenia.axd>.
62. The AMO, 'Usmernenie Protimonopolného úradu Slovenskej republiky o prednotifikačných kontaktoch v procese posudzovania koncentrácií', <http://www.antimon.gov.sk/165/smernice-ausmernenia.axd>.
63. The AMO, 'Usmernenie Protimonopolného úradu Slovenskej republiky o podrobnostiach pri zjednodušenom oznámení koncentrácie', <http://www.antimon.gov.sk/data/files/399_nove-usmernenie-pmu-sr-o-podrobnostiach-pri-zjednodusenom-oznameni-koncentracie-16092014.pdf>.
64. The AMO, 'Usmernenie k výpočtu obratu', <http://www.antimon.gov.sk/data/files/387_usmernenie-protimonopolneho-uradu-slovenskej-republiky-k-vypoctu-obratu.pdf>.
65. The AMO, 'Usmernenie Protimonopolného úradu Slovenskej republiky o podrobnostiach udelenia výnimky zo zákazu implementácie koncentrácie', <http://www.antimon.gov.sk/data/files/398_nove-usmernenie-protimonopolneho-uradu-slovenskej-republiky-o-podrobnostiach-udelenia-vynimky-zo-zakazu-implementacie-koncentracie-16092014.pdf>.

(14) Guideline on business secrecy and confidential information assessment.[66]

In addition to these documents, the AMO follows guidelines and recommendations issued by the European Commission, as well.

It is worth to mention that one of the recent decisions of the Constitutional Court questioned the possibility of undertakings to require from the AMO to follow its guidelines during the decision-making process. The principles of legitimate expectations and legal certainty has been treated as irrelevant by this decision. The Constitutional Court stated that:

Modification of the Constitution that would exist, if each executive, freely at its discretion and independently from authorisation to issue an implementing generally binding legal regulation, amended the Constitution, indicated everything considered by it to be purposeful or useful for modification of its own power and exercise thereof as constitutional, is incompatible with a material legally consistent state. A practical consequence of such treatment of the Constitution would be 'a different Constitution with each executive', while the principle of a material legally consistent state is only such legal protection that is provided by public authorities under a generally binding legal regulation effective at the time of resolving an individual dispute of right.[67]

This opinion is not in line with the several judgment of the European Court of Justice (ECJ) and may cause problems with further application of the soft-law in competition law cases in the future.

§4. Sources' Relation and Hierarchy

25. Even though the Slovak Constitution does not include specific provisions from which it could be possible to derive a hierarchy of acts, norms and other generally legally binding regulations, the Slovak Constitution and constitutional acts are jointly at the highest level of the hierarchy of national legal sources. This conclusion follows from Article 152(4) of the Slovak Constitution according to which 'Constitutional laws, laws and other generally binding legal regulations shall be interpreted and applied in conformity with this Constitution.' This article is deemed to be a constitutional basis for the hierarchical system of the Slovak legal order.

Doubts as to whether the constitutional acts do possess the same status as the Slovak Constitution were overturned by the Constitutional Court decision according to which:

> Laws of the majority of states currently differentiate between the Constitution and laws. The Constitution represents the topmost layer of laws, its top: The adoption, amendment, and cancellation thereof require a number of votes bigger

66. The AMO, 'Usmernenie k posudzovaniu ochrany obchodného tajomstva, dôverených informácií a osobných údajov', <http://www.antimon.gov.sk/data/files/454_usmernenie-protimonopolneho-uradu-sr-k-posudzovaniu-ochrany-obchodneho-tajomstva-dovernych-informacii-a-osobnych-udajov-pdf.pdf>.
67. Resulution of the Constitutional Court, I ÚS 505/2015-27, 18 Nov. 2015, <https://www.ustavnysud.sk>.

than the adoption, amendment, or cancellation of laws. From this point of view, no difference between the Constitution and constitutional laws exists in the system of sources of law of the Slovak Republic.[68]

26. The theory further divides constitutional acts into several groups, but basically, these are represented by constitutional acts which amend or supplement the Slovak Constitution and thus have become an integral part of it. Further on, there are constitutional acts which regulate the code of conduct in 'less than constitutional relations' and the legal force of the constitutional acts they have for political reasons – to guarantee a higher stability level of legal regulations.[69] The constitutional acts which do not amend or supplement the Slovak Constitution and regulate in 'less than constitutional relations' are deemed to be subordinated to the Slovak Constitution.[70] The difference between the constitutional acts and other acts is represented not only by the fact that they regulate different relations but also by the fact that they are adopted by a different number of parliament members' votes.

27. Basically, the hierarchal system of the Slovak legal order thus comprises:

(1) The Slovak Constitution and constitutional acts which amend or supplement the Slovak Constitution or the constitutional acts which regulate constitutional relations for exceptional circumstances.
(2) The constitutional acts which regulate code of conduct in 'less than constitutional relations'.
(3) The laws.
(4) The other generally binding legal regulations, for example, By-laws.[71]

28. It must be borne in mind that according to Article 7(2) and (5) of the Slovak Constitution, legally binding acts of the European Communities and of the European Union; international treaties on human rights and fundamental freedoms; international treaties for whose exercise a law is not necessary, and international treaties which directly confer rights or impose duties on natural persons or legal persons, do have precedence over laws of the Slovak Republic. The international treaties take precedence only if they are ratified and promulgated in a way laid down by a law. Furthermore, according to Article 154c of the Slovak Constitution, international treaties on human rights and fundamental freedoms which the Slovak Republic has ratified and that were promulgated before the coming into force of the constitutional Act No. 90/2001 Coll. (it concerns mainly the amendment of the Article 7 of the Slovak Constitution) are part of the Slovak legal order and do have precedence over laws if they provide a

68. Ruling of the Constitutional Court No. I.ÚS 39/93, 2 Jun. 1993, CFR 1993, translation by author; *see* J. Drgonec, *Ústava Slovenskej republiky, Komentár*, 2nd edn (Šamorin, Slovak Republic: Heuréka, 2007), 34.
69. J. Drgonec, *Ústava Slovenskej republiky, Komentár*, 2nd edn (Šamorin, Slovak Republic: Heuréka, 2007), 40.
70. J. Drgonec, *Ústava Slovenskej republiky, Komentár*, 2nd edn (Šamorin, Slovak Republic: Heuréka, 2007), 40.
71. For more detailed classification of sources of law, *see* J. Drgonec, *Ústava Slovenskej republiky, Komentár*, 2nd edn (Šamorin, Slovak Republic: Heuréka, 2007).

greater scope for constitutional rights and freedoms. Also, other international treaties which the Slovak Republic has ratified and that were promulgated in the manner laid down by law before the taking effect of the constitutional act in 2001 are part of the Slovak legal order, if so provided by the law.

§5. Role and Authority of Precedents

29. The Slovak legal order comes under a system of continental law. The basic legal source is represented by the law / the legal act. Precedents do not represent the source of the Slovak legal order as it is, for example, in the Anglo-American legal practice, which means that courts are not bound by decisions of other courts (mainly higher courts).[72] The judge in Slovak Republic is thus not obliged to take into consideration decisions issued in similar cases by the court of the same level or higher level, whereas the decisions as such cannot create a 'new binding law'. This arises from the strict division of the state powers into legislative power, executive power and judicial power.

Judicial decisions are thus binding only for respective parties, that is, they have and can have only *inter partes* effect. Nevertheless, according to the principle of legal certainty, courts, as well as state administration bodies are obliged to assess similar legal situations equally. This conclusion was made in several rulings of the Slovak Constitutional Court,[73] and moreover, the Constitutional Court declared an approach according to which equal or similar situations were treated differently, without objective and justified reason as discriminatory.[74]

30. In addition, the Supreme Court of the Slovak Republic according to section 22(1) of the Act on Courts[75] makes public judicial decisions of cardinal importance and also issues statements on unification of the interpretation of generally binding legal acts with the aim to ensure their uniform interpretation. This approach is also connected to the principle of legal certainty and to the predictability of the law; the basic principles of the state governed by the rule of law.

31. It can be thus concluded that a judicial decision does not represent a source of law in the Slovak legal order; it is only a tool for assurance of uniform interpretation of legal norms,[76] even though different opinions also exist. According to these opinions, it is not necessary to strictly adhere to the division of the legislative power and the

72. For example, the role of a 'common law' was reversed by a Civil Code No. 141/1950 which in its s. 568(1) stated that the 'common law' followed from judicial decisions or other sources was cancelled.
73. Ruling of the Constitutional Court of the Slovak Republic No. I.ÚS 87/93, 23 Sep. 1993, <http://www.concourt.sk>; Ruling of the Constitutional Court of the Slovak Republic No. II.ÚS 243/05, 9 Nov. 2006, <http://www.concourt.sk>.
74. Ruling of the Constitutional Court of the Slovak Republic, No. IV.ÚS 14/07, 17 May 2007, <http://www.concourt.sk>.
75. Act No. 757/2004 Coll. on Courts and on amendments and supplementations of some acts as further amended.
76. Conclusion mentioned in, Ludislav Dudiš, 'Sudcovská tvorba práva – je súdne rozhodnutie prameňom práva?', <http://www.upjs.sk/public/media/4518/LD%20Sudcovsk%C3%A1%20 tvorba% 20pr%C3%A1va.doc>.

judicial power represented by courts, as the judicial power may represent effective completion of the former.[77]

Nevertheless, the precedents are a useful tool for the interpretation of legal regulations, and their role is increasing. It is not unusual that natural or legal persons use in their arguments a previous courts' or public authorities' reference to precedents, as moreover, it is not rare to also find references to judicial decisions in a courts' judgments. Also from the AMO's and the court's decisions, it is evident that they take EU case law into consideration, even in cases decided solely according to the national law. This approach is particularly evident in competition law cases.

77. L. Hanuš,*Právní argumentace nebo svévole, úvahy o práve, spravedlnosti a etice* (C.H. Beck, 2008), 89 mentioned in Stanislav Demčák, 'O závaznosti judikatúry v podmienkach Slovenskej republiky',*Bulletin slovenskej advokácie* 6 (2009) (Slovenská advokátska komora).

Chapter 2. Scope of Application

§1. Territorial Reach

32. The CA applies to behaviour and activities conducted on the territory of the Slovak Republic having effect on the Slovak territory, that is, activities conducted on the domestic market with an impact on the domestic market as well as to all activities which take place abroad, and lead or may lead to restriction of competition on the domestic market.[78]

The decisive factor for the territorial application of the CA is thus the existence of the effect of respective activities on Slovak territory. According to the mentioned principle (principle of the presence of the effect or potential effect on the domestic market), activities whose effects are present only on foreign markets are not covered by the CA, provided that the international treaties do not provide otherwise.[79]

The jurisdiction of the AMO over the case must be reviewed in each case independently, taking into account the circumstances of the individual case. If the reviewed conduct has an effect on domestic market as well as on other Member States' markets, the AMO will also use community material law.[80]

33. The jurisdiction in merger control cases must be assessed in connection with section 10(1) of the CA, as each concentration meeting threshold criteria must be notified to the AMO. These transactions, provided that they are not covered by the Merger Regulation,[81] (transactions with a community dimension) are dealt by the AMO within a merger control proceeding.

§2. Special Sectors

34. The CA applies to all undertakings and to all sectors irrespective of whether these undertakings or sectors are subject to *ex-ante* regulation. The only principle by which the AMO is bound by appraisal of conduct of special sectors' undertakings is the *ne bis in idem* principle, that is, the obligation to avoid imposing of double sanctions for the same conduct. The AMO will assess only such conduct which is not at the same time a breach of obligations defined by special sector legislations or imposed pursuant special regulations. This approach was acknowledged by the AMO in the proceedings against the monopoly distributor of energy concerning the abuse of a dominant position. The AMO finally stated that:

Thus, the Office is authorised to interfere in case of a suspicion of a potential abuse of the dominant position in any sector, including sectors that are subject to

78. Section 2(4) of the CA.
79. Section 2(5) of the CA.
80. Section 2(3) of the CA.
81. Council Regulation (EC) No. 139/2004 of 20 Jan. 2004, on the control of concentrations between undertakings (the EC Merger Regulation), OJ L 24, 29 Jan. 2004, 1–22.

regulation. Even in cases where a certain specific activity is regulated by a sector-specific regulator's measure, it applies that the Office has the possibility to interfere, here, however, provided that the undertaking has had a certain autonomous space to act within the regulation set. All the more, the Office has the competence to act in case that certain acting would potentially be subject to regulation but no specific regulatory measure would be taken. The fact whether an undertaking has determined its acting in the market autonomously is decisive for the possibility of interference by a competition authority. Such interpretation of competences of the competition authority and specific regulator's sectors represents an interpretation officially applied at the European level.[82]

35. However, the CA, till its amendment became effective in June 2009, had included a disputable provision that was limiting powers of the AMO concerning application of competition rules to specific sectors such as electronic communications, energy sector and post services.[83] This provision of the CA was attacked by the European Commission in a formal infringement procedure[84] (*see* Part I, Chapter 5, §1, III).

§3. State-Owned Enterprises and Public Utilities

36. As already mentioned above, the CA applies to all subjects which come under the term 'undertaking' defined in section 3(1) of the CA, thus also to state-owned enterprises or public utilities.

The exemption from this rule is covered in section 2(2) of the CA. Activities and conduct that restrict or may restrict competition conducted by undertakings providing services in the public interest according to special legislations are not covered by the antitrust rules, provided that the application of the CA factually or legally prevents them from fulfilling their tasks. This provision protects the same interests as protected by Article 106(2) of the TFEU (ex Article 86(2) of the EC Treaty).

Basically, the CA requires the fulfilment of two conditions – the provision of services in the public interest and the fact that application of the antitrust rules hinders such provision of services.

Neither the CA nor the Slovak legal order include a general definition of the term 'public interest'.[85] However, the CA, for example, refers to the Collective Bargaining Act,[86] specifically in respect to conclusion of collective labour agreement. The Explanatory report to the CA[87] states that the notion of 'public interest' is included

82. Decision of the Council, No. 2012/DZ/R/2/030, 29 Jun. 2012, <http://www.antimon.gov.sk/2012dzr2030/>.
83. Section 2(6) of the CA is valid before the amendment of the Competition Act, effective as of June 2009. According to the respective provision, the Competition Act 'does not apply to cases of restrictions of competition which appraisal falls under the competence of another body ensuring protection of competition according to a special regulation', such as the ECA or NIRA.
84. *See* European Commission's press release IP/09/200, 2 Feb. 2009.
85. The definition of the notion 'public interest' is included in the Act No. 552/2003 Coll. on Performance of Work in Public Interests and is defined as the interest which provides material benefit or other benefit to all citizens or majority of citizens, s. 2(1).
86. Act No. 2/1991 Coll. Collective Bargaining Act, ss 5–7.
87. The Explanatory Report, published in Slovak at: <http://www.antimon.gov.sk/69/105/dovodovasprava.axd>.

or follows from respective legal regulations by which the state imposes on some undertakings the obligation to provide services in public interest. If the undertaking also performs other activities, the antitrust rules apply to these activities, without an exception.

The second condition means that the application of competition rules is excluded if it hinders the provision of public services. This is, for example, the case of so-called postal reservation, according to which some postal services are exclusively reserved for the universal service provider.[88]

§4. Sensible Effect and De Minimis

37. The CA does not include any provisions, which would eliminate the scope of its application except the already-mentioned exemption concerning undertakings providing services in public interest (*see* Chapter 2, §3).

38. However, the general clause of agreements restricting competition (section 4(1) of the CA) stipulates that only the behaviour of undertakings which are at least capable of restricting competition on the market is prohibited. The general clause thus supposes that a certain level of materiality must be present whereby it is represented either by the aim to restrict competition (agreements restrictive 'by object') or by the potential for a negative impact on competition (agreements restrictive 'by effect').

The CA thus in section 4(2) provides the negative definition of an appreciable effect on competition based on the market share criteria defined by the *De minimis* decree. An example of an agreement that would not be prohibited because it does not meet at least material conditions of a potential restriction of economic competition according to the general clause, is an agreement concluded between members of a legitimate association of undertakings; typically between companies that are grouped in a holding structure. The companies under the terms of a holding structure do not look like 'typical' undertakings in their mutual relations; the expression of their will to behave in a certain manner in the market is replaced by a decision of the mother company, and if it is not replaced directly, it is realized according to the intention of the mother company. The competition between these companies does not exist, thus it is not possible to distort it. This understanding issues from the so-called *intra-enterprise doctrine*, according to which subjects, between whom relations of real control exists, form one economic entity. This approach was used by the AMO in Case *Škoda*;[89] the AMO assessed the import agreement concluded between Škoda Auto (a car producer) – a mother company and its Slovak subsidiary – Škoda Auto Slovensko, whereby it concluded that:

> The contract under consideration therefore represents agreement between the parent company and subsidiary, regulating and providing for terms and conditions of their activities and acts based on control within the framework of a single economic group. The Authority states that the companies pursuing their business

88. For example, a postal reservation applies to distribution of items of correspondence and direct mail items up to 50g of weight.
89. Decision of the AMO No. 2002/ZK/1/1/070, 4 Apr. 2002, <http://www.antimon.gov.sk>.

> within the framework of a single economic group based on control relations are entitled to coordinate their activities and mutually create such links and relations, which allow an optimum development of the business activity of the whole group, without restricting competition. For this reason, the Authority has reviewed the Contract as an agreement within the framework of a single economic group and not as an agreement restricting competition pursuant to section 4(1) of the Act.[90]

The notion of 'one economic entity' has been incorporated to the CA by its amendment in 2014. The definition states that the 'one economic entity' is made up of companies whose relationships are based on relations of direct or indirect control as defined in section 9(4) of the CA.[91]

39. To conclude that any behaviour on the market represents an agreement restricting competition, the AMO at first examines whether the aim to restrict competition, though not expressed, is present. If it is proved, no further analysis of a negative impact of the agreement on the market is required; the negative impact is supposed by itself. The Council in the *GIS* cartel case[92] stated that if the aim of the agreement is anticompetitive 'agreements among undertakings are prohibited regardless of their possible effects.... Where its aim is to restrict competition, the agreement cannot be justified by any analysis of its economic context, in which it takes place'.[93] Furthermore, the AMO in the Case *Chamber of Geodesists and Cartographers*[94] quoted:

The evaluation of the issue, whether a decision is aimed at a restriction of competition, depends on several factors. The aim of the competition restriction itself may be deduced from circumstances/subject matter of the decision, contemplated aim of the decision, from the legal and economic contexts of the behaviour of the parties.[95]

If the existence of the cartel agreement's aim was not proved, the AMO would have to concentrate on proving negative consequences of the agreement on the market by means of an economic analysis. During the evaluation of the anticompetitive impact, the AMO reviews an agreement in its legal and economic context, whereas it evaluates mainly the nature of products, which are the subject of the agreement, the position of agreement's participants on the market, a wider economic context, in which the agreement was made, context of the whole relevant market, relationship in which the

90. Decision of the AMO No. 2002/ZK/1/1/070, 4 Apr. 2002, <http://www.antimon.gov.sk>, translation by author.
91. Section 9(4) of the Competition Act states that control is the ability to exercise a controlling influence on the activities of an undertaking, especially by means of: (a) ownership rights or other rights; (b) rights, contracts or other facts allowing the exercising of a controlling influence on the composition, voting or decisions of the undertaking's bodies.
92. Decision of the Council No. 2009/KH/R/035, 14 Aug. 2009, challenged by the administrative complaint at the Regional Court in Bratislava – pending procedure, <http://www.antimon.gov.sk>.
93. Decision of the Council No. 2009/KH/R/035,14 Aug. 2009, §621, <http://www.antimon.gov.sk>, translation by author.
94. Decision of the AMO No. 2007/KH/1/1/108, 21 Dec. 2007, <http://www.antimon.gov.sk>.
95. Decision of the AMO No. 2007/KH/1/1/108, 21 Dec. 2007, <http://www.antimon.gov.sk>, translation by author.

agreement was made, impact on 'inter-brand' and the 'intra-brand' competition, and the existence of similar agreements in the market.

Prevailing examples of agreements, which generally can almost always have an object to distort competition particularly include horizontal price-fixing agreements, horizontal agreements on production and selling quotas, horizontal market-partitioning agreements, bid-rigging, horizontal exchange of price-sensitive information, vertical agreements containing Resale Price Maintenance (RPM), and vertical agreements determining absolute territorial protection of distributors.

40. Even though an agreement that is anticompetitive by object or by effect is regarded as prohibited, it still can be exempted in legitimated cases from the ban following the *de minimis* rule (section 4(2) of the CA and *De minimis* decree).

The *de minimis* rule is applicable to agreements restricting competition with minor relevance. This rule provides that agreements with an insignificant impact on the market are not prohibited, whereby the rule follows from the application of the doctrine *de minimis* included in the Commission Notice on agreements of minor importance which do not appreciably restrict competition under Article 81(1) of the Treaty establishing the European Community (*de minimis*),[96] (*De minimis* Notice).

The assessment of whether an agreement can be exempted based on the *de minimis* rule, is linked to the determination of the market shares of the agreement's participants. The effects '*de minimis*' are valid *ex tunc* (from the beginning itself).

Nevertheless, the CA in section 4(2) stipulates that the *de minimis* rule does not apply if the agreement has its aim restriction of competition.

41. The review of whether an agreement restricting competition is prohibited includes also an appraisal of possible exemptions:

(1) *de minimis* rule as defined by the section 4(2) of the CA *and De minimis* decree (*see* the quotation of section 4(2) of the CA – Part I, Chapter 3, §1);
(2) *block* exemptions regulations (section 5 of the CA refers to the EU Block Exemptions Regulations);
(3) *ex lege* exemption defined in section 4(5) of the CA including three cumulative conditions (*see* Part I, Chapter 3, §1 and Part I, Chapter 3, §5, II).

42. Furthermore, the CA involves limitation of powers of the AMO over the assessment of concentrations under the merger control provisions. The powers are limited by the defined threshold criteria (section 10(1) of the CA) meaning that only transactions meeting the stipulated thresholds (*see* Part III, Chapter 3, §1, I) must be notified to the AMO.

96. Commission Notice on agreements of minor importance which do not appreciably restrict competition under Art. 81(1) of the Treaty establishing the European Community (*de minimis*), OJ C 368, 22 Dec. 2001, 13–15.

Chapter 3. Overview of Substantive Provisions

§1. Restrictive Agreements

43. Definition of the agreement restricting competition (section 4(1) and (3) of the CA):

> (1) Agreement between undertakings and concerted practice between undertakings, as well as decisions of their associations, objective or effect of which is or may be restriction of competition … are prohibited, unless this Act provides otherwise.
>
> (3) For the purpose of this Act:

(a) an agreement between undertakings means any verbal or written positive expression of the will of the parties thereto, as well as any other positive expression of will derived from their conduct;
(b) a concerted practice between undertakings means any coordination of their activities that does not bear signs of agreement between undertakings referred to in (a) and cannot be identified as the natural consequence of the behaviour of another undertaking;
(c) a decision by an association of undertakings is any legal act of the association's body, as well as a recommendation of the association's body.[97]

According to the general clause (section 4(1) of the CA), the notion of an 'agreement restricting competition' covers three forms of conduct: 'Agreements', 'Concerted Practices', and 'Decision of Associations'. These are prohibited provided that their object or potential impact is an exclusion, restriction or distortion of economic competition. The definition of an agreement restricting competition incorporated in the CA is in line with Article 101(1) of the TFEU (ex Article 81(1) of the EC Treaty). The CA in addition involves individual definitions of the 'agreement', 'concerted practice' and 'decision of associations' as quoted above.

The general clause does not comprise any distinction between horizontal agreements (entered by undertakings that are for the purpose of this agreement on the same level of the market that means between competitors) and vertical agreements concluded among undertakings that are not mutual competitors. The CA applies to both of these basic types uniformly. The factual difference which is currently present in the decision-making practice of the AMO, is linked to the appraisal of their impact on the market, as horizontal agreements are deemed to be more harmful to competition than vertical agreements. This approach is also reflected in the higher amount of fines imposed for horizontal cartels.

97. At http://www.antimon.gov.sk/.

The term 'Agreement' covers any verbal or written positive expression of the will of the parties to the agreement, as well as any other positive expression of will, derived from their conduct.[98] The notion 'Agreement' thus covers offences that are the most similar ones to the making of a standard, legally enforceable contract according to the national private law. On the other hand, the 'Concerted Practices' are not based on a pre-determination of the behaviour on the market; they are based on a coordination and cooperation of business activities because of the expectation of another undertaking's behaviour on the market. A 'Decision of Associations' has, unlike the two previous forms, the nature of an order or recommendation, unilaterally determined, set or at least recommended as a rule, towards those undertakings who are the association's participants. The order or the recommendation is qualified to identify future competitive behaviour of either the association's members or undertakings that are outside the association.

In 2007, the AMO issued a decision by which it concluded that the Chamber of Geodesists and Cartographers[99] had restricted competition by the adoption of a price list involving recommended prices. The recommended prices were applied in practice by members of the Chamber, in contracts with clients, and at the same time the Chamber monitored their adherence; in fact, the Chamber imposed sanctions for a violation of the recommended prices. The AMO reviewed whether coordination of the activities in the market in the pricing area was necessary for a high-quality performance of their profession, for geodesists and cartographers, whereby it came to the conclusion that such coordination was not indispensable. Describing the violation of the antitrust rules by the decision of association, the AMO used argumentation from the EU case law as it stated:

> The evaluation of the issue, whether a decision is aimed at a restriction of competition, depends on several factors. The aim of the competition restriction itself may be deduced from circumstances/subject-matter of the decision, contemplated aim of the decision and from the legal and economic contexts of the behaviour of the parties.... It results from the established case law of the European Court of Justice (ECJ) that a decision of the association of undertakings consisting in a recommendation may be in conflict with Article 81(1) of the Treaty, specifically, provided that the recommendation at issue coordinates behaviour of members of the association on the relevant market, even despite its recommendatory nature. ... The European Court of Justice states in its next decision that despite the fact that the determined prices have not been applied in practice, the decision of the association of undertakings in the matter of the determination of prices is aimed at competition restriction. ... The decision of the association of undertakings does not have to be legally binding, if it factually binds its members. Even such recommendation, which contains no sanctions for a failure to observe it, may be considered to be a decision of the association of undertakings being in conflict with Article 81(1) of the Treaty. Such recommendation of the association of undertakings, which demonstrates the will of the association

98. Section 4(2) letter a) of the CA.

99. Decision of the AMO No. 2007/KH/1/1/108, 21 Dec. 2007, <http://www.antimon.gov.sk>.

of undertakings to coordinate behaviour of its members on the respective relevant market, may also be in conflict with Article 81(1) of the Treaty.[100]

The AMO so far issued only one guideline concerning the assessment agreements restricting competition. It is the Vertical agreements restricting by object guideline[101] which provide also information concerning the assessment and evaluation of RPM agreements. There is no other guidance or recommendations concerning the assessment of individual 'forms' and 'types' of agreements restricting competition; thus, the rules followed by the AMO for the assessment are included in the EU guidelines, recommendations, notices or in the EU case law.

44. The invalidity of the cartel agreement can be derived directly from the prohibition of the general clause.[102] Nevertheless, the only authority that can declare the invalidity of a contract for sure is a civil court on the basis of a private law action. The invalidity can be established only in relation to those agreements that meet conditions of a legal act in the sense of the civil law. In principle, it is thus excluded to claim invalidity of the 'concerted practices'.

An agreement restricting competition can be invalid either as a whole or only partially. If only a part of an agreement is prohibited, it is possible to separate it from the rest of the agreement, if the rest of the agreement is individually capable of its 'next life' as such.[103]

45. Appreciable effect on competition

As an agreement restricting competition will not be treated behaviour which has only negligible impact on competition on the market. According section 4(2) of the CA 'Agreement between undertakings, concerted practice and decision by association of undertakings does not constitute an agreement restricting competition if its effect on competition is not appreciable. Agreement between undertakings, concerted practice and decision by the association of undertakings does not constitute an appreciable effect on competition if the market shares of undertakings being parties to the agreement, concerted practice or decision by the association of undertakings do not exceed the thresholds set by the Office in the generally binding legal regulation. If the agreement between undertakings, concerted practice or decision by the association of undertakings has the restriction of competition as its object, it does constitute an appreciable effect on competition.'

46. Prohibitions (section 4(4) of the CA):

---

100. Decision of the AMO No. 2007/KH/1/1/108 21 Dec. 2007, <http://www.antimon.gov.sk>, translation by author.
101. The AMO, in Slovak: 'Cieľové vertikálne dohody (Pohľad PMÚ SR)', <http://www.antimon.gov.sk/data/files/422_cielove-vertikalne-dohody-pohlad-pmu-sr.pdf>.
102. Section 4(1) of the CA.
103. Section 6(2) of the CA: 'If the reason for prohibition pursuant section 4(1) is only related to part of an agreement between undertakings or decision by an association of undertakings, then only that particular part shall be deemed prohibited, provided that it follows from the content of this agreement or the content of this decision by the association that the aforementioned part can be separated from the remaining content.'

The non-exhaustive list of section 4(4) of the Competition Act demonstrates such types of undertakings' activities which can be highly supposed to belong under the prohibition defined by the general clause; possibly concerning the 'most common' types of restrictive agreements. According to section 4(4) of the Competition Act:

Agreements restricting competition that involve:

(a) direct or indirect fixing of prices or other trade conditions;
(b) commitment to limit or control production, sales, technical development, or investments;
(c) division of the market or sources of supply;
(d) commitment by the parties to the agreement that different conditions relating to an identical or comparable performance will be applied to individual undertakings, which will or may disadvantage these undertakings in competition;
(e) conditions stipulating that the conclusion of contracts will require the parties to accept further obligations that are not related to the subject of these contracts in terms of their nature or according to customary commercial practice; or
(f) signs of collusive behaviour as a result of which undertakings coordinate their behaviour in the process of public procurement, in public tender or in other similar tendering procedure, in connection with public procurement, public tender or other similar tendering procedure;

shall be prohibited in particular.

47. *Ex lege* exemption (section 45) of the CA):

(3) The section 4(1) prohibition shall not apply to agreements restricting competition which at the same time:

(a) contribute to improving the production or distribution of goods or to promoting technical or economic progress whereby allow consumers a fair share of the resulting benefit;
(b) do not impose on the parties to the agreement restricting competition such restrictions that are not indispensable to the attainment of the objectives of the agreement;
(c) do not afford the parties to the agreement restricting competition the possibility of eliminating competition in respect of a substantial part of the goods in question on the relevant market.

§2. Dominant Undertakings

48. Definition of dominance (section 8(1) of the CA):

A dominant position on the relevant market is held by an undertaking or several undertakings that are not subject to substantial competition or can act independently as a result of their economic power.

49. Subject matter (section 8(2) of the CA):
Abuse of a dominant position on the relevant market is defined mainly as:

(a) direct or indirect enforcement of excessive prices or other unfair trading conditions;
(b) restriction of production, sale or technological development of goods to the detriment of users;
(c) application of dissimilar conditions to identical or comparable transactions with individual undertakings through which these undertakings are or may be placed at a competitive disadvantage;
(d) tying in the conclusion of a contract with the condition that the other party accepts supplementary obligations unrelated to the subject of the contract by their nature or according to commercial usage.

§3. Concentrations

50. The definition of concentration and the notion of control (section 9(1) to (5) and (8) of the CA):

(1) For the purpose of this Act, concentration means the process of economic combining of undertakings on a lasting basis through:

(a) a merger or amalgamation of two or more separate undertakings; or
(b) acquiring of direct or indirect control by an undertaking or several undertakings over another undertaking or part of another undertaking or undertakings.

(2) For the purpose of this Act, a merger or amalgamation within the meaning of subsection 1(a) means a merger or amalgamation pursuant to special legislation,[104] as well as a merger or amalgamation whereby the undertakings concerned become economically combined, while retaining their legal independence, especially in the case of the existence of joint economic management.
(3) For the purpose of this Act, a part of an undertaking within the meaning of subsection 1(b) means assets from which turnover may be attained.
(4) Control within the meaning of subsection 1(b) means the ability to exercise controlling influence over the activities of an undertaking, especially by means of:

(a) ownership or other rights to the undertaking or part thereof;
(b) rights, contracts or other facts allowing the exercise of controlling influence on the composition, voting or decisions of the decision-making bodies of the undertaking.

104. Section 69(3) of the CC.

(5) Concentration within the meaning of subsection 1(b) also means the establishment of a joint venture jointly controlled by two or more undertakings if the respective joint venture on a lasting basis performs all functions of an independent economic entity.

(6) Concentration does not arise when:

(a) banks, branches of foreign banks, other financial institutions or insurance companies, the normal activities of which include trading in securities on their own account or on the account of others, temporarily acquire securities with an intention to resell them, which enables them to acquire control over another undertaking or part thereof, if they do not exercise voting and other rights with the intention to influence competitive behaviour of that undertaking, or if they exercise these voting rights only with the intention of preparing the sale of the entire undertaking or part thereof or the sale of securities, provided that this sale is effected within one year counted from the date of acquisition of the securities; based on an undertaking's request, the Office shall issue a decision by which the one-year time limit may be extended if it is proven that the sale of securities was not possible within this time limit;

(b) temporary acquisition of control over another undertaking or part thereof ensues from special legislation.[105]

51. The threshold criteria for notification of a concentration as well as principles of turnover calculation are specified in sections 10(1) to (7) of the CA (for details *see* Part III, Chapter 3, §1).

52. The notion of 'one single group' is defined in section 10(4) of the CA. In order to determine whether undertakings belong to the same economic group, the AMO examines relations of direct or indirect control defined in section 9(4) of the CA (*see* the point 50 above).

53. Prohibition to exercise the rights and obligations arising from concentration (section 10(1+) to (14) of the CA):

(14) An undertaking may not exercise the rights and obligations resulting from a concentration, before the decision on the concentration becomes legally valid.

(15) The prohibition pursuant to subsection 11 does not preclude the right of selected bidders in a public tender[106] to make their bid, provided that the acquirer does not exercise its voting rights arising in connection with the implementation of the bid.

(16) The prohibition pursuant to subsection 11 also does not preclude the realization of an acquisition bid or realization of more transactions with securities at the

105. For example, ss 70–75 of the CC; s. 8 of Act No. 328/1991 Coll. on Bankruptcy and Settlement as amended.

106. Sections 281–288 of the CC.

securities market,[107] through which a control pursuant to section 9(1)(b) is acquired from various subjects, provided that:

(a) such a concentration is immediately notified to the Office, pursuant to section 7;
(b) the acquirer of the control does not exercise its voting rights connected with these securities or it only does so to maintain the full value of these investments based on the exemption granted by the Office pursuant to section 14.

54. Decisions on concentration (sections 12(1) to (3), 12(9) and (11) of the CA):

(1) The Office shall issue a decision approving concentration if the concentration does not significantly distort effective competition in the relevant market, mainly due to the creation or strengthening of dominant position.

(2) The Office shall issue a decision approving concentration pursuant to section 9(6) if the concentration complies with subsection 1 and coordination of competitive behaviour is not prohibited according to section 4(1).

(3) The Office shall also issue a decision approving concentration if the condition imposed in the decision ensures that the concentration complies with subsection 1 or 2. In its decision, the Office may impose on the parties to the proceedings an obligation related to that condition, especially in order to ensure the fulfilment of the imposed condition, the achievement of its purpose, or control its fulfilment.

(9) The Office shall prohibit a concentration which would significantly distort competition in the relevant market mainly due to the creation or strengthening of dominant position.

(10) The Office shall prohibit a concentration within the meaning of section 9(6) if the concentration would significantly distort competition in the relevant market mainly due to the creation or strengthening of dominant position or the coordination of competitive behaviour was inconsistent with the provisions of Article 4(1).

(11) A decision referred to subsections 1–3 shall be deemed to cover competition restrictions that are directly related to a concentration and essential for implementing the concentration.

107. For example, Act No. 566/2001 Coll., Act No. 429/2002 Coll. on the Stock Exchange as amended.

§4. Other Prohibitions

55. Other forms of unlawful restrictions of competition (section 39 of the CA):

> State administration authorities in the exercise of state administration, local government authorities in the exercise of self-administration and transferred exercise of state administration, and special interest bodies in the exercise of transferred exercise of state administration must not provide evident support giving advantage to certain undertakings or otherwise restrict competition.

56. The AMO is also entitled to assess and fine activities of public entities, state administration authorities, local government authorities as well as special interest bodies, if they restrict competition. Anticompetitive measures of state administration bodies and municipalities are thus assessed according to section 39 of the CA, within a formal administrative proceeding. If any restriction of competition is proved, all these public authorities can be fined up to EUR 66,000 according to section 38(2) of the CA.

The Regional Court in Bratislava in its judgment[108] related to the breach of section 39 by the City of Zvolen concluded that: 'any activity of state administration authorities, or local government authorities or special interest bodies is subject to an assessment power of the Office. It therefore concerns also the issuance of generally binding regulations of local government, regardless of whether it concerns the exercise of state administration or transferred state administration'.[109] In this case, the City of Zvolen gave, by its generally binding regulation, the priority to the connection of customers to a central heat source, whereby it discriminated other alternative sources of heat.

The AMO concluded that also only a potential restriction of competition by public authorities was covered by section 39 of the CA and that for the assessment of any behaviour, it was decisive that a certain subject distorted conditions of competition by its administrative act.[110] Additionally it is not for determining whether any undertakings were excluded from the market or not.[111]

Pursuant to section 39 of the CA, the AMO assessed activities of public authorities such as:

(1) The municipality of the city district Bratislava Nové Mesto issued a negative opinion to the company *Enotrade*, which planned to open a pharmacy in the premises of the *Tehelná Polyclinic*. The reason for the negative opinion was that another pharmacy already provided its services in the premises of the respective polyclinic. The AMO concluded that the behaviour of the Municipality led to an

108. Judgment of the Regional Court in Bratislava No. 2S 11/2007-57, 18 Sep. 2009, <http://www.antimon.gov.sk>.
109. Judgment of the Regional Court in Bratislava No. 2S 11/2007-57, 18 Sep. 2009, <http://www.antimon.gov.sk>, translation by author.
110. Decision of the Council No. 2009/39/R/2/027, 15 May 2009, <http://www.antimon.gov.sk>.
111. Decision of the Council No. 2009/39/R/2/027, 15 May 2009, <http://www.antimon.gov.sk>.

artificial restriction of competition and an elimination of the customers' possibility to choose between several suppliers.[112]

(2) The City of Stará L'ubovňa issued a generally binding regulation related to the heat supply, by which it precluded the chance of customers to disconnect from the central source of heat and restricted the possibility to be supplied by individual sources of heat.[113]

(3) The municipality of the city district of Bratislava Staré Mesto restricted competition by concluding a long-term contract with the company *Bratislavská parkovacia služba* (a company leases parking places in the centre of the City of Bratislava) allowing this company to provide parking places amounting to nearly 50% of all places in the centre of the City of Bratislava.[114]

§5. Test of Illegality

I. Per se Prohibitions and Naked Restraints

57. The rule of per se prohibition does not directly result from the CA. However, the case law evently incorrectly and by simplification resorts to this term referring to the EU case law, according to which a restriction of competition is automatically supposed in relation to some types of agreements, mainly hard-core cartels such as price-fixing, market-partitioning or bid-rigging.

The structure of the CA, however, supposes the application of the object/effect doctrine also in assessing the so-called hard-core cartels; that is, the CA does not assume that hard-core cartels are, per se, illegal and prohibited. All agreements, concerned practices, as well as decisions of associations, must be reviewed in line with the legal definition of the general clause (section 4(1) of the CA). Even if an agreement restricting competition is defined as a hard-core agreement, the AMO is obliged to describe its effect on economic competition in terms of the object/effect doctrine every time. This means that only a brief statement that the agreement is by its nature restrictive is not sufficient, even though it is the current practice of the AMO not to provide any relevant reasoning of the conclusion that the agreement is restrictive by object and the AMO continues to use more formalistic approach during the assessment;[115] the competition authority must present which specific effects in the terms of the object/ effect doctrine the agreement invokes (*see* Part I, Chapter 3, §1).

112. Decision of the Council No. 2008/39/R/2/018, 7 Mar. 2008, <http://www.antimon.gov.sk>.
113. Decision of the Council No. 2009/39/R/2/027, 15 May 2009, <http://www.antimon.gov.sk>.
114. Decision of the AMO No. 2008/39/1/1/103, 27 Nov. 2008, <http://www.antimon.gov.sk>.
115. Decision of the AMO No. 2014/KH/1/1/041, 19 Dec. 2014 repealed by the decision of the Council No. 2016/KH/R/2/003, 4 Feb. 2016 and final Decision of the AMO on suspension of the proceedings No. 2016/Z/1/1/051, 8 Nov. 2016.

II. Balancing Test

58. The *ex lege* exemption defined by section 4(5) of the CA represents one of the exemptions from the ban to conclude an agreement restricting competition, defined by the CA (prohibition of section 4(1) of the CA). The assessment of the criteria defined by section 4(5) of the CA (these are in line with Article 101(3) of TFEU, ex Article 81(3) of the EC Treaty) for the application of the *ex lege* exemption could be treated as a Balancing test sui generis. However, balancing is not made in relation to pros and cons of the agreement in general, but the review is focused on the fulfilment of advantages and disadvantages described directly in section 4(5) of the CA, which stipulates as follows:

The section 4 (1) prohibition shall not apply to agreements restricting competition which at the same time:

(a) contribute to improving the production or distribution of goods or to promoting technical or economic progress whereas allow consumers a fair share of the resulting benefit;
(b) do not impose such restrictions on the parties to the agreement restricting competition that are not indispensable to the attainment of the objectives of the agreement;
(c) do not afford the parties to the agreement restricting competition the possibility of eliminating competition in respect of a substantial part of the goods in question in the relevant market.

59. In 2007, the AMO assessed several types of distribution agreements concluded between *Heineken Slovensko* (the Slovak beer producer) and operators of Hotel/ Restaurant/Café (HORECA).[116] One of the assessed agreements was the investment agreement on mutual cooperation which is one of basic agreements, which Heineken Slovensko concludes with operators of HORECA. The cooperation according to the assessed agreement includes provisions based on which *Heineken Slovensko* provides operators of HORECA with equipment such as cooling systems, beer parlour equipment, fridges, equipment for summer terraces and marketing and promotional materials. On the other hand, the operator of HORECA accepts provisions, by which it is bound to buy products exclusively from *Heineken Slovensko*. The AMO assessed the fulfilment of four cumulative criteria defined by the CA, whereby it came to the conclusion that (i) the mentioned agreements are treated under the competition rules as special agreements taking into consideration particularities of the beer distribution market, distribution to HORECA, (ii) the agreement provides financial, material and commercial benefits to operators of HORECA and facilitates the establishment, modernization and maintenance of HORECA, (iii) moreover the agreement facilitates coordination between the parties to the business relation and can lead to a decrease of costs of distribution on both sides.

The AMO further stated that the obligation to buy products exclusively from *Heineken Slovensko* has been imposed with the aim of not allowing competitors of *Heineken Slovensko* to use benefits provided to the operator of HORECA and to

116. Decision of the AMO No. 2007/ZK/1/1/084, 10 Oct. 2007, <http://www.antimon.gov.sk>.

safeguard the return of investments made by *Heineken Slovensko* by regular supplies to HORECA. The AMO concluded that the exclusivity provisions are allowed because they handle the so-called free-riding problem. The exclusivity is also justified by the fact that the incurred investments (investments in equipment, summer terrace, services improving quality of sale) made by *Heineken Slovensko* in each supplier-buyer relation are specific, relate to respective HORECA premises and are asymmetric, whereas it is the supplier who invests more than the buyer. The AMO came to the conclusion that these investments were so specific that upon a termination of the contract, they cannot be used elsewhere. Based on these findings, the AMO drew the conclusion that the criteria defined by section 6(3) letters a), b) and c) of the CA are met; however, a deep economic analysis of the said criteria is missing in the AMO's decision.

The AMO assessed also the last criterion according to which the *ex lege* exemption can be granted, provided that it does not eliminate competition in respect of a substantial part of goods (section 6(3) letter d) of the CA). The AMO concluded that despite the high market share of *Heineken Slovensko* which has been above 30% and the existence of a cumulative effect of similar agreements, the position of *Heineken Slovensko* and its distribution network is compensated by the fact that operators of HORECA could terminate the respective contract any time. Furthermore, the risk of an elimination of 'intra-brand' competition is compensated by a strong position of other beer supplier, and moreover, the exclusivity included in the contract does not represent any barrier for the entry of potential competitors. The AMO concluded that all the above-mentioned criteria for the exemption of the exclusivity in the investment agreement on mutual cooperation are met.

III. Merger Test

60. The definition of the merger test in Slovak Republic is based on the significant impediment of competition test and including the dominance test. According to section 12(1) of the CA, 'The Office shall issue a decision approving concentration if the concentration does not significantly distort effective competition in the relevant market, mainly due to the creation or strengthening of dominant position. Test of dominance is now still the leading test as it is presumed that if the dominant position is created or strengthened by the concentration, this automatically means that the concentration would negatively affect competition, i.e. significantly lessen, impede or distort competition.' The merger test was changed several times during the last decade.

Initially the merger test was based purely on the test of dominance as the AMO approved the concentration only if it did not create or strengthen dominant position resulting in significant barriers to effective competition on the market. The AMO was obliged first of all to review whether a concentration creates a dominant position on the market or it at least strengthens the already existing market dominance. The second part of the legal clause supposes that the created dominant position or strengthened dominant position results in significant barriers to effective competition. This wording of the legal sentence invoked discussions on whether it is sufficient for the AMO to prove only the dominance on the market, which automatically supposes the existence of 'significant barriers to effective competition', or an additional deep analysis of barriers to effective competition must be made. The second opinion would assume the existence of two-step assessment, that is, performance of the dominance test and at the same time of the test similar to the Substantially Lessening of Competition test, based on a purely competition-based test. Finally, the leading opinion concerning initial merger test definition was that if the creation or strengthening of the dominance on the market is determined, the 'significant barriers to effective competition' are assumed. The above-mentioned discussions were stopped by the adoption of a new merger test in January 2012 according to which the AMO could approve the concentration, if the concentration does not significantly distort effective competition in the relevant market, particularly due to creation or strengthening of the dominant position.

Chapter 4. Overview of Main Notions

§1. Undertaking

61. The term 'undertaking' is defined directly by the CA.[117] It covers any entrepreneur according to the CC:[118]

(1) any person registered in the Commercial register;
(2) person which undertakes business based on the trade permission;
(3) person which undertakes business based on other permission according to special legislation; or
(4) a natural person, sole agricultural producer registered in the evidence based on special legislation.

In addition, the term 'undertaking' under the CA comprises any natural and/or legal person, their associations and associations of these associations, with respect to their activities and conduct that are, or may be, related to competition, regardless of whether or not these activities and conduct are aimed at making profit.

62. Despite the fact that the Slovak competition law is in line with the EU competition rules, the current legal definition of the term 'undertaking' under the Slovak law does not fully correspond with the EU 'undertaking' doctrine. Even though the term 'undertaking' according to the CA is linked to all activities and conducts that are or may be related to the competition, the term 'undertaking' is at the same time limited by the fact that it covers only entities with legal personality. The only non-subject covered by the definition of 'undertaking' is the association of legal or natural persons created based on the articles of association according to the respective provisions of the Civil Code (CvC).[119] The term 'undertaking' under the CA thus involves only a person (natural or legal), but it does not cover a 'group' of individual persons forming a single economic group. This explanation was acknowledged by the Council in its decision concerning Case *GIS cartel,*[120] arguing that the concept of an undertaking under the Slovak law is understood in a different way from the EC law. The Council accepted objections of parties to the administrative proceedings related to the different understanding of the term 'undertaking' under the Slovak competition law and came to the conclusion that this difference hindered the AMO from applying joint and several liability for the breach of competition rules of the companies belonging to the same economic group, as was applied by the Commission in the same case.[121]

117. Section 3(1) of the CA.
118. Section 2(2) of the CC.
119. Sections 829–841 of the CC.
120. Decision of the Council No. 2009/KH/R/2/035, 14 Aug. 2009, §185, <http://www.antimon.gov.sk>.
121. Decision of the Commission, Case COMP/F/38.899-Gas insulated switchgear cartel, 24 Jan. 2007, <http://ec.europa.eu/competition/elojade/isef/index.cfm?fuseaction=dsp_result>.

However, the present position of the AMO is that whereas national competition law must be interpreted in conformity with EU law, the term 'undertaking' also needs to be interpreted as it covers also non-subject. Moreover, this opinion is also supported by the fact that in a last three years nearly all proceedings of the AMO were carried out in parallel according national substantive law as well as community law.

Finally, it must be noted that the amendment 2014 to the CA has included definition of 'one economic group' to the act. Even though the definition is presented in a part of the CA which concerns only merger control, it is commonly used also in cases of the breach of cartel prohibition[122] and the ban to abuse a dominant position. The definition 'one economic group' is defined by the relations of direct or indirect control pursuant section 9(4) of the CA.[123]

63. The CA also applies to professional services provided, for example, by lawyers, notaries, pharmacists and architects, and to activities of these persons. All these professionals are entrepreneurs pursuant to the CC because they undertake businesses based on permission, according to special legislation. The case law of the AMO is related mainly to the assessment of agreements restricting competition, concluded in the form of a decision of association. The assessment of the anticompetitive conduct thus covers the review of rules regulating the performance of professional services applied by professional associations or chambers. The case law of the AMO as well as Slovak courts acknowledged that autonomous professional associations had to be treated as undertakings under the CA.

The Slovak Bar Association (the SBA) claimed, within the administrative proceedings[124] concerning the imposition of a penalty for a breach of the obligation to submit information to the AMO, that it could not be treated as an undertaking according to the CA. It reasoned that the SBA was neither an entrepreneur according to the CC, nor any entity whose activities were connected to competition. Moreover, the SBA claimed that it only grouped all advocates listed in its register, whereby, these advocates could not be treated as competitors since conditions of the provision of legal services were determined by the state in the public interest with the aim of safeguarding their quality. At the same time, the SBA reasoned that the amount of remuneration for legal services was determined by the general legal regulation or by an agreement between the advocate and client; thus, the economic competition influenced by price or advertisement was not present.

The Council disagreed with the reasoning of the SBA by concluding that: (i) advocates were entrepreneurs pursuant to section 2(2) letter c) of the CC, (ii) the SBA was, pursuant to the Act on Advocacy, an autonomous professional organization grouping all advocates, and so it represented an association of undertakings according to section 3(2) of the CA.

---

122. For example s. 38d(6) of the CA concerning the Leniency programme.
123. 'Control ... means the ability to exercise a controlling influence on the activities of an undertaking, especially by means of: a) ownership rights or other rights; b) rights, contracts or other facts allowing the exercising of a controlling influence on the composition, voting or decisions of the undertaking's bodies.'
124. Decision of the Council No. 2005/SP/2/139, 21 Dec. 2005, <http://www.antimon.gov.sk>.

The Council supported its arguments by the Judgment of the ECJ,[125] in which the ECJ ascertained that the Dutch Bar Association was treated as an association of undertakings under competition rules whereas its members carried on economic activities.

The Regional Court in Bratislava acknowledged the opinion of the AMO that an autonomous organization of professionals was treated as an undertaking according to the CA in its Judgment concerning the imposition of a penalty on the Chamber of Notaries for its failure to submit required documents.[126]

64. Furthermore, public entities also fall under the term 'undertaking', provided that their conduct may be related to competition. This is, for example, usual in merger control cases when public entities (such as, for example, the Ministry of Transport, Post and Telecommunications, Ministry of Economy, National Property Fund of the Slovak Republic) exercise sole or a joint control over private entities. However, it is more common that the AMO reviews activities of public entities according to section 39 of the CA (*see* Part I, Chapter 3, §4).

In the '*Humbel and Edel*' case,[127] the Court of Justice stated that the establishment and maintenance of a public education system is one of the tasks of the State, the goal of which is not to achieve profit but to serve citizens. The conclusions made be the competition authorities in relation to health insurance companies in the performance of the public health insurance activity, which are, according to the AMO, only a kind of managers of entrusted public funds, should also be seen in this context. This opinion has been established by the AMO when reviewing the notified concentration of the health insurance companies Dôvera and Apollo,[128] while referring to the decision-making practice of the Court of Justice when stating that:

> economic activity consists in an offer of goods and services in a market, whereby it differs from a sovereign activity performed within the framework of the 'exercise of public authority', while the criterion decisive for differentiation is the nature of the activity being performed. It is therefore necessary to analyze a specific activity on a case-by-case basis in order to determine in which category the specific activity belongs. Thus, the identification of a certain entity as an enterprise under the European Law depends on the nature of the activity being performed by it. A certain entity may thus be considered during the performance of certain activities to be an enterprise under the competition law, while it will not be subject to the competition law during the performance of other activities.[129]

125. Judgment of the European Court of Justice, C-309/99, 19 Feb. 2002, <http://www.curia.europa.eu>.
126. Judgment of the Regional Court in Bratislava No. 1S 431/2005-43, 2 Oct. 2008, <http://www.antimon.gov.sk>.
127. Judgment of the Court of Justice, C-263/86 *Belgian State v. René Humbel and MarieThérèseEdel*, (1988) ECR I-05365, point 18, <http://www.curia.europa.eu>.
128. Decision of the AMO No.2009/ZK/3/1/059, 14 Dec. 2009, <http://www.antimon.gov.sk>.
129. Decision of the AMO No. 2009/ZK/3/1/059, 14 Dec. 2009, p. 11, <http://www.antimon.gov.sk>.

In relation therewith, it is possible to refer also to other services, the provision of which has not been considered to be the performance of an economic activity, such as, for instance, sickness funds and social insurance system,[130] or pension funds.[131]

§2. Relevant Market

65. The relevant market must be properly defined in each antitrust case and also in merger control cases. The CA contains the definition of the relevant market[132] as well as the individual definitions of the product[133] and geographical relevant markets.[134] All definitions introduced by the CA are in accordance with the principles and rules presented by the Commission's Notice on relevant market.[135] The relevant market is determined with respect to its product and the geographical aspect as a geographical and temporal concurrence of the supply of and demand for goods that are identical or mutually interchangeable with respect to the satisfaction of certain needs of users. The term 'goods' covers any products, performances, works and services.

Consequently, a product relevant market comprises identical or mutually interchangeable goods (according to the legal definition, mutually interchangeable goods are goods that are interchangeable among themselves, especially from the viewpoint of their physical and technical characteristics, price, and purpose of use) that can satisfy certain needs of users. The product aspect of the relevant market is thus defined on the basis of the assessment of the demand substitution (assessment of the price and cross-elasticity of demand, application of Small but Significant Non-transitory Increase in Prices (SSNIP test) and supply substitution (mainly assessment of potential competition and the ability and the likelihood of the potential competitors supplying the market with competing products in a relatively short time-period and free of substantial costs). The relevant market is determined on a case-by-case basis, and its definition might also be very narrow. For example, the AMO, in the case *Slovenské aerolínie*[136] (Slovak Airlines), defined individual product markets such as the regular domestic air passenger transport relevant market or the regular international air passenger transport relevant market. In the case *Slovenské telekomunikácie*[137] (Slovak fixed line telecommunication incumbent), the AMO defined the relevant market from the product aspect as the relevant market of specific users' programmes (tariffs plans) of three telecom operators (incumbent and two mobile operators), and sustained the narrow definition of the product relevant market by the fact that the respective

130. Judgment of the Court of Justice, joined cases C-264-01, C-306/01, C-354/01 a C-355/01 *AOK Bundesverband*, (2004) ECR I-02493, point 18, <http://www.curia.europa.eu>.
131. Judgment of the Court of Justice, C-67/96 *AlbanyInternational BV v. StichtingBedrijfspensioenfondsTextielindustrie*, (1999) ECR I-05751, <http://www.curia.europa.eu>.
132. Section 3(2) of the CA.
133. Section 3(3) of the CA.
134. Section 3(4) of the CA.
135. Commission Notice on the Definition of the Relevant Market for the Purposes of Community Competition Law, OJ C 372, 9 Dec. 1997, 5–13.
136. Decision of the AMO No. 2003/FK/3/1/133, 2 Jul. 2003, <http://www.antimon.gov.sk>.
137. Decision of the AMO No. 2003/ZK/2/1/157, 12 Nov. 2003, <http://www.antimon.gov.sk>.

tariff plans were used only by a specific group of persons such as old age pensioners, people with lower income or students.

66. Relevant geographical market represents a territory in which conditions for competition are homogeneous and which can be separated from other territories with different conditions for competition. The geographical definition of the relevant market can be local – covering only some regions of Slovak Republic[138] or even defined by the telecommunications network or electric energy distribution network,[139] or a regular bus line,[140] nationwide or even broader.

67. The temporal aspect of the relevant market is determined in the AMO's decision only if the supply and the demand on the market are influenced by seasonality (e.g., a sugarbeet season)[141] or by other terminable circumstances.

68. It is necessary to mention that the AMO, in its decision-making practice concerning the hard-core cartels, does not specify the relevant market in detail. Pursuant the opinion of the AMO, in cases of agreements restricting competition by object, it is sufficient to provide even wider relevant market definition as negative impact of the hard-core cartel on competition is presumed, so the further analysis of the relevant market is not necessary. Similarly, in merger control cases in which the deeper analysis of the impact on the market is not necessary, the AMO applies to only a wider market definition.

69. The relevant markets are also defined for the purpose of *ex-ante* regulation of the electronic communications networks and/or services. The list of relevant markets which are subject to *ex-ante* regulation is defined by the decision of Regulatory Authority for Electronic Communications and Postal Services of the Slovak Republic (TO SR) based on the Commission's recommendation and in line with the competition law principles.[142] The TO SR is obliged to consult its relevant market definition with the AMO[143] whereas the AMO is not bound by the relevant market definitions for *ex-ante* regulation, that is, it is authorized to depart from the relevant market definition determined by the TO SR's decision on relevant markets.

§3. Market Power/Dominant Position

70. The definition of the dominant position on the market can be the most complicated aspect of the assessment of behaviour of the undertaking in cases of the abuse of a dominant position, and could be also a complicated question in appraisals of concentrations and their impact on the market.

71. The definition of the dominant position is included directly in the CA, according to which an undertaking, or several undertakings, that are not subject to substantial competition or can act independently, has a dominant position as a result

138. Decision of the Chairman No. 2002/ZK/P/2/033, 28 Feb. 2002; Decision of the AMO No. 2001/DZ/B/1/214, 25 Jun. 2001, <http://www.antimon.gov.sk>.
139. Decision of the AMO No. 2002/FH/3/1/175, 28 Aug. 28, <http://www.antimon.gov.sk>.
140. Decision of the AMO No. 2003/ZK/1/1/162, 18 Jun. 2003, <http://www.antimon.gov.sk>.
141. Decision of the AMO No. 2002/KH/1/2/087, 15 Feb. 2002, <http://www.antimon.gov.sk>.
142. Section 11(3) of the Act No. 351/2011 Coll. Electronic CommunicationsAct, (ECA).
143. Section 8(1) letter c) of the ECA.

of its economic power. The definition of the dominance is based on the concept of 'economic strength/economic power' and its determination is subject to assessment of several criteria such as: structure of the relevant market (market concentration, market transparency, product homogeneity),[144] barriers to entry,[145] level of innovations (manufacturing and technological),[146] stability of market shares of main competitors,[147] strategic aims of competitors on the market,[148] differences in costs and cost structure,[149] market shares of the undertakings, number of rivals as well as their position and market shares, size of the distribution network, possession of the essential facility, ownership of strategic premises (e.g., storage capacities),[150] vertical integration of the undertaking, access to financial resources, contractual relations with customers, ease to switch to substitute products, etc. These criteria are not included in the CA but issued from the AMO's case law. The former Economic Competition Act No. 188/1994 contained rebuttable presumption, according to which an undertaking has a dominant position if it possesses 40% market share on the relevant market. This presumption is not currently included in the CA; nevertheless, it is still used as a rule of thumb along with the proper consideration of all above-described relevant factors.

72. Based on the CA, the dominant position can be held by one undertaking individually as well as by several undertakings – a collective dominance. The Supreme Court in the judgment[151] by which it confirmed the AMO's negative decision on concentration of companies Südzucker AG and Saint-Luis Sucre, S.A.[152] acknowledged that the AMO is entitled to follow EU case law in assessing the existence of collective dominance on the market. According to its statement:

> Administrative authorities as well as the claimant depart from the definition of this notion in the case law of the European Commission or from the one lately rendered in the decision by the European Court of Justice revising the Commission decision prohibiting the planned merger between Airtours and First Choice ... as follows:

(a) each member of the dominant oligopoly must have the ability to knowhow the other members are behaving in order to monitor whether or not they are adopting

144. Decision of the AMO No. 2002/FH/1/3/046, 19 Mar. 2002, 21–24, <http://www.antimon.gov.sk>.
145. Decision of the AMO No. 2002/FH/1/3/046, 19 Mar. 2002, <http://www.antimon.gov.sk>.
146. Decision of the AMO No. 2002/FH/1/3/046, 19 Mar. 2002, <http://www.antimon.gov.sk>.
147. Decision of the AMO No. 2001/FH/4/1/104, 27 Mar. 2001; Decision of the AMO No. 2001/FH/4/1/294, 12 Oct. 2001, <http://www.antimon.gov.sk>.
148. Decision of the AMO No. 2001/FH/4/1/104, 27 Mar. 2001; Decision of the AMO No. 2001/FH/4/1/294, 12 Oct. 2001, <http://www.antimon.gov.sk>.
149. Decision of the AMO No. 2001/FH/4/1/104, 27 Mar. 27; Decision of the AMO No. 2001/FH/4/1/294, 12 Oct. 2001, <http://www.antimon.gov.sk>.
150. Decision of the AMO No. 2006/DZ/2/1/140, 22 Dec. 2006; Decision of the Council No. 2007/DZ/R/2/102, 7 Dec. 2007, <http://www.antimon.gov.sk>.
151. Judgment of the Supreme Court of the Slovak Republic No. 4 Sž 122-123/03, 29 Apr. 2004, <http://www.antimon.gov.sk>.
152. Decision of the Council No. 2003/KH/R/2/121, 19 Jun. 2003; Decision of the AMO No. 2002/FH/3/1/272, 12 Dec. 2002, <http://www.antimon.gov.sk>.

the common policy. It is not enough for each member of the dominant oligopoly to be aware that interdependent market conduct is profitable for all of them but each member must also have a means of knowing whether the other operators are adopting the same strategy and whether they are maintaining it. There must, therefore, be sufficient market transparency for all members of the dominant oligopoly (duopoly) to be aware, sufficiently precisely and quickly, of the way in which the other members' market conduct is evolving; and at the same time;

(b) the situation of tacit coordination must be sustainable over time, that is to say, there must be an incentive not to depart from the common policy on the market. It is only if all the members of the dominant oligopoly (duopoly) maintain the parallel conduct that all can benefit. The notion of retaliation in respect of conduct deviating from the common policy is thus inherent in this condition. For a situation of collective dominance to be viable, there must be adequate deterrents to ensure that there is a long-term incentive in not departing from the common policy, which means that each member of the dominant oligopoly (duopoly) must be aware that highly competitive action on its part designed to increase its market share would provoke identical action by the others, so that it would derive no benefit from its initiative; and at the same time;

(c) to prove the existence of a collective dominant position to the requisite legal standard, the Commission (in this case the Office) must also establish that the foreseeable reaction of current and future competitors, as well as of consumers, would not jeopardize the results expected from the common policy.

From the content of the contested reasoned decisions, it ensues that administrative authorities analysed the situation that would occur in case the concentration also resulted from the point of view of collective dominance. From their conclusions, it follows that:

(a) the concentration would create such structure and character of the relevant market as would facilitate the coordination of behaviour among independent players on the market. The market after the concentration is sufficiently transparent and allows both undertakings to survey the situation on the market and the activities of competitors. The product being the object of concentration is homogenous, which contributes to higher transparency on the market and facilitates the coordination of behaviour;

(b) the relevant market in question is on the whole a depressed one, with a low level of innovation and high barriers to enter the sector, so significant changes in competition conditions are not likely to occur. […] The structure and the character of the relevant market in question, after concentration the likelihood is of both undertakings creating a natural incentive to give preference to a long-term mutual coordination on the market over competitive struggle because their eventual competition would lead to a loss of profit;

(c) this possibility is at the same time a sufficient argument to deter the undertakings from departing from their policy on the market.

73. According to the AMO's case law concerning the merger control (the AMO has not determined a collective dominant position in any case of the abuse of a dominant position so far) and the EU case law, the following factors will mainly be taken into consideration in determining the joint dominance by the AMO: product homogeneity, market transparency, market concentration, maturity of the market, level of innovations, similarity of cost structure, multi-market contacts, economic and structural links between undertakings.

§4. Agreements and Concerted Practices

74. 'Agreements between undertakings', 'concerted practices' and 'decisions of associations of undertakings' are referred to by the CA under the legislative expression 'agreements restricting competition' and if their objective or effect is or may be a restriction of competition, then are prohibited, unless the CA provides otherwise. All three types of agreements restricting competition are defined by the CA and from their definitions as well as from the AMO's case law results, we see that:

- The 'agreement between undertakings' can be any written or even a verbal agreement, formalized (having all essentials required by the law or even lacking the formalities prescribed by the law for certain types of contracts) or not precise, legally enforceable[153] or only a gentleman's agreement, by which parties express their will/consent to behave in a certain manner on the market, that is, there is a common understanding ('meeting of minds') to achieve a common result. The agreement between undertakings may comprise not only a single isolated act but also a series of acts.[154]
- The 'concerted practice' represents a certain level of coordination of the market activities which still does not bear signs of the 'agreement between undertakings' which replaces independent market behaviour. It must be borne in mind that the existence of parallel behaviour among undertakings on the market is not sufficient to arrive at a conclusion regarding prohibited conduct. The Council of the Office, in its decision concerning the GIS cartel, described 'concerted practice' as follows: 'Concerted practice can be at a place even where, although not subscribing to a common plan determining their market behaviour, the parties consciously adhered or adapted to collusive intention that facilitates the coordination of their common commercial behaviour ... Thus, an agreement restricting competition in the form of concerted practice is a form of coordination between undertakings, without having reached the stage where a so-called proper agreement has been concluded,

153. The Council in the GIS cartel decision stated that the concept of an 'agreement' does not require the same degree of legal certainty as it is needed for the purposes of civil or business law. Decision of the Council No. 2009/KH/R/2/035, 14 Aug. 2009, §474, <http://www.antimon.gov.sk>.

154. Decision of the Council No. 2009/KH/R/2/035, 14 Aug. 2009, §475, <http://www.antimon.gov.sk>.

knowingly substituting practical cooperation between them for the risks of competition.'[155]

- Furthermore, the Council concluded that the actual contents of the concept of 'agreement' and 'concerted practice' may overlap, and that is why it is not always necessary to characterize such conduct exclusively as an agreement or a concerted practice.[156]
- The 'decision of associations of undertakings' comprises any legal act of the association's body (constitution of the Associations, internal rules, guidelines or directives) by which common future behaviour on the market of members of the association is determined. Furthermore, it comprises also any non-binding recommendation of the association (of the body or person which is authorized to act on behalf of the association) to its members.

75. All mentioned types of agreements restricting competition are prohibited only if their objective or their effect is, or may be, the restriction of competition on the market. If the agreement is restricting by objective, it is not necessary to provide evidence on its potential or actual effect on the market. It is assumed that 'an agreement by object' such as, for example, horizontal price-fixing or bid-rigging (this is considered based on its legal and economic context) has a negative impact on the market.

76. The section 4(2) of the CA foresees that there are agreements of minor importance which effect on the market is not appreciable and thus are excluded from ban to conclude agreement restrictive competition as specified by section 4(1) of the CA (*de minimis* rule). The effect on the marker is not appreciable if the market shares of undertakings being parties to the agreement, concerted practice or decision by the association of undertakings do not exceed the thresholds of the AMO set by the generally binding legal regulation. The current threshold is defined by the *De minimis* decree[157] for both vertical and horizontal agreements. However, if the agreement restricting competition has the restriction of competition as its object, it is presumed that it always has an appreciable effect on competition.

77. The section 4(1) of the CA stipulates that agreements restricting competition are prohibited. It arises from the CvC[158] that a legal act which is by its content or by its object in contradiction with the law, or it evades the law or is contrary *bonos mores* (contrary to good morals), is null and void. The Slovak regulation is in this respect similar to Article 101(2) of the TFEU (ex Article 81(2) of the EC Treaty) according to which prohibited agreements are null. According to the Slovak regulation, nullity

155. Decision of the Council No. 2009/KH/R/2/035, 14 Aug. 2009, §472, <http://www.antimon.gov.sk>.
156. Decision of the Council No. 2009/KH/R/2/035, 14 Aug. 2009, §§474 and 476, <http://www.antimon.gov.sk>.
157. Decree No. 169/2014 Coll. on Laying down thresholds for determining whether an agreement between undertakings, a concerted practice between undertakings or decision of an association of undertakings have a negligible effect on competition 'Vyhláška č. 169/2014 Z.z., ktorou sa ustanovujú prahové hodnoty na určenie, či dohoda medzi podnikateľmi, zosúladený postup podnikateľov alebo rozhodnutie združenia podnikateľov má zanedbateľný účinok na hospodársku súťaž', <http://www.antimon.gov.sk/data/files/368.pdf>.
158. Section 39 of the CvC.

can be declared only in cases of agreements which fulfil requirements of legal acts according to the CvC. This means that it is not possible to declare the nullity of the concerted practice. It must be borne in mind that the only authority that can declare a nullity of the agreement is the competent civil court.

§5. Restriction of Competition

78. The term 'restriction of competition' was defined directly by the CA till its amendment in 2014 as 'any restriction placed upon the freedom of an undertaking to act in the relevant market, especially an exclusion of existing or potential competitive activities, the actual, or potential reduction of the scope of competitive activities, or distortion of conditions for competition'.[159] Even though the definition is not incorporated in the law anymore, in practice the term is used likewise.

The term 'restriction of competition' is treated as an objective category irrespective of whether a factual or a potential restriction is subject to proofs, that is, whether it is in terms of the object/effect doctrine, an agreement by which the aim to restrict competition is proved or an agreement which has an anticompetitive impact.

Section 4(1) of the CA requires that each agreement must be assessed in line with the object/effect doctrine individually and that a certain level of materiality is needed to come to the conclusion that an agreement restricts competition. The level of restriction is not defined directly by the CA, but it is supposed that if the AMO proves the existence of the aim to restrict competition or proves the existence of a potential to restrict competition, it declares the agreement as prohibited, provided that such agreement does not have only negligible effect on competition, i.e. cannot appreciably effect the competition (defined by *De minimis* decree) or is not exempted based on exemptions defined by the CA (block exemption or *ex lege* exemption).

According to the CA, a restriction of competition may be caused also by an act of state administration authorities, self-administration authorities or special interest bodies if they exercise state administration. The restriction of competition also comprises the provision of a support, giving an advantage to certain undertakings by any measures of these authorities (decisions, regulations or other legal acts) (*see* Part I, Chapter 3, §4).

§6. Monopolization and Abuse of Dominance

79. The CA does not treat the existence of the dominant position (including a monopoly, *see* Part I, Chapter 4, §3) as automatically being prohibited. The dominance as such is not prohibited because 'The existence of a dominant position does not necessarily completely exclude competition on the market; it only allows an undertaking in this position, if not to determine, than at least to affect conditions on the market, in a sensitive manner and in each case, to act regardless of any competitive pressures.'[160]

159. Section 3(1) of the Competition Act valid till its amendment by the Act No. 151/2014 Coll.

160. Decision of the Council No. 2006/DZ/R/2/055, 12 May 2006, <http://www.antimon.gov.sk>, translation by author.

However, any commercial practices and market behaviour of the dominant undertaking which has a negative impact or even a potential negative impact on the market and on the effective competition is prohibited. The Slovak competition law thus includes limits restricting the behaviour of dominant undertakings on the market and also applies the so-called special responsibility doctrine concerning the behaviour of a dominant undertaking. This was expressed by the AMO, for example, in its 2004 Annual report in this way:

Unlike other players, undertakings in a dominant position 'carry' special responsibility for their market output. [...] Control and intervention against the endeavour of undertaking possessing market strength – dominants to abuse their position and hinder new competition, is among important activities of the Office.

The Council in the case *Slovnaft* (Slovak refinery company) concluded that:

> Any undertaking that has the position of a dominant player on the defined relevant market bears a special responsibility for its actions. ... it is obliged not to discriminate its business partners, i.e. it is obliged to apply the same conditions for identical or comparable fulfilment towards its consumers. That obligation does not involve that a dominant is forced to apply uniform pricing. Nevertheless, it means that the dominant player who possesses a special responsibility for its behaviour due to its position cannot have such nontransparent system of pricing that practically allows unjustified application of different trading terms.[161]

Under Slovak competition law, any abuse of a dominant position is prohibited without a possibility of exempting such behaviour from the prohibition, as in the case of agreements restricting competition (*block exemption* or *ex lege* exemption, based on the fulfilment of the criteria defined in the law).

80. The CA comprises (section 8(2) of the CA) a demonstrative list of conducts which are treated as the abuse of a dominant position. These conducts mainly refer to pricing of the dominant undertaking (unreasonable prices[162] including predatory pricing, price discrimination or fidelity rebates), to inappropriate commercial conditions, refusal to cooperate[163]/to deal or to anticompetitive tying of products.[164]

As the autonomous subject matter, the CA until its amendment in July 2014 comprised the practice of refusal to grant access to the essential facility.[165] Currently, this abusive practice is covered by section 8(2) letter b) of the CA as one of the possible refusal to deal practices.

Even though the CA does not comprise division of abusive conduct to exclusionary or exploitative behaviour, the AMO, in its case law, uses both mentioned terms[166] (*see* Part III, Chapter 2).

161. Decision of the Council No. 2007/DZ/R/2/102, 7 Dec. 2007, <http://www.antimon.gov.sk>.
162. Decision of the Council No. 2009/DZ/R/2/017, 9 Apr. 2009, <http://www.antimon.gov.sk>.
163. Decision of the Council No. 2014/DZ/R/2/035, 5 Nov.2014, <http://www.antimon.gov.sk>.
164. Decision of the Council No. 2009/DZ/R/2/017, 9 Apr. 2009, <http://www.antimon.gov.sk>.
165. Section 8(3)–(5) of the Competition Act valid till its amendment by the Act No. 151/2014 Coll.
166. For example, Decision of the Council No. 2007/DZ/R/2/102, 7 Dec. 2007; Decision of the AMO No.2007/DZ/2/1/111, 21 Dec. 2007, <http://www.antimon.gov.sk>.

Moreover, it is worth to mention that the AMO decided some cases only based on the general clause without exact defining the anticompetitive behaviour according to the demonstrative list of section 8(2) of the CA.[167]

81. The assessment of the abuse of a dominant position in relation to network industries (telecommunications and energy sector) under the competition rules is influenced by the existence of a special sector regulation. Till the amendment of the CA in June 2009,[168] the CA comprised provisions according to which the CA did not apply to restrictions of competition, the assessment of which belonged to other administrative bodies (e.g., the TO SR and the NIO SR) that ensured protection of competition according to special regulations. Even though the respective provision is no longer valid, there is an open question for the AMO to define its competence in each individual case concerning the regulated industries, that is, to define limits between *ex-ante* and *ex-post* regulation.

§7. Concentrations

82. The term 'concentration' under the CA comprises several forms of transactions. First of them is the acquisition of direct or indirect control over another undertaking or of its part, gained by one undertaking (a single control) or by several undertakings (a joint control). The second form is the merger and the third form is a creation of full-functioned joint venture.

The concentration is subject to the merger control, provided that turnover criteria stipulated directly by the CA are met. The undertakings can submit to the AMO either a pre-notification or a notification of the concentration. Pre-notification means that undertakings notify of the transaction prior to its establishment. The notification needs to be submitted to the AMO prior to executions of rights and obligations arising from the concentration.

83. The CA stipulates that the undertakings cannot execute rights and obligations ensuing from the concentration until validation of the decision on concentration. Nevertheless, it is possible to request an exemption from this prohibition. The exemption is granted by an individual decision.

84. The merger test represents the assessment of whether a concentration significantly distort effective competition on the relevant market mainly by creating or strengthening dominant position (*see* Part I, Chapter 3, §5, III).

§8. Joint Ventures

85. The CA explicitly deals with joint ventures under the merger control provisions. There are no specific rules defined by the law for the assessment of partially functioning joint ventures. These types of joint ventures and cooperative joint ventures are reviewed under agreements restricting competition rules. The review will consist mainly of the appraisal of the horizontal effects of the cooperation and their impact

167. Decision of the Council No. 2010/DZ/R/2/049, 6 Aug. 2010, <http://www.antimon.gov.sk>.
168. Amendment of the Competition Act No. 165/2009 Coll.

on actual and/or potential competition on the market. The possibility of applying all valid exemptions (block exemptions as well as *ex lege* exemption – section 6(3) of the CA) is unaffected.

86. The CA determines that establishment of a joint venture is deemed to be a concentration if the joint venture is under the joint control of two or more undertakings and it performs all the functions of an independent economic entity, on a lasting basis.

The factors, which the AMO takes into consideration to decide on whether a notified transaction fulfils the criteria to be declared as a full-function joint venture, are listed in Part II. Chapter 3, §5 below.

Even though the joint venture is declared as a concentration, the coordination of the business behaviour of undertakings controlling the joint venture is assessed under the rules regulating agreements restricting competition. This means that the assessment of the establishment of a fully functioning joint venture comprises two tests – one is a general merger test and the second is a review of the impact of the cooperation of mother companies on the market. The concentration is approved only if this coordination is not prohibited as an agreement restricting competition.[169]

169. Section 12(2) of the CA.

Chapter 5. Consequences of Violations and Enforcement Institutions

87. The competition law in Slovak Republic is primarily enforced by the AMO within the administrative proceedings governed by the Administrative Procedure Code (APC) and the CA. Even though there are many discussions concerning the private enforcement and as well as new national legislation has been adopted[170] in line with the Directive 2014/104/EU of the European Parliament and of the Council on certain rules governing actions for damages under national law for infringements of the competition law provisions of the Member States and of the European Union, it is still underdeveloped. The same applies to the criminal enforcement.

§1. Administrative Enforcement

88. The antitrust rules are enforced by the AMO (in the Slovak language: *Protimonopolný úrad Slovenskej republiky*) the powers[171] of which are determined by the CA. The AMO is the only authority in Slovak Republic that can issue decisions on agreements restricting competition or an abuse of a dominant position, and is also responsible for merger control.

I. The Antitrust Authorities

89. As already mentioned, the AMO, independent from the Slovak government ('Government'), is the only administrative body responsible for the administrative enforcement of competition rules. Its seat is in the City of Bratislava.[172] It is the central administrative body for assuring protection and promotion of competition,[173] and it is not subordinated to any other central administrative body. The AMO was established by Act No. 347/1990 Coll. on the Organization of Ministries and Other Central Bodies of State Administration of the Slovak Republic[174] and its position as a central administrative body is governed by the Act No. 575/2001 Coll. on the Organization of the Activities of the Government and Organization of Central State Administration.[175]

170. Act No. 350/2016 Coll. on Certain Rules Concerning the Claims for Damages Caused by the Breach of Competition Rules Effective as of 27 Dec. 2016 (Act on Damages).
171. Sections 22–23 of the CA.
172. Section 14(3) of the CA.
173. Section 14(1) of the CA in connection with s. 21 letter b) of the Act No. 575/2001 Coll. on Organization of the Operation of the Government and Organization of Central State Administration.
174. Section 23 of the Act No. 347/1990 Coll. on Organization of Ministries and Other Central Bodies of State Administration of the Slovak Republic.
175. Section 21 letter b) in connection with s. 25 of the Act No. 575/2001 Coll. on Organization of the Operation of the Government and Organization of Central State Administration.

The AMO can establish permanent or temporary branch offices outside Bratislava, however there are currently none.

The AMO is also the only administrative authority which is empowered to apply EU legislation in the field of economic competition[176] (Articles 101 and 102 of the TFEU, ex Articles 81 and 82 of the EC Treaty).

A. Formation, Composition

90. The AMO is headed by the Chairperson[177] and in the case of his absence by the Deputy Chairperson, appointed and recalled by the Chairperson.[178]

The Chairperson is the statutory body of the AMO who acts on behalf of the AMO in all matters, manages and supervises the activities of the AMO[179] and participates in the regular meetings of the Government even though he is not a member of the Government and he has no right to vote.

The Deputy Chairperson, as an employee of the AMO, in case of the absence of the Chairperson, acts on his behalf, to the extent determined by the AMO's internal rules.[180] The Deputy Chairperson is at the same time responsible for submission of factual statements to the Government concerning draft materials submitted by other central administrative bodies for review (such as proposals of generally binding legal regulations). These activities are conducted by the AMO within the so-called competition advocacy. The Deputy Chairperson represents the first-degree decision-making body and is responsible for issuing of the approval to conduct inspection in business premises of an undertaking (a written authorization).

91. The Chairperson is appointed and can be recalled by the President of the Slovak Republic based on the proposal of the Government.[181] Its term of office is five years and can be appointed for a maximum of two consecutive terms of office.[182]

The Chairperson can be recalled[183] only if one of the following circumstances occurs:

(1) the Chairperson has been sentenced for an intentional criminal act or crime of negligence directly related to the performance of his function;[184]
(2) the Chairperson's legal capacity has been terminated on the basis of a legally valid court decision;[185]

176. Section 14(2) of the CA.
177. Section 22(2) of the Act No. 575/2001 Coll. on Organization of the Operation of the Government and Organization of Central State Administration, s. 15(1) of the CA.
178. Section 22(5) of the Act No. 575/2001 Coll. on Organization of the Operation of the Government and Organization of Central State Administration, s. 15(3) of the CA.
179. Organizational structure – description, in Slovak available at: <http://www.antimon.gov.sk/organizacna-struktura/>.
180. Organizational Structure, <http://www.antimon.gov.sk/organizacny-poriadok/>.
181. Section 15(2) of the CA.
182. Section 15(2) and (4) of the CA.
183. Section 16(3) of the CA.
184. Section 16(3) letter a) of the CA.
185. Section 16(3) letter b) of the CA.

(3) the Chairperson has begun to perform a function or activity incompatible with the position of the Chairperson of the AMO;[186]
(4) the Chairperson has not performed the function for a period exceeding six consecutive months due to his own fault or his health condition prevented him from doing so.[187]

The Chairperson may resign from office, and after resignation, his term of office terminates upon the appointment of a new Chairperson.[188]

92. The organizational structure of the AMO is further determined by the internal order, which specifies scope of authorizations of chief employees as well as activities and internal relations of individual departments of the AMO.[189] Activities of the AMO concerning the enforcement of antitrust rules are covered basically by three executive divisions which represent the first-degree decision-making process. These are the Cartel Division dealing only with horizontal agreements restricting competition, the Division of Abuse of a Dominant Position and Vertical Agreements and the Division of Concentrations. The executive divisions are supported by the Legislative, Legal and European Affairs Division (Legal Department), which provides internal legal services through official opinions, issues legal advice and offers consultations necessary in the decision-making process. The Legal Department acts on behalf of the AMO before courts and other state administration bodies, including public prosecution authorities.

In needs to be mentioned, that by Act No. 358/2015 Coll. on State aid, the AMO has become responsible for coordination of state aid in Slovakia and thus the separate Division of State Aid became part of the AMO.

93. The second-degree decision-making process is represented by the Council of the Office (the 'Council', in the Slovak language *Rada úradu*). The Council was established by the CA as an independent decision-making body. The Council is empowered particularly to decide on appeals, it reviews decisions outside appellate proceedings and it decides on the reopening of proceedings.[190] Before the creation of the Council, the second-degree process was represented by the Chairperson of the AMO.[191] The AMO's first-degree decisions, issued by the respective division and signed by the Deputy Chairperson as the first-degree body, can be appealed to the Council. However the two-phase decision-making process (the first instance and the second instance of the process) represent one single administrative proceeding within the AMO. All administrative support for the Council is provided by the AMO's employees, and whole communication with the parties to the administrative proceedings is handled by the administrative staff of the AMO and case handlers of the Division of Second-Instance Proceedings. The director and case handlers of this division study all materials submitted by parties to the administrative proceedings as well as third

186. Section 16(3) letter c) of the CA; s. 15(5) of the CA; Act No. 357/2004 Coll. on Protection of Public Interest at Discharge of Office of Public Officials.
187. Section 16(3) letter d) of the CA.
188. Section 16(2) of the CA.
189. In Slovak at: <http://www.antimon.gov.sk/organizacna-struktura/>.
190. Section 18(1) of the CA.
191. Section 61(2) of the APC.

parties within the first instance phase; they prepare documents for members of the Council and report on information and data included in administrative files during the Council's meetings. The meetings of the Council are irregular and their periodicity depends on the availability of the Council's members to be present in the meetings and on the amount of the submitted cases. They take place on the AMO's premises.

The Council is a collective body of seven members involving the Chairperson of the AMO (he holds the position of the Council Chairperson)[192] and six members – not employees of the AMO, appointed and recalled by the Government – based on the Chairperson's proposal.[193] At least two of the appointed persons must have a degree in law and at least two persons must have a degree in economy.[194] The term of the office of the Council's members is five years.[195] The Council makes decisions by voting at closed meetings.[196]

94. Even though the Council is established as an independent appellate body not linked to the first-degree decision-making process of the AMO, there are still discussions on whether its independence is reflected in actual practice when the Chairperson as a representative of the AMO has a right to vote on decisions and in the case of the legality of votes, the vote of the Chairperson is decisive.[197] It is not unusual that the parties to the proceedings in this respect claim breach of the principle of independence before the Council trying to exclude the Chairperson from a decision-making process. The reasoning behind this approach is based on the fact that in the past the Chairperson commented cases that have been decided on first-degree, sometimes also in the press or in its public speeches.

B. *Investigating Powers*

95. The investigative powers of the AMO are executed by the respective executive division within either a general investigation (sector inquiries or general investigations aimed at a specific undertaking) or a formal administrative procedure. These powers are specified directly by the CA (*see* Part III, Chapter 1, §2, II).

All evidence necessary for the appraisal of a specific conduct of undertakings, in line with the provisions of the CA, can be gathered only by the AMO, which means that the AMO is not empowered to delegate its investigative powers to third persons such as, for example, another administrative authority, police or a public prosecutor. However, this does not prevent the AMO to cooperate with other administrative bodies (*see* Part III, Chapter 1, §2, III).

96. The formal administrative proceedings (*see* Part III, Chapter 1, §1) is usually initiated based on the findings and evidence gathered by the AMO within a general investigation or more often within an investigation aimed at behaviour of a respective undertaking. Concerning the cartel cases, the AMO usually begins the investigation against respective undertakings by execution of inspection in business premises (so-

192. Section 18(1) of the CA.
193. Section 18(3) in connection with s. 19 of the CA.
194. Section 19(3) of the CA.
195. Section 18(4) of the CA.
196. Section 20(3) of the CA.
197. Section 20(2) of the CA.

called down-raid). When the AMO concludes, following an investigation, that the competition rules might have been breached it starts a formal administrative proceeding terminated either by a penalty decision, or by a decision in which the AMO approves measures proposed by undertakings[198] or by a decision issued according to the outcome of a Settlement procedure.[199]

97. The usual practice of the AMO at the time the Settlement has not been regulated by the CA was to award the willingness of the respective undertaking to settle by reduction of the fine with application of mitigating circumstances. For example, the AMO used the Settlement procedure in the case of a vertical distribution agreement concluded between a producer of electronic cash registers – the company ELCOM – and its distributors.[200] ELCOM applied direct (defined a minimum price for a further supply) as well as indirect price-fixing (a maximum level of discounts, which could be provided by distributors to its dealers) in its contract. The settlement was based on the fact that parties to the prohibited agreements accepted the findings of the AMO and refrained from exercising the right to file an appeal against the AMO's decision. Furthermore, the parties to the agreement accepted the AMO's findings submitted in the Statement of Objections, they acknowledged their breach of competition rules by identified behaviour and declared restrictive agreements invalid at the time of issuing the AMO's decision announcing that they were in the process of preparation of a new contract, and they did not ask the AMO to submit its statement to all their argumentation provided during the procedure. The AMO acknowledged all these declarations as mitigating circumstances which eventuated in a 50% decrease of the fine.

Nowadays, the Settlement and its conditions are directly involved in section 38f of the CA and further defined by the Decree on laying down details on Settlement.[201]

The AMO may accede to the Settlement in case of a breach of the CA (save for breaches for which disciplinary sanctions are imposed), if it is in the interest of cost-efficiency or achievement of expeditious and effective remedy, even if on one´s own initiative. In such a case, the AMO delivers a proposal to commence negotiations to a party to the proceedings. It may, however, be primarily assumed that the request for the Settlement shall be filed actively to the party to the proceedings. Negotiations regarding the Settlement may be conducted during the pending proceedings, specifically, before the party to the proceedings becomes familiar with conclusions of the proceedings pursuant to section 33 of the CA or only after the party to the proceedings receives a call prior to the decision pursuant to the said provision. In the first case, if the Settlement negotiations commence before the party to the proceedings is made familiar with results of the proceedings, the AMO shall submit preliminary conclusions to the party to the proceedings during the Settlement negotiations, to which the party to the proceedings provides its statement within a specified period. During the negotiations, the AMO shall state a breach in the proposal for the Settlement for which the party to the proceedings is blamed and description and duration of the breach, while stating an amount of the sanction planned to be imposed by the AMO. In case of consent with

198. Section 8a of the CA.
199. Section 38f of the CA.
200. Decision of the AMO No. 2009/KV/1/1/038, 21 Aug. 2009, <http://www.antimon.gov.sk>.
201. Decree No. 171/2014 of the AMO laying down details on Settlement, <http://www.antimon.gov.sk/legal-norms-in-force/>.

the proposed Settlement, the party to the proceedings shall deliver a written statement to the AMO that it has participated in the objected anticompetitive practices to the extent to which it is objected and admits its responsibility for such practices. If the content of the statement conceived in such a manner corresponds to the proposal for the Settlement, the AMO shall notify the party to the proceedings that it considers its statement to be accepted, whereby the negotiations are deemed to be completed by the Settlement. If the situation where the negotiations are not completed by the Settlement (e.g., by expiration of the period within which the party to the proceedings has been supposed to provide its statement to the proposal submitted by the AMO in vain) appears, no further requests of the party and no statements made by the party within the framework of the negotiations shall be taken into account. Despite this 'guarantee', it may only hardly be assumed that it is fully possible during further proceedings to depart from the fact that the party to the proceedings has already been ready to agree with the Settlement and admit its guilt. Failure to accede to the Settlement in the final stages of administrative proceedings may thus subsequently affect its position in further defence in the proceedings.

In cases of hard-core cartel agreements, a cartel member may be recognized a discount of a 30% sanction reduction only. In less serious cases of breaching the CA, the sanction may be decreased by up to 50%. However, following from the fact that hard-core cartel arrangements are encumbered by the highest possible sanctions, the reduction of the sanction even at the level of 30% could be sufficiently motivating. The AMO applied Settlement in an agreement restricting economic competition case concluded by the Association of Estate Agents[202] in a real estate service market. The subject matter of review was the acting consisting in the determination of prices and restriction of demand, where cartel members committed to observe the specified amount of commission and amount of an arranger fee for the provided services related to the preparation of a proposal for registration with the Properties Register. The restriction of demand consisted in the obligation that members of the Association of Estate Agents were not entitled to enter into a similar contract with the same client. The agreement restricting competition at the same time contained the obligation according to which a member of the Association was not allowed to knowingly contact a client of another association with an offer of services which had already been provided to the client by another member of the Association. For two of the parties to the proceedings, the sanction was decreased on the basis of the procedure under soft-law, while applying the then mitigating circumstance, by 30% from the sum that would otherwise be imposed on them.

C. Adjudicating Powers (Ascertaining and Sanctioning)

98. The AMO, namely its executive divisions (*see* the text above) is the only administrative authority in Slovak Republic responsible for the administrative enforcement of competition rules (except *ex-ante* regulation executed by special sector regulators, *see* Part I, Chapter 2, §2 above).

99. The administrative proceedings at the AMO consist of two-instance decision-making process. The respective executive division conducts investigations against the

202. Decision of the Council No. 2010/KH/R/2/010, 26 Feb. 2010, <http://www.antimon.gov.sk>.

respective undertaking as well as formal administrative proceedings. It is the respective division of the AMO which ascertains facts relevant for the case and subsequently the Deputy Chairperson who is a decision-making body entitled to decide whether the breach of the CA or EU Competition Law took place.

The executive division may conclude, in its decision, that an infringement of competition rules did not occur; thus, in this case, it will terminate the administrative proceedings. If the violation is proved, it imposes a penalty along with obligations (remedies) if necessary or it can approve commitments submitted by the parties to the procedure[203] or the administrative proceedings may be concluded by a settlement.

100. Each and every administrative proceeding must be terminated by a formal decision, the essentials of which are defined by the APC.[204] The decision contains the verdict, reasoning and the instruction on the possibility of challenging the decision. The lack of these prescribed essentials is one of the reasons for a revocation of the decision by the court. The decision needs to be delivered to all the parties to the administrative proceedings. The notification is made by serving a record of the decision on each party to the proceedings, if the law does not provide otherwise. The day of the delivery of the decision is deemed to be the day its record was served on the party to the proceedings.[205] The decision is valid if it cannot be appealed and it is enforceable if it cannot be appealed or the appeal does not have a suspensive effect[206] (*see* Part III, Chapter 1, §3, IV).

101. In its judgment concerning the abuse of a dominant position by the company Slovnaft (the Slovak refinery)[207] in relation to the verdict of the decision finding an infringement, the Regional Court in Bratislava stated that:

> The definition of the matter of the proceedings in the verdict of the decision must contain such a specification of the infringement as it could not be interchanged with other behaviour. This finding directly ensues from section 47 subsection 2 of the Administrative Procedure Code and requires that, in administrative decisions of a punitive character, it is essential to specifically define the conduct the person is sanctioned for. This is only possible by specifying the data describing the act with determination of the place, the time and the manner of committing it, eventually also other facts necessary to individualize the illegal behaviour. This degree of detail is essential for the proceedings mainly for the reason of determining litispendence, excluding double sanctioning for the same infringement, observing the ne bis in idem principle, determining the extent of evidence needed and also for granting the right of defence … The importance of the verdict lies in the fact that only this part of the decision is able to influence the rights and obligations of the parties to the proceedings. The verdict formulated in the appropriate manner, and specifically the description of the act contained in it, e.g. what type of behaviour, at what time and in what manner caused the infringement of a

203. Section 8a of the APC.
204. Section 47 of the APC.
205. Section 51(1) of the APC.
206. Section 52(1) of the APC.
207. Judgment of the Regional Court in Bratislava No. 3 S 9/2008, 15 Dec. 2009, 8 and 9, translation by Mgr. Bc. Daniel Uherek, Ph.D.

specific duty, is the inseparable part of the decision that should provide the information on the sanctioned actions and the sanctions imposed.

102. The AMO is also entitled to impose obligations – remedies – on undertakings with the aim of providing for effective competition on the market, assuring the status of competition before the infringement took place or preventing further anticompetitive behaviour. These remedies are imposed according to section 22(1) letter d) of the CA based on which the AMO decides on imposing the obligation to refrain from the anticompetitive conduct and the obligation to remedy the unlawful status. Due to the fact that the AMO is obliged to fine each infringement[208] (the CA includes only one exception which is the approval of commitments),[209] these remedies are always imposed along with a fine in a penalty decision. These remedies can be in general divided into behavioural remedies and structural remedies. While behavioural remedies[210] aim at determining the behaviour of the undertaking on the market (e.g., the obligation to provide access to a production capacity, or the obligation to grant the license to intellectual property rights (IPR), or the obligation to eradicate conclusion of exclusive contracts), the structural remedies aim directly at structural changes in the business of the respective undertaking (e.g., changes in the internal structure of the undertaking or changes in the organization of its business activities).

103. The first-degree decisions are prepared by case handlers of a respective executive division, under the supervision of the director of this division and signed by the Deputy Chairperson. The decisions of the AMO can be challenged by an appeal[211] submitted to the first-degree decision-making body[212] and decided on by the Council (exceptions concern mostly the procedural decisions by which the administrative proceeding is suspended or the decisions on termination of the administrative proceeding, Part III, Chapter 1, §3, IV below).

Neither the CA or the APC include details of second-degree proceedings, but despite this, the administrative proceedings from its initiation till the delivery of the Council's decision on appeal represents one whole,[213] and thus, the respective provisions of the CA[214] concerning the administrative proceeding and the APC apply accordingly to appellate proceedings as well.

208. This is the difference between the Competition Act (s. 38(1)) and the Regulation 1/2003 (Art. 23(2)). The AMO cannot use the discretion, and it is obliged to fine any discovered and proved infringement, provided that the proceeding does not end by approval of commitments (s. 8a of the CA).
209. Section 8a of the CA.
210. For example, Decision of the AMO No. 2003/DZ/P/2/052, 24 Mar. 2003 in the case *TASR/SITA* in which the AMO imposed on TASR, the obligation to provide SITA (its competitor) with price proposals and conditions for off-take of press services, within fifteen days from the validity of the decision.
211. Section 34 of the CA.
212. Section 54(1) of the APC.
213. For example, Judgment of the Regional Court in Bratislava No. 3 S 9/2008, 15 Dec. 2009, 7, <http://www.antimon.gov.sk>.
214. Section 34(2) of the CA specifies that in the appellate procedure ss 22, 22a, 25(3)–(6), 27–33, 40 and 41 of the CA apply accordingly.

The APC allows the appeal against the first-degree decision to be heard by the division that issued it, if the appeal is admitted in its integrity and, at the same time, the decision challenged by the appeal concerns only one party to the administrative proceedings (the appellant), or if it concerns more parties and all these parties agree with such an approach.[215] If the first-degree division does not decide on the appeal, it is obliged to submit the appeal to the Council.[216]

The Council reviews the first-degree decision *in extenso*, it may also gather evidence if necessary.[217] However, the general rule of the two-instance procedure is that the second-degree proceedings cannot supersede the first-degree proceedings. The Council may modify[218] the decision if there are reasons for such an approach, for example, if the fine exceeded the limit set by the CA[219] or a different legal qualification of the contested behaviour is justified. If the decision is issued in line with the law, the Council confirms the decision and rejects the appeal.[220] Furthermore, the Council may recall the first-degree decision and terminate the proceedings[221] or recall the decision and refer the case back to the first-degree division for further proceedings,[222] whereby the first-degree division is bound by the legal opinion of the Council. The decision on the appeal cannot be further appealed;[223] however, it is subject to judicial review (*see* the Part III, Chapter 4 below).

104. The AMO is obliged to publish non-confidential versions of legally valid decisions, notifications of concentrations as well as notices on the commencement of administrative procedure, provided that the nature of the matter does not exclude this approach.[224] The obligation is fulfilled if the publication is made in the Commercial Bulletin and on the AMO's official website.[225]

D. *Other Institutional Tasks (Consultancy to Parliament/Government)*

105. The AMO mainly actively participates on commenting and analysing of draft laws and generally binding regulations.

II. Government Direct Enforcement Activities

106. The Government itself has no direct powers concerning the enforcement of antitrust rules, and it cannot intervene in any antitrust proceedings. Even though the direct enforcement activities of the Government are not present, the AMO is obliged

215. Section 57(1) of the APC.
216. Section 57(2) of the APC.
217. Section 59(1) of the APC.
218. Section 59(2) of the APC.
219. Section 38(1) of the CA.
220. Section 59(2) of the APC.
221. Section 59(2) of the APC.
222. Section 59(3) of the APC.
223. Section 59(4) of the APC.
224. Section 40(11) of the CA.
225. Section 40(13) of the CA.

to provide the Government with a report of its activities[226] at least once a year, and the Government is involved in the Chairperson's appointment.[227]

III. Other Administrative Agencies Applying Antitrust Rules

107. As already mentioned above in the text, the AMO is currently the only administrative body applying rules on protection of economic competition in all business sectors, irrespective of whether, in some sectors, *ex-ante* regulation is conducted by special sector regulators.

However, the CA, till its amendment effective as of June 2009, included disputable provision according to which the powers of the AMO to apply competition rules to specific sectors such as electronic communications, energy sector and post services were limited.[228] This provision of the CA was attacked by the European Commission in a formal infringement procedure[229] as a provision preventing the application of competition rules in special sectors. The AMO, in its statement submitted to the European Commission, argued that despite the existence of this provision, the AMO applied competition rules also in special sectors and that the respective provision had only a declaratory character and was exclusively linked to the *ne bis in idem* principle.[230] For example, in 2006 the Council, in its decision concerning a generally binding regulation of the city of Zvolen by which the city of Zvolen restricted competition in the area of heat-power engineering (by preferring connection to a central source of heat), concluded:

> the Competition Act does not cover the cases of restricting competition that should be assessed by another authority protecting competition according to special legislation. The behaviour of the city of Zvolen, assessed by the Office in the present proceedings, does not, however, fall into the range of application of the NIRA statute, which means that the Network Industries Regulation Office is not empowered to proceed in this matter. These are the reasons why the behaviour of the city of Zvolen needs to be assessed according to the general regulation on the protection of economic competition, which is the Competition Act.[231]

226. Section 14(5) of the CA.
227. Section 15(2) of the CA.
228. Section 2(6) of the CA valid before the amendment of the Competition Act effective as of June 2009. According to the respective provision, the Competition Act 'does not apply to cases of protection of competition the appraisal of which falls under the competence of other body ensuring the protection of competition according to special regulation' such as ECA or NIRA.
229. *See* European Commission's press release IP/09/200, 2 Feb. 2009.
230. The AMO's press release, <http://www.antimon.gov.sk/134/3278/podla-protimonopolneho-uradu-srzakon-o-ochrane-hospodarskej-sutaze-je-v-sulade-s-pravidlami-europskej.axd>.
231. The administrative proceedings was conducted according to s. 39 of the Competition Act (provisions concerning other forms of unlawful restrictions of competition); Decision of the Council No. 2006/39/R/2/127, 24 Nov. 2006, <http://www.antimon.gov.sk>, translation by Mrg.Bc. Daniel Uherek, Ph.D.

108. Currently there are still disputes linked to the dividing line between the *ex-ante* regulation applied by special sector regulators and *ex-post* regulation. Disputes arise mainly in respect of antitrust proceedings. In several cases, the AMO came to the conclusion that it has no competence to decide the case that concerns *ex-ante* price regulation. The Council in the Case *BD Humenné* (Housing association in the city of Humenné claimed excessive prices applied by the regional water-works) stated that:

> The Office is not competent to review the adequateness of creating prices for drinking and sewage water ..., as this competence belongs to the responsibility of a price regulator. The first-degree division had, in the opinion of the Council of the Office, to terminate the proceedings due to the lack of competency of the Office. [...] The price regulator for the given range of activities ... is the Ministry of Finance of the Slovak Republic and from 11/01/2002 The Office of Network Industries Regulation.[232]

109. In its decision in the case *Slovenské telekomunikácie* (Slovak fixed line telecom operator), the Council excluded its competence in the case of regulated prices when it concluded:

> After a repeated analysis of the case, the Office came to the conclusion that even though the behaviour of the Slovenské telekomunikácie, a.s. might have had the character of discrimination or tying, which are practices of dominant undertakings and as such are subject of the Office's control, the submission is primarily concerned about prices – the prices required by Slovenské telekomunikácie, a.s. for some telecommunication services. [...] The basic problem of the submission and the primary reason allowing further continuance of the behaviour of the Slovenské telekomunikácie, a.s. described in the submission, lies in the problematic of prices – requiring certain prices from the part of the Slovenské telekomunikácie, a.s. for some telecommunication services – which is regulated by section 32 subsection 1 of the Telecommunications Act. According to this statute, in relation to general price regulation legislation, the price and tariff regulation of telecommunication services is exercised by the Telecommunication Office of the Slovak Republic. [...] The interpretation of these provisions is such that the price and tariff regulation belongs to the Telecommunication Office of the Slovak Republic. [...] The stated provisions prove that the obligation to review a submission indicating a problem in pricing telecommunication services by their suppliers with important effect on the telecommunication market does not belong to the competence of the Antimonopoly Office of the Slovak Republic ... but to the competence of the Telecommunication Office of the Slovak Republic, a special price regulator whose function is, among others, the ex-ante regulation of prices with the aim of creating condition for competitive environment on the telecommunication market and eventually, by timely regulation, preventing the

232. Decision of the Council No. 2004/ZK/R/2/147, 25 Jun. 2004, <http://www.antimon.gov.sk>, translation by Mgr.Bc. Daniel Uherek, Ph.D.

abuse of a dominant position of a telecommunication operator with a significant position on the market.[233]

110. In its recent decision concerning the behaviour of *Slovak Telekom*[234] (previously Slovenské telekomunikácie, a.s., fixed line telecom operator) the Council confirmed the first-degree decision on the refusal to grant access to an essential facility (local loop access) and accepted conclusions in the decision of the first-degree division concerning the competence of the AMO[235] to decide the case. Slovak Telekom, as a party to the administrative proceedings, claimed that the competence of the AMO is not given due to the fact that the obligation to provide an access to local loop is exclusively a tool of a sector-specific regulation. The Council defined the competence of the AMO as follows:

The Office, as the general authority of competition protection, has always the competence to intervene with the aim that effective competition works on the market. It has this obligation even in a situation where a regulatory decision was imposed by a sector-specific regulatory authority. The basic goal, the Office is obliged to pursue, is to eliminate the competition problem, as well as to punish the entity for its unlawful behaviour. The determination of competence of the Office shall be thus based on the real state of the market and is found by concluding whether in each individual case, a competition problem, able to be pursued by the Act, has occurred on the market.[236]

The Council supported its findings by the judgment of the Supreme Court[237] according to which:

> Behaviour of undertakings active in the telecommunication sector (and other sectors) fulfilling the content of terms defined only by the Act on Protection of Competition (in cases of agreements restricting competition, in cases of control of concentrations and also in cases of abusing a dominant position) shall be judged in terms of this Act by the Office established thereby. This Office may not divest itself of this obligation as its empowerment results from its position of cross-branch regulatory authority.[238]

Furthermore, the Council in the respective case stated that the AMO and the specific sector regulators protect different interests, and that the preferred aim of the regulation is to create conditions simulating competitive environment on specific markets whereas the aim of competition rules is to secure undisturbed competition on the market in

233. The decision of the Council No. 2003/ZK/2/1/054, 27 Mar. 2003, <http://www.antimon.gov.sk>, translation by Mgr.Bc. Daniel Uherek, Ph.D.
234. The decision of the Council No. 2009/DZ/R/2/026, 15 May 2009, mainly the s. 1.1 concerning the competence of the AMO to decide the case. <http://www.antimon.gov.sk>.
235. The decision No. 2008/DZ/2/1/066, 5 May 2008, points 13–28, <http://www.antimon.gov.sk>.
236. The decision of the Council No. 2009/DZ/R/2/026, 15 May 2009. The decision of the Council was revoked by the Regional Court's in Bratislava judgment dated 3 Dec. 2010. The judgment not published yet. <http://www.antimon.gov.sk>, translation by Mgr.Bc. Daniel Uherek, Ph.D.
237. Judgment of the Supreme Court No. 2 Sž 14/2004, 28 Feb. 2005.
238. Decision of the Council No. 2009/DZ/R/2/026, 15 May 2009, <http://www.antimon.gov.sk>, translation by Mgr.Bc. Daniel Uherek, Ph.D.

general 'not only on specific markets, while it is necessary to intervene always when behaviour of a certain entity fulfils the subject matter of offences encompassed in the Act. Specific sector regulation and competition rules exist alongside, however, regulation may not substitute competition policy'. Also, this conclusion was supported by the already-mentioned judgment of the Supreme Court[239] according to which:

> In this relation, according to the court's opinion, it is necessary to differentiate between realization of state regulation policy by means of the respective industry sector regulatory authority (TO SR), with the emphasis on enforcing the ex-ante principle (i.e., setting such conditions in advance that ensure the environment corresponding to effective competition), and regulation by means of penalizing anticompetition practices by a cross-sector regulatory authority (the Antimonopoly Office of the SR), based on the ex-post principle (i.e., on retrogressive sanctioning of entities committing conduct contravening competition rules).[240]

Furthermore, the Council supported its conclusions also by the judgment of the Supreme Court[241] according to which:

> The TA (Telecommunication Act), also in the case of such regulation, has not directly allowed the plaintiff applicant (note – ST, a.s.) as a provider of telecommunication services, to behave against the rules of free competition. Even when such interpretation of the TA would be nevertheless possible, the APC (note – the Act on Protection of Competition) shall prevail. The latter is more in conformity with … the Constitution of the SR, since observance of the rules of competition and not practices hampering it should be a part of a free market economy.[242]

The last time the issue of the lack of competence of the AMO to decide the case arose in the case *ZSE Distribúcia*[243] concerning abuse of a dominant position by excessive pricing. The competence of the AMO to decide the case also in the area of regulated industries has been finally acknowledged also by the Supreme Court.[244]

111. There are several sector regulators with competencies for conducting *ex-ante* regulation such as:

239. Judgment of the Supreme Court No. 2 Sž 14/2004, 28 Feb. 2005.
240. Decision of the Council No. 2009/DZ/R/2/026, 15 May 2009, <http://www.antimon.gov.sk>, translation by Mgr.Bc. Daniel Uherek, Ph.D.
241. Judgment of the Supreme Court No. 4 Sž 23/03, 16 Sep. 2009.
242. Other recent decisions in which the AMO supported its competence to appraise anticompetitive behaviour in the telecom sector: Decision of the Council No. 2009/DZ/R/2/017, 9 Apr. 2009, points 1–31 (competence of the AMO in margin squeeze and anticompetitive bundling); Decision of the Council No. 2009/DZ/R/2/011, 27 Mar. 2009, <http://www.antimon.gov.sk>.
243. Decision of the Council, No. 2012/DZ/R/2/030, 29 Jun. 2012, č. 2012/DZ/R/2/030, <http://www.antimon.gov.sk/2012dzr2030/>.
244. Judgment of the Supreme Court, No. 4Sžh/2/2015, 1 Dec. 2015.

(1) the Regulatory Authority for Electronic Communications and Postal Services of the Slovak Republic as an independent sector and price regulator for the area of electronic communications[245] and for regulation of and supervision over the postal services;[246]
(2) the Regulatory Office for Network Industries of the Slovak Republic;[247] empowered to regulate activities in the field of network industries.[248]

Despite the fact that the AMO is the only administrative authority entitled to apply the national and the EU competition laws, in Slovak Republic, some competencies of special regulators might be aimed at assessment of the same or similar conduct as the competition law.

112. Besides the competences of special sector regulators concerning price regulation of specific areas of business, the general rules of price regulation are defined by the Act on Prices.[249] This Act does not however apply to price regulation of electronic communications services and network industries.[250] The Act on Prices defines several forms of price regulation[251] and one of the reasons for applying it is the threat of market deterioration caused by an insufficiently developed competitive environment. In this case, the AMO submits its assessment of the competitive environment on the respective market[252] to the Ministry of Finance of the Slovak Republic.

113. The AMO acknowledged its competence concerning the assessment of excessive prices imposed by a dominant undertaking after the amendment of the CA in 2005,[253] which amended its section 8(2) letter a) as follows: 'The abuse of a dominant position on the relevant market shall be defined as: (a) direct or indirect enforcement of excessive prices or other unfair trade conditions ...' Before this amendment the AMO claimed that it is entitled only to review enforcement of unfair trade conditions excluding prices.

114. In 2008, the controversial Act on Inappropriate Conditions in Business Relations[254] was adopted, according to which the Ministry of Agriculture of the Slovak Republic and the Ministry of Economy of the Slovak Republic were entitled to assess and fine inappropriate conditions applied in business relations between a supplier of products and a buyer if one of the parties in this relation was economically dependent on the other one.[255] The aim of the legal regulation was to 'regulate' the behaviour of supermarket chains, control their business relations with suppliers, and finally, to fine an imposition of inappropriate conditions in business relations as the abuse of economic

245. Section 6(1) letter b) of the ECA.
246. Section 12 letter b) of the Postal Services Act.
247. Section 4 of the NIRA.
248. Section 2 letters a) and b) of the NIRA.
249. Act No. 18/1996 Coll. on Prices as amended.
250. Section 1(4) of the Act on Prices.
251. Section 5 of the Act on Prices.
252. Section 4a(2) letter b) of the Act on Prices.
253. Act No. 68/2005 Coll. on the Amendment and Supplementation of the Act on Prices, the press release of the AMO at: <http://www.antimon.gov.sk/375/1712/nove-kompetencie-protimonopolnehouradu-sr.axd>.
254. Act No. 172/2008 Coll. on Inappropriate Conditions in Business Relations.
255. Article I, s. 1 letter a) of the Act on Inappropriate Conditions in Business Relations.

dependence. The 2008 Act was cancelled and replaced by the Act on Inappropriate Conditions in Business Relations between a Supplier and Buyer of Products Being Foodstuffs.[256] Neither the former 2008 Act, nor the new 2010 Act operates with the notion of dominance (as it is in the CA). The notion of 'economic dependence' defined by the 2008 Act was cancelled as vague. The reason for the adoption of these regulations was to assess behaviour consistent with inappropriate practices of supermarkets claimed by suppliers, which was not covered by the CA. For instance, financial performance for listing of a supplier and its goods to the register of suppliers, for using of the buyer's distribution network or for placing goods at certain places on the buyer's premises are treated as inappropriate conditions.

IV. Administrative Fines

115. The AMO is obliged to impose a fine every time it comes to the conclusion that the infringement of national or EC competition rules occurred, provided that the administrative proceeding is not finished by a decision on an approval of commitments submitted by undertakings.[257]

A fine can be imposed only by a decision issued according to the APC and the CA after a formal administrative proceeding is conducted. The CA allows the AMO to impose fines either for the breach of competition rules (for the abuse of a dominant position or the conclusion of an agreement restricting competition) as well as fines of a procedural nature (e.g., a fine for submission of incomplete information or for refusal to submit required data).

The fine for the breach of competition rules can be imposed only on the undertaking that is a party to the administrative proceedings and possesses a legal personality. The CA enables the AMO to impose fines of up to EUR 66,000 also on state administration authorities, territorial self-government authorities and on special interest bodies, if they restrict competition.[258]

116. The CA does not include the exact amount of the fine which can be imposed on undertakings; it only defines the maximum limit, which cannot be exceeded.[259] The final amount of the fine is thus the result of the AMO's discretion after considering all relevant circumstances stipulated by the CA.[260] The imposed fine has two functions. The first is its repressive function where the fine represents the punishment for the competition rules violation, the second is its preventive function consisting of individual prevention (discouraging the undertaking from the breach of competition rules in the future) and general prevention (discouraging other undertakings from infringing competition rules). The AMO in its decision concerning the GIS cartel stated that:

256. Act No. 140/2010 Coll. on Inappropriate Conditions in Business Relations between a Supplier and Buyer of Product Being Foodstuffs.
257. Section 8a of the CA.
258. Section 39 in connection with s. 38(2) of the CA.
259. Section 38(1), s. 38a (1) and (2) of the CA.
260. Section 38(3) of the CA.

> As a form of sanction, the fine is the principal instrument of enforcement of competition law and remedy. Its purpose is to ensure that anticompetitive behaviour is no longer perpetrated and to punish the infringing party (repressive effect) and to prevent its reoccurrence (preventive effect). The preventive effect influences the actual addressee of the decision, and ... raises general awareness of competition ... towards other undertakings. [...] General prevention ensures educatory influence of third parties through sanction, to prevent their possible actions contra legem.[261]

117. Even though the AMO is entitled to use its discretion in determining the amount of the fine, the Supreme Court stated that the administration is bound by the basic principles of administrative decision-making, including the obligation to ensure that similar cases are adjudicated in a similar manner.[262]

118. The CA stipulates that in determining the amount of the fine, the AMO has to take into consideration the gravity and the duration of the violation. When assessing the gravity of the infringement, the following factors are relevant: its character, actual impact on the market, and where appropriate, also the size of the relevant market.[263] Other factors that the AMO shall take into account are particularly: repeated violation, refusal to cooperate, the position of the undertaking as a leader or an instigator of the violation, financial benefit from the violation, non-performance of an agreement restricting competition in practice.[264] In 2008, the AMO issued a non-binding Guideline on the Imposition of Fines,[265] which further specifies all factors relevant for determining fines in agreements restricting competition and abuse cases. In 2014, along with the amendment of the CA, the AMO issued a new Guideline on Imposition of Fines[266] which specified in details calculation of the basic amount of fine taking into consideration duration and the gravity of an anticompetitive behaviour.

119. On the issue of assessment of the real impact of the violation on the market as defined by section 38(3) of the CA, the AMO in its *GIS* cartel case stated that:

> quantifying, in detail, the market impacts of anticompetitive behaviour is not indispensable ... particularly when considering that a number of other external factors can simultaneously influence, e.g. the prices or inputs, which makes a conclusion of an exact influence of all possible factors on the situation at the market excessively difficult. ... the actual impacts on the market of a specific practice do not have to be necessarily quantified or specified; it is sufficient to

261. Decision of the Council No. 2009/KH/R/2/035, 14 Aug. 2009, §797 challenged at the Regional Court in Bratislava – procedure pending, <http://www.antimon.gov.sk>, translation by Mgr. Bc. Daniel Uherek, Ph.D.
262. Judgment of the Supreme Court No. 8 As 5/2005, 29 Jun. 2005.
263. Section 38(3) of the CA.
264. Section 38(3) of the CA.
265. 'Metodický pokyn o postupe pri určovaní pokút v prípadoch zneužívania dominantného postavenia a dohôd obmedzujúcich súť až', <http://www.antimon.gov.sk>.
266. The AMO, 'Metodický pokyn o postupe pri určovaní pokút v prípadoch zneužívania dominantného postavenia a dohôd obmedzujúcich súťaž', 1 Jul. 2014, <http://www.antimon.gov.sk/data/files/396_metodicky-pokyn-o-postupe-pri-urcovani-pokut-v-pripadoch-zneuzivania-dominantneho-postavenia-a-dohod-obmedzujucich-sutaz.pdf>.

demonstrate, with reasonable probability, how the market was or could have been affected as a result of the anticompetitive conduct.[267]

120. Nevertheless, the Regional Court in Bratislava, in its judgment concerning the abuse of a dominant position by the company Slovnaft (Slovak refinery company),[268] contested this approach and concluded that the AMO is obliged to take into consideration all factors specified by the CA when imposing a fine.

121. The first step in imposing a fine is the determination of the basic amount of the fine which is the result of three criteria:

(1) the turnover achieved from sale of products directly or indirectly linked to the breach of competition rules ('the relevant turnover');
(2) the gravity of the violation where the maximum percentage of gravity is 30%;
(3) the duration of the infringement.

According to the Guideline on Imposition of Fines 2014, the basic amount of the fine is determined as multiplication of the relevant turnover by the percentage of the gravity and the sum total is multiplied by the duration of the anticompetitive behaviour.

The relevant for the calculation of the fine is the turnover from activities on the market in which the breach of competition rules took place. The maximum percentage of the gravity is 30%.

It must be mentioned that it is not unusual for the AMO to impose the fine at the maximum statutory limit when it comes to the breach of competition rules committed by hard-core cartels. The second step is the appraisal of aggravating and mitigating factors based on which the basic amount of the fine is increased or decreased.

Mitigating factors taken into consideration when assessing an infringement of competition rules are mainly: a passive role in the infringement or a role of a follower; cooperation of the undertaking with the AMO, which significantly contributes to the detection or proving the violation; cooperation of the undertaking with the AMO to the extent of exceeding its legal obligations;[269] non-implementation of the cartel in practice or a breach of competition rules by negligence.

The aggravating factors are, for example, an intentional breach of competition rules, repeated violation and financial benefit. For example, in the GIS cartel decision, the Council declared the fact that some participants of the cartel acted as secretaries of the cartel helping the implementation of the cartel in practice as an aggravating factor.[270]

---

267. Decision of the Council No. 2009/KH/R/2/035, 14 Aug. 2009, §811 challenged at the Regional Court in Bratislava – procedure pending, <http://www.antimon.gov.sk>, translation by Mgr. Bc. Daniel Uherek, Ph.D.
268. Judgment of the Regional Court in Bratislava No. 3 S 9/2008-783, IčS 1008200074, 15 Dec. 2009, <http://www.antimon.gov.sk>.
269. For example, the AMO in the case of 'highway cartel' did not acknowledge the fact that the undertaking cooperated with the AMO as a mitigating factor because this cooperation was its legal duty. Decision No. 2006/KH/R/2/116, 16 Oct. 2006, <http://www.antimonon.gov.sk>.
270. Decision of the Council No. 2009/KH/R/2/035, 14 Aug. 2009, §828, <http://www.antimonon.gov.sk>.

122. As already mentioned above, the AMO applies the Guideline on Imposition of Fines only in antitrust proceedings, when imposing the fine for other violations of the CA (such as the breach of the obligation to notify a concentration to the AMO prior to execution of rights and obligations resulting from the concentration, breach of the obligation to submit correct and complete data) it proceeds in line with the respective provisions of the CA (section 38(3)).

123. As already mentioned, the CA determines the maximum limit for the imposition of a fine which is defined alternatively either as a fixed amount or as a percentage from the turnover. A breach of antitrust rules as well as a failure to fulfil conditions, obligations or commitments imposed by a decision and a violation of a prohibition to exercise rights and obligations ensuing from a concentration without an exemption, failure to comply with a decision of the AMO and violation of the prohibition to enter the public procurement can be fined by the AMO by up to 10% of the undertaking's turnover achieved in the preceding closed accounting period. If the turnover of the undertaking did not exceed EUR 330 or the undertaking attained no turnover or the turnover cannot be calculated, a fine can be imposed of up to EUR 330,000.

The CA defines a limitation period for imposing a fine.[271] The AMO can impose a fine within four years from the commencement of the administrative procedure (subjective limitation period, *see* Part III, Chapter 1, §1 below); however, a fine must be imposed within eight years from the day of the violation of the competition rules (objective limitation period). If a breach of competition rules is of a continuing or lasting character, the time limit begins on the day of the last occurrence of the violation. The day of the beginning of the objective limitation period is dependent on a characteristic of the particular breach of competition rules (e.g., in case of prohibited exclusive agreements, it is the day when the prohibited provision was excluded from the agreement). The limitation period means that within the stipulated time limit, the decision of the AMO needs to be not only issued, but the decision has to be valid. The Slovak legal regulation enables the interruption of the limitation period only in case of judicial review of the decision of the AMO;[272] however, the CA does not provide for such suspension of the limitation period as it is stated, for example, in the Article 25 of the Regulation 1/2003.

124. The CA further enables to the AMO to fine undertakings or legal persons for a failure to submit required documents and data within a stipulated time limit, for submitting incorrect or incomplete information. In these cases, the AMO is entitled to impose a fine up to 1% of the undertaking's turnover achieved in the preceding closed accounting period and to impose a fine to a natural person in the amount up to EUR 1,650. The AMO will impose a fine to an undertaking for not allowing entry to its business premises up to 5%.[273] The natural person who does not allow inspection in its private premises can be fined up to EUR 80,000.[274] Furthermore, the undertaking

271. Section 38c(4) of the CA.
272. Section 71(1) of the CPAC.
273. Section 38(2) letter a) of the CA.
274. Section 38a(3) letter a) of the CA.

can be fined if it does not participate in oral hearings without justified reasons or otherwise interferes with the progress of the procedure.[275]

125. All sanctions, except the sanction for the breach of the seal of the AMO, can be imposed by the AMO, also repeatedly.[276]

126. Sometimes a fine cannot be imposed on the undertaking which concluded the cartel agreement due to the fact that the respective undertaking does not exist at the time of the administrative proceedings or it does not exist in the form in which it existed at the time of the breach of competition rules. The AMO used the *Economic Continuity Test* for the first time in 2005[277] in the case of the abuse of a dominant position by the company Železničná spoločnosť ('ŽS', Railroad Company). During the administrative proceedings, the Government decided on the division of ŽS into two successors. Subsequently, the first-degree division decided to stop the proceedings. The Council disagreed with this approach and in its decision recalling of the first-degree decision, stated that the AMO had to proceed against one of the ŽS's successors. The Council of the AMO further stated:

> In certain cases concerning the public interest in functional competition, it is possible to hold an economic successor responsible for the illegal conduct of its legal predecessor and impose a fine on it. Two conditions must be met in this case: firstly, the new company continues the activity of the entity that has committed the violation, i.e., the continuity of economic activities of these two companies exists, and, secondly, the original entity has ceased to exist. If the successor company, which acquires material and personnel units of the business and continues the economic activities of the dissolved company, still takes part in competition on the market and benefits from a possible anticompetitive behaviour in the event of its predecessor's illegal conduct, it is necessary to make sure that the illegal conduct does not remain unpunished as a result of organizational or structural changes in these undertakings. Regarding the aim to protect competition, succession in the legal sense of the word is not as important as the involvement in economic activities of the undertaking, that is, succession in the economic sense of the word.[278]

---

275. Section 38b of the CA.
276. Section 38c(3) of the CA.
277. The decision of the Council No. 2005/65/R/1/093, 9 Sep. 2005, <http://www.antimon.gov.sk>; *see* the AMO's press release <http://www.antimon.gov.sk/391/2105/abuse-of-a-dominant-position-zeleznicnaspolocnost-railroad-company-a-s-application-of-the-economic.axd>; Decision of the AMO No. 2006/DZ/2/1/067, 3 Jul. 2006 confirmed by the decision of the Council No. 2006/DZ/2/144, 22 Dec. 2006; the final amount of the penalty imposed by the AMO was substantially decreased by the Regional Court in Bratislava, *see* the press release <http://www.antimon.gov.sk/427/2858/theantimonopoly-office-of-sr-will-submit-an-appeal-against-judgment-of-the-county-court-inbratislava.axd>; the AMO used the Economic Continuity Test also in its recent *GIS* cartel case – Decision of the Council No. 2009/KH/R/2/035, 14 Aug. 2009, challenged at the Regional Court in Bratislava – pending procedure, <http://www.antimon.gov.sk>.
278. The AMO's press release published at <http://www.antimon.gov.sk/391/2105/abuse-of-a-dominant-position-zeleznicna-spolocnost-railroad-company-a-s-application-of-the-economic.axd>.

127. The AMO may reduce the fine or even grant immunity from the fine in cartel cases, provided that leniency conditions stipulated by the CA[279] are fulfilled. The Leniency Programme applies to any agreement restricting competition according section 4(1) of the CA and Article 101(1) of the TFEU concluded between undertakings in a position of competitors, not only in cases such as price-fixing cartels, market-partitioning or bid-rigging as it was valid the amendment of the CA in 2014. The CA recognizes two levels of the Leniency Programme's application. At the first level, the undertaking may benefit from total immunity, if it provides the AMO with the decisive evidence on the cartel or provides information or evidence enabling to conduct inspection in business premises of an undertaking.[280] At the second level, even the undertaking that does not fulfil criteria for total immunity can benefit from a reduction of the fine of up to 50%, provided it submitted to the AMO evidence with added value in relation to evidences already gathered in administrative files.[281] Neither the CA nor the Leniency Guideline[282] include the definition of the 'decisive evidence' or 'an added value evidence', but it can be concluded that major relevance will be given to evidence which is directly linked to the appraised behaviour or evidence which is confirmed by other sources. In practice, as the added value evidence will be treated also the evidence which confirms information that the AMO has in disposal already.

The basic precondition for the application of the Leniency Programme is a systematic and full cooperation of the undertaking with the AMO, namely from the moment of the submission of the request for leniency and throughout the investigation as well as the administrative proceedings.

Total immunity from a fine[283] can be granted only if following cumulative conditions are fulfilled:

(1) the applicant terminated its involvement in the agreement restricting competition at the time when it provided evidence to the AMO at the latest, except involvement in the agreement restricting competition based on AMO´s approval if it is necessary for preserving the integrity of inspections;[284]
(2) the applicant did not force another undertaking to participate in a cartel or was not an instigator of a cartel;[285]
(3) the applicant provided the AMO with all the evidence that comes into the applicant's possession and properly cooperated with the AMO throughout the entire investigation and subsequent administrative proceedings;[286]

279. Section 38d of the CA.
280. Section 38d(1) of the Competition Act.
281. Section 38d(2) of the Competition Act.
282. 'Program zhovievavosti podľa § 38d zákona o ochrane hospodárskej súťaže (Leniency program) Non-imposing or reducing a fine in some types of agreements restricting competition pursuant to the Art. 38 paras 11 and 12 of the act (Leniency Programme)', Leniency programme pursuant s. 38d of the Act on Protection of Economic Competition, <http://www.antimon.gov.sk/data/files/388_program-zhovievavosti.pdfwww.antimon.gov.sk/files/ 30/2009/Leniency5(k)-en.rtf> (Leniency Guideline).
283. Decision of the Council No. 2009/KH/R/2/035, 14 Aug. 2009, <http://www.antimon.gov.sk>.
284. Section 38d(3) letter a) of the CA.
285. Section 38d(3) letter b) of the CA.
286. Section 38d(3) letter c) of the CA.

(4) the applicant did not inform the other parties of the cartel about the Leniency submission.[287]

The reduction of the fine up to 50% can be granted to the applicant for leniency if at the same time conditions under points (i), (iii) and (iv) are met.[288]

The AMO's Leniency Guideline[289] specifies that the decisive evidence needs to be sufficient to prove a cartel; it needs to be specific whereby direct evidence is preferred.[290] If an undertaking submits information decisive to perform an inspection, the AMO assesses only whether the information convincingly justifies the execution of the inspection, during which decisive evidence should be found.[291] Total immunity is granted only to the undertaking which is the first to submit the decisive evidence and the evidence was submitted on the own initiative of the applicant. If the AMO comes to the conclusion that the undertaking was not first in the line when submitting evidence, the AMO will assess its application under the criteria for reduction of fine (the second level of leniency).[292]

If several undertakings submit applications for leniency, the AMO will assess these requests in the order that they have been delivered.[293]

According to the Leniency Guideline, the applicant for immunity may ask the AMO for reservation of an order – a marker.[294] The marker thus guarantees to the undertaking, the order during a reasonable period within which the undertaking is able to fill in the application and to collect evidence. If the application is amended within a stipulated time limit, the undertaking's application is considered to be delivered on the day the marker was granted. Otherwise, the undertaking loses its reservation.

The applicant can also file a so-called hypothetical request for leniency. In this case, the identity of the applicant and identities of other participants of the cartel do not have to be revealed until the submission of the described evidence. However the applicant is obliged to provide the AMO with information on the relevant market on which the supposed cartel behaviour took place, description of the supposed agreement restricting competition, list and description of evidence which can be subsequently submitted to the AMO, the period within which the anticompetitive behaviour took place and the time limit within which the applicant plans to provide the AMO with evidence. The application must be marked as the 'hypothetical request'.[295]

Based on the submitted list of evidence the AMO assesses whether submitted information may constitute decisive evidence or provide enough information to perform inspection. If the subsequently submitted information and documents correspond to

287. Section 38d(3) letter d) of the CA.
288. Section 38d(4) of the CA.
289. The AMO, 'Program zhovievavosti podľa § 38d zákona o ochrane hospodárskej súťaže (Leniency program)', Leniency programme pursuant s. 38d of the Act on Protection of Economic Competition, <http://www.antimon.gov.sk/data/files/388_program-zhovievavosti.pdf> (Leniency Guideline).
290. Leniency Guideline, §§11, 12.
291. Leniency Guideline, §13.
292. Leniency Guideline, §16.
293. Leniency Guideline, §24.
294. Leniency Guideline, §§41–46.
295. Leniency Guideline, §§47–53.

the hypothetical application, the AMO grants a conditional exemption from a fine to the applicant.

Even though that the hypothetical request can be submitted by the representative of the applicant and the applicant is not obliged to submit any business names of cartel participants, submission of the hypothetical request can be risky on the markets where only a few competitors are present, on the markets with special products or services, as the applicant has to provide the AMO with the information on product concerned and on the geographic area touched by the supposed cartel. In such a case the AMO is able easily recognize the respective parties of the supposed cartel.

Finally, the hypothetical application cannot be combined with the marker.[296]

The fine can be reduced to only one and also to several undertakings. The CA does not recognize several levels of fine reduction dependent on the order of submissions for leniency as it is stated in the EU Immunity Notice.[297] In deciding on the amount of the reduction, the AMO considers the value of the provided evidence in proving a cartel as well as the time at which they were provided. As already mentioned, the AMO assesses applications in the order they have been delivered.

128. The application for leniency can be filed at any time, that is, prior to or during the investigation, or during the formal administrative procedure; nevertheless, it is advisable to submit the request for leniency as soon as possible because at later stages of the procedure, the AMO might have enough evidence proving the violation, at its disposal.[298]

The leniency application can be submitted jointly also by several undertakings who belong to the one economic group. However, conditions for leniency need to be met by each undertaking within the group individually.[299]

Finally, it is worth to mention that the applicant seeking for the leniency in several EU Member States has to submit the leniency application in each Member State separately as the leniency application submitted in Slovakia cannot be used by competition authorities in other Member States. However, the applicant can submit the summary application for immunity in each Member State and the complete leniency application to the Commission should the Commission be the best-placed authority for dealing with the case.[300]

129. The reduction of fine based on leniency can be further combined with the reduction of fine granted in the Settlement procedure. The fine can be further reduces up to 30%.[301]

Further details of the leniency process are described in the Leniency Guideline.

296. Leniency Guideline §53.
297. Commission Notice on Immunity from Fines and Reduction of Fines in Cartel Cases, OJ C 298, 8 Dec. 2006, 17–22.
298. Leniency Guideline, §37.
299. Section 38d (6) of the Competition Act.
300. Leniency Guideline, §§54–60.
301. Leniency Guideline, §68.

V. Administrative Injunctions and Other Restrictive Orders

130. The AMO's decision finding an infringement, always includes the verdict on fine along with the verdict on specification of the prohibited conduct, and may include the verdict by which the AMO prohibits the undertaking from continuing the violation of competition rules.

The decision on fine in cartel cases concerning the bid-rigging will always include the verdict on prohibition to participate in public procurement. The AMO prohibits participating in public tenders to all participants of the cartel within three years from the validity of its decision.[302] If the undertaking benefits from the leniency, the ban to participate in public procurement will not apply.[303] If the undertaking settles with the AMO based on the rules on Settlement, the AMO prohibits to participate in public procurement for the period of one year.[304]

The AMO may further include remedies to the penalty decision (behavioural or structural) as mentioned in Part I, Chapter 5, §1, I (ii) above).

VI. Interim Measures

131. According to the APC,[305] the AMO has powers to impose interim measures if they are essential for assuring the respective administrative procedure, that is, there is a need to arrange legal relations before the issue of the final decision in the matter. By the interim measure, the AMO is entitled in the necessary extent to impose the obligation:

(1) to perform something (e.g., to continue to supply customers);
(2) to cease from some operations (to refrain from dissolution); or
(3) to endure something.

In the decision, the AMO can also order the securing of things necessary for the execution of evidence (*see* Part III, Chapter 1, §3, IV below). The granted interim measure ceases to be effective, at the latest, on the day the decision on the matter becomes valid.

§2. Civil Enforcement

132. The observance of the prohibition of cartel agreements and prohibition on abuse of a dominant position is primarily enforced by public law means. Private law protection then supplements this enforcement by public law means; it consists in the assertion of competition rules by national courts within the framework of an 'ordinary' civil procedure, that is, in proceedings regarding the application of specific private

302. Section 38h(1) of the CA.
303. Section 38h(2) of the CA.
304. Section 38h(2) of the CA.
305. Section 43 of the APC.

law claims arising out of a breach of economic competition rules. This type of protection plays, so far, a minor role in Slovak Republic. However, in future, its importance should increase also due to new legal regulation – the Act on Damages.[306]

133. Both lines of the assertion of the observance of competition rules (public as well as private law) are distinguished by several differences. The first difference consists in the object, and extends to the protection of what they intend. Public assertion of competition law, which is institutionally covered in Slovak Republic by the AMO, leads to the protection of effective economic competition as an existing phenomenon against its restriction. The object of the private law assertion is then primarily an individual's interest and protection of its specific private rights, whether the individual is another competitor (competitor, client, contractor), that is, an entity being a direct participant of relationships incurring economic competition, or the end consumer. Public law assertion may be characterized as the application of specific recourses by injured entities against those entities, which have breached competition rules, in the way of private law.

The clearest function of the private law assertion is to reach compensation of the injured party for negative consequences, which have been demonstrated against it, by a breach of competition rules; typically, it concerns compensation for damage, which has been caused to an individual entity by a breach of competition rules; however, through this private law assertion, it is also possible to claim that a delinquent refrains from an illegal action and removes the defective (illegal) condition.

The private law assertion may function as a sufficient deterrent against those who breach competition rules, and an authoritative (court) imposition of the obligation to remedy the damage caused may serve for these entities to more forcefully realize their liability for their action in economic competition and potential and material negative impact. Subsequently, the private law assertion of the observance of competition rules indirectly leads towards the provision of an object primarily protected by public law, specifically, towards the creation and protection of an effective competitive environment.

The essential difference between both lines of enforcement of observance of antitrust rules follows from the fact that in case of the imposition of a sanction (penalty) under the public competition law regulations, it shall probably be sufficient, especially in cases of agreements restricting competition, to prove that the behaviour of a competitor has at least been capable of impairing economic competition. Within the framework of the private law line, that is, typically, in cases of civil procedures on compensation for damage caused by an anticompetitive acting, it shall be necessary to prove that:

(1) a specific competitor has acted in a specific way;
(2) its action has breached economic competition rules;
(3) a specific entity has been caused damage;
(4) a causal relation between the specific competitor's action, which has breached economic competition rules, and the incurred damage exists.

306. The Act No. 350/2016 Coll. on Certain Rules Concerning the Claims for Damages Caused by the Breach of Competition Rules effective as of 27 Dec. 2016. .

134. The action for damages according to the Act on Damages can be filed by any person (natural or legal entity) who has suffered damage caused by the breach of the ban to conclude agreement restricting competition (section 4(1) of the CA and Article 101(1) of TFEU) or the ban to abuse a dominant position (section 8(2) of the CA and Article 102 of TFEU).

135. It is supposed, by the Act on Damages, that the breach of competition rules causes the damage. Moreover, it is supposed that by conclusion of an agreement restricting competition the damage was caused provided the defendant proves the contrary.

136. Under section 3(2) of the Act on Damages, damage consists of compensation of: (i) an actual damage, (ii) a loss of profit and (iii) an interest from the amount of actual damage and loss of profit. There is no need to prove and to calculate the exact amount of damage as the court may determine the damage by estimate.

In order to prove the amount of damage, the court may order an undertaking or third parties to disclose evidence in its possession if this evidence can be relevant for the case. The undertaking is entitled to mark documents and information as trade secret or confidential. It should be mentioned that limited access to the documents present in the administrative files of the AMO concerns only the information and statements provided within a leniency application process and during the Settlement.

137. The undertaking who has caused the damage can claim that the plaintiff transferred the damage to the third party, particularly to its own customers by increasing the final price. Thus, the principle of passing on effect applies.

138. The action for damages can be brought to the court within five years limitation period which starts to run when the claimant knew or ought to have known that the anticompetitive conduct occurred.

139. It is worth to mention that stand-alone claims as well as follow-up actions for damages shall be allowed. The only competent court to decide the case is the Bratislava II District Court. However, the court is bound by a final decision of the AMO concerning the infringement, as the decision of the AMO constitutes the evidence for the court on the breach of competition rules.

140. Even though the stand-alone claims shall be permitted, the current wording of the CPAC does not support this conclusion. According to the respective provisions of the CPAC, the court is obliged, in all matters concerning the administrative sanctioning, which also include the breach of competition rules, to turn to the respective authority and request a decision on the matter. The available commentary to the CPAC provides the explanation that in such case the court is not entitled to decide the matter on the breach of administrative rules alone and it shall ask the AMO to issue a decision. Subsequently, the court will stay the proceedings on damage compensation and wait for the decision of the AMO. However, this approach would make stand-alone claims impossible and only the future practice will verify relevance of this opinion.

141. Finally, it needs to be mentioned that the proceedings on damages compensation can be terminated by the out-of-court settlement or by mediation. The compensation of the damage based on the amicable settlement or mediation will be treated as the mitigating factor when imposing the fine for the breach of antitrust rules by the AMO.

I. Competent Civil Courts

142. Private enforcement of competition law, mainly disputes regarding the compensation for damage, are conducted based on a filed petition in proceedings before a civil court, under the standard civil proceedings governed by the Civil Procedure Code (CvPC). The claims for damage may result either in a rejection of the petition or recognition of the claim for compensation for damage according to the request of the petitioner.

The Bratislava II District Court has jurisdiction (for proceedings in matters of protection of rights from economic competition); an appeal shall then be decided by the Regional Court in Bratislava.[307]

II. Sanctions

A. Nullity

143. A separate question concerning civil enforcement is that of petitions for the determination of invalidity of contracts containing cartel agreements. According to section 4(1) of the CA, agreements restricting competition are prohibited, while the invalidity of such agreements is derived from section 39 of the CvC, under which a legal act being in conflict by its content or purpose, with law, is invalid. The only authority, which may declare invalidity of a contract or invalidity of a part of the contract, is the court, which may do so based on a petition. The result of the dispute shall be demonstrated especially in a potential liberation from the performance of contractual obligations by the parties to a contract containing a cartel agreement.

B. Damages

144. The compensation of the damage caused by the breach of competition rules is governed by the Act on Damages. Please *see* Part I, Chapter 4, §2.

C. Interim Measures

145. A court may issue a preliminary measure (in Slovak *neodkladné opatrenie*) prior to the trial, provided that the situation of the parties must be temporarily adjusted or if the execution of the judgment could be endangered.[308] The preliminary measure is issued based on the petition of a party to the proceedings, whereby the proposal for the issuing of a preliminary measure must be justified, that is, the petitioner must properly describe the situation and give reasons for the issuing of a preliminary measure.[309]

By the preliminary measure, the court may particularly order the party not to dispose of certain assets or rights; to do something or to suffer something to be done

307. Section 27(1) of the Civil Proceedings Code.
308. Section 324 of the CPAC.
309. Section 326 of the CPAC.

or may order that an amount of money be deposited into court custody.[310] The preliminary measure ceases to be in effect, for example, if the claimant does not submit a petition to commence judicial proceedings within a specified time limit,[311] the reason for the issuing of the preliminary measure ceases to exist;[312] or the period for which the interim measure was issued expired.[313]

§3. Criminal Enforcement

146. The criminal enforcement in Slovak Republic is governed by Act No. 300/2005 Coll. Criminal Code (CrC),[314] and the criminal procedure by Act No. 301/2005 Coll. Criminal Procedure Code (CPC) as further amended ;[315] both legal regulations came into force in January 2006. Criminal enforcement is limited by the fact that under Slovak criminal law, only a natural person[316] has a criminal liability. Thus, the anticompetitive conduct to be assessed as a criminal act needs to be attributed to the natural person.

I. Criminal Sanctions for Antitrust Violations

147. The CrC defines the criminal act connected to the anticompetitive behaviour in section 250 under the title 'Abuse of participation in economic competition'.

A natural person commits a crime when that person: (i) by an unfair competition in economic relations impairs the reputation of a competitor, or (ii) by a conduct contrary to the CA causes to the other competitor considerable damage or threatens ruin of its business. The notion of a competitor must be perceived in a broad sense, not only as it is known in the antitrust law covering only undertakings competing on the same relevant market. The considerable damage is defined directly by the CrC[317] as a sum which represents at least a 100-fold of the damage. Currently, the basic sum of the damage is EUR 266.

148. The natural person will be punished by imprisonment for up to three years for committing this crime. However, if the natural person by its behaviour causes a great damage (which is at least 500 fold of the damage), or causes bankruptcy of a competitor's business, or the criminal act is caused because of particular initiative[318]

310. Section 325 of the CPAC.
311. Section 336 of the CPAC.
312. Section 334 of the CPAC.
313. Section 333 of the CPAC.
314. Act No. 300/2005 Coll. CrC as further amended.
315. Act No. 301/2005 Coll. CPC as further amended.
316. Section 19(2) of the CrC.
317. Section 125(1) of the CrC.
318. Section 140 of the CrC.

or committed by a major proceeding,[319] that person will be punished by imprisonment for between two and six years.[320]

The definition thus allows imposing imprisonment for any breach of competition rules which causes at least a considerable damage or threatens ruin of the other undertaking's business, that is, it covers all types and all forms of agreements restricting competition (not only cartels (or hard-core cartels) concluded between undertakings operating on the same relevant market) as well as, hypothetically, any abuse of a dominant position, provided that the breach can be attributed to a natural person and is proved. Seeing that a criminal act can be committed only by a natural person, the criminal prosecution under section 250 of the CrC concerns mainly managers, members of boards or executive officers.

149. The authors are not aware of any case law concerning the criminal act connected to the breach of the antitrust rules even though the AMO fulfils its obligation arising from section 3(2) of the CPC and notifies authorities active in a criminal procedure on the potential breach of the CrC.

The application of the Leniency Programme under the section 38(11) and (12) of the CA does prevent the application of the CrC and sanctioning of respective natural persons under the CrC, provided that a respective person enabled by its action to fulfil conditions for a lenient treatment.[321] It is also necessary to note that a criminal court is not bound by the AMO's decision on the violation of the CA when it comes to the assessment of the guilt of the person accused.[322]

150. It is necessary to mentioned that the Act No. 91/2016 Coll. on the Criminal Liability of Legal Persons and on Amendments to Certain Laws has been adopted in 2016. The natural person can be responsible for the crime committed, for example, by its statutory body or a member of the statutory authority. There is an exhaustive list of crimes for which the natural person can be responsible; however, none of them is related to the breach of the competition law.

II. Other Application of Criminal Law to Relevant Conducts

151. The Criminal Law – The CrC also covers, as a separate crime, the behaviour of an undertaking which can be treated according to the CA as hard-core cartel-bid-rigging. The bid-rigging is covered by section 266(1) and mainly section 267 of the CrC.

Any behaviour of a natural person acting in the process of public procurement who acts in contradiction with generally binding legal regulations providing for the public procurement process with the aim to gain benefit for itself or for another person is treated under section 266 of the CrC.

Any behaviour, which can be treated as bid-rigging according to section 4(4) letter f) of the CA, is covered mainly by section 267 of the CrC. Any crime under this provision is committed by a person which commits machinations concerning public

319. Section 138 of the CrC.
320. Section 250(2) of the CrC.
321. Section 86 letter d) of the CPC.
322. Section 7(1) of the CPC.

procurement by forcing another person (in a more compelling manner of acting) not to participate in the public procurement; makes offers, or promises any financial or other benefit for not participating in the public procurement process or requires or receives any financial or other benefit for not participating in the public procurement.

152. The person who commits a crime defined by section 267 of the CrC can be sentenced for between one and five years of imprisonment. Depending on the circumstances of committing the crime under section 266 of the CrC, the person can be sentenced with up to twelve years of imprisonment.

III. Role of Prosecutors

153. According to Article 149 of the Slovak Constitution, the Public prosecution is an authority for the protection of law. Its organizational structure corresponds to the organizational structure of the Slovak courts.

154. Criminal prosecution under the CPC is a rather complicated process consisting of two main parts which are the 'pre-trial proceedings'[323] (this includes so-called preparatory proceedings[324] within which respective evidence is collected) and the 'trial proceedings'[325] (this begins based on a criminal charge or an Agreement on Settlement (in Slovak *dohoda o vine a treste*); both can be submitted only by a public prosecutor).[326] In each individual part of the criminal prosecution, the public prosecutor plays a role specified by the law, whereas in general, the public prosecutor represents the state in a criminal prosecution and is obliged to pursue all criminal acts about which it has knowledge.[327]

155. A complaint (in Slovak *trestné oznámenie*) can be submitted by any natural or legal person either to a police or to a public prosecutor.[328] The criminal prosecution begins based on the Decision on the commencement of the criminal prosecution (in Slovak *uznesenie o začatí trestného stíhania*) issued by a policeman.[329] In the course of the preparatory proceedings, the police gathers evidence based on which it is decided whether the public prosecutor will bring a criminal charge to the court. In the state of the preparatory proceedings, the public prosecutor executes legal steps concerning a person which is under suspicion of committing a crime (an accused person, in Slovak *obvinený*) such as conclusion of the Agreement on Settlement,[330] whereas at the same time, the public prosecutor executes supervision of the legality of the preparatory proceedings and supervision over investigators. The public prosecutor is also entitled to issue decisions related to supervision (e.g., a decision by which the public prosecutor dismisses an illegal decision of the policeman).[331] The public prosecutor reviews files

323. Sections 196–236 of the CPC.
324. Sections 199–229 of the CPC.
325. Sections 237–405 of the CPC.
326. Section 237(1) of the CPC.
327. Section 2(5) of the CPC.
328. Section 196(1) of the CPC.
329. Section 199(1) of the CPC.
330. Section 231 letter b) of the CPC.
331. Section 230(2) letter e) in connection with s. 230(3) of the CPC.

submitted by the police, the scope and nature of evidence, legality of the proceedings and decides on whether it is possible to submit a criminal charge to the court or it is required to collect additional evidence by the police. Only the public prosecutor is entitled to submit a criminal charge (in Slovak *obžaloba*) or an Agreement on Settlement, to the court.[332] The person against whom the criminal charge is submitted is in the position of a culprit (in Slovak *obžalovaný*), whereas the CrC distinguishes between the accused person (in Slovak *obvinený*) and the culprit. The accused person/culprit is represented in the course of the criminal prosecution by an advocate.[333]

IV. Competent Criminal Courts

156. The court system in the Slovak Republic does not separately distinguish 'criminal courts'; thus, all steps and actions concerning criminal prosecution are conducted by the general courts. There is only one exception represented by a so-called Specialized Criminal Court (in Slovak *Špecializovaný trestný súd*) whose activities cover the prosecution of major crimes. Section 250 of the CrC (the criminal acts connected to a breach of the CA) is not covered by the Specialized Criminal Court's jurisdiction; however, crimes of machinations committed in a public procurement process (*see* II above) are covered by the jurisdiction of the Specialized Criminal Court.[334]

157. The Slovak Republic has a two-level court system whereas criminal acts concerning violation of antitrust law are in the first instance decided by district courts.[335] The competent court is the district court of the area in which the respective crime was committed. If it is not possible to determine such place, the competent court is the court to which a prosecutor submits a criminal charge.[336] The first-degree decision can be appealed to the regional court in which district the first instance court is placed.

158. The judgment which is already in force can be challenged by the appeal on points of law[337] (in Slovak *dovolanie*) which is decided by the Supreme Court of the Slovak Republic;[338] it may be filed also by the Minister of Justice.[339] Another extraordinary remedy is a claim for a renewal[340] (in Slovak *obnova konania*) which is in general admitted when new evidence that could not have been presented before issuing a judgment, emerge.

332. Section 237(1) of the CPC.
333. Section 36(1) of the CPC.
334. Section 14 of the CPC.
335. Section 15 in connection with s. 17(1) of the CPC.
336. Section 20 of the CPC.
337. Section 368–395 of the CPC.
338. Section 377 of the CPC.
339. Section 371 of the CPC.
340. Section 393–405 of the CPC.

Part II. The Application of the Prohibitions

Chapter 1. Restrictive Agreements

§1. Horizontal Agreements

159. The agreement is regarded as horizontal if concluded between undertakings that operate on the same level of the same relevant market, that is, concluded between competitors. The CA includes neither the definition of the horizontal agreement/the horizontal relationship nor the definition of the competitor. However, the AMO's case law is consistent with the EU case law and follows a definition of 'competitor' included in respective block exemptions.[341] The notion of a competitor thus involves a real competitor (factual, existing) as well as a potential competitor (future, prospective).

160. When evaluating these agreements, it is necessary to take into account not only the restriction of competition between parties to the agreement, but also its negative influence on prices, innovations or a number of types or a quality of products or services.

161. The horizontal agreements are traditionally divided into two categories. First of these agreements are those considered in practice automatically as anticompetitive – the proof of the breach of the antitrust rules is based on the existence of such agreement itself and these are usually treated as prohibited 'per se' (even though the CA does not involve categories of 'per se' prohibited agreements and agreements assessed based on the 'rule of reason' and it requires assessment in line with the object/effect doctrine, *see* Part I, Chapter 3, §5, I).

162. However, it should not be forgotten that the AMO has to prove its conclusion that an agreement restricting competition is the agreement 'by object'; the 'aim' to restrict competition has to be evident and present. The 'aim' to restrict competition has to be seen as an objective conception, while having a relation to the nature of the agreement under review in its economic context.[342] The subjective motivation of cartel participants towards restricting competition will play an important role in making a decision on the amount of a sanction and may simplify the competition authority's

341. For example, Art. 1(1) of the Commission Regulation No. 1217/2010 of 14 Dec. 2010 on the application of Art. 101(3) of the Treaty on the functioning of the European Union to categories of research and development agreements, OJ L 335, 18 Dec. 2010, 36.
342. Kindl, J., 'Protisoutěžní cíl a účinek ve světle poslední judikatury Soudního dvora EU', Antitrust 4/2014, p. 136.

evidence position.[343] In the *Groupement des CarteBancaire* case,[344] the Court of Justice sent a kind of a warning of an exaggerated assessment of cases according to the 'object-based agreement' rule and automatic concluding on a breach of competition rules.

163. The possible anticompetitive impact of other agreements is reviewed in relation to the circumstances of an individual case.

Among the agreements that the AMO considers as 'per se' illegal belong particularly those ones that fix prices, restrict the production's capacities, impose conditions for the participation in tenders, and divide markets. On the contrary, agreements containing restrictions that do not belong to the list of 'always prohibited agreements' have to be considered individually on the basis of the actual circumstances of the case, both in the economic and the legal context in which the agreement was made. The consideration is based mainly on the assessment of the nature of the agreement, character of goods and of the relevant market touched by the agreement, position of parties to the agreement on the market and a combined market share of participants. Agreements which are in general treated by the AMO according to the 'rule of reason' are particularly agreements on fixing of a uniform standard of products, joint selling and promotion activities.

I. Cartels

A. Price Fixing

164. The prohibition to conclude price-fixing cartels is included in the section 4(4) letter a) of the CA and is expressed as the prohibition of 'direct and indirect price-fixing'. The respective prohibition refers to all types of agreements (such as horizontal, vertical or mixed) and to all three forms of agreements restricting competition, assumed by the general clause ('Agreements', 'Concerted practices' and 'Decision of associations').

165. The substance is the prohibition of any actions characterized by the coordination of the competitive behaviour in the area of prices, without the necessity that such cooperation would necessarily lead to identical or similar competitive policy in the pricing area applied on the market. The coordination may also be obscure and can be aimed, or can even lead to absolutely different competitive pricing behaviour. The usual target of the price cartel is to reach the same price of certain goods delivered to customers (in case of horizontal agreements) or to fix price for further selling (in case of vertical agreements). In the first case, the behaviour represents so-called price-fixing, in the second one it is so-called RPM.

166. The 'price-fixing' cartels represent the most serious form of the breach of competition rules because they clearly and directly eliminate the price competition on the market and simultaneously, also the possibility of customers to choose the best price. These types of cartels constantly belong to hard-core cartels.

343. Kindl, J., 'Protisoutěžní cíl a účinek ve světle poslední judikatury Soudního dvora EU', Antitrust 4/2014, p. 136.

344. Judgment of the European Court of Jusctice, case C-67/13 P, *Groupement des cartesbancaires (CB) v Commission*, 11 Sept. 2014, https://curia.europa.eu/.

167. The price-fixing cartel on the horizontal level was, for example, assessed by the AMO in Case *Association of University Hospitals,*[345] whereby the association intervened with the negation of the price for terminated hospitalization which had to be covered in university hospitals by individual public-health insurance companies. The Council in its decision, in relation to the materiality condition of the general clause, concluded (referring to the EU case law) that:

> The aim of the agreement has to be evaluated objectively according to the intentions of the agreement and it is not necessary to review subjective intentions of the parties. In general, if an obvious consequence of an agreement is a restriction or impairment of competition, from the legal evaluation aspect, this is its 'aim', even though the parties to the agreement declare that it has not been their intention or that the agreement has other aims. As regards horizontal agreements, courts of the Community have repeatedly confirmed that agreements, which follow the goal of a competition restriction and fall under the category of agreements directly prohibited by Article 81(1) of the Treaty, may not be justified by an analysis of the economic context of the anticompetitive behaviour. This means that if an agreement is undoubtedly aimed at a competition restriction, for example, by a determination of prices, restriction of sales or distribution of clients, it is not necessary to prove that the price competition has actually been affected or imports have been restricted, in order for it to involve a breach of Article 81(1).[346]

168. Price cartel can be described as a way for coordination of business behaviour when suppliers of certain goods, in the position of mutual competitors, directly agree on prices for delivery of goods to the market (selling price cartels), or agree on prices for buying of goods (purchasing price cartels), or they agree on factors by which the price is fixed or at least influenced (system of discounts, coordination when setting payment terms, system of surcharges to price). A price cartel is also the coordination of determination of a minimal price or a maximal price at both an 'on sale' and an 'on purchase' level.

169. However, a price cartel can have a lot of other forms such as indirect price-fixing,[347] when the price-fixing of certain goods can be realized also by means of the same calculating pricing formula, of the same system of discounts, of the same price range and of an agreed differential between prices and discounts.

The existence of a price cartel is apparent if the price range or other components of prices proposed by single undertakings to their business partners are obviously similar or show changes around a certain date. The problem with discovering such cartel behaviour can be connected to the fact that prices can be very similar both even on a highly competitive market (where an undertaking has the possibility to 'study'

345. Decision of the AMO No. 2008/KH/1/1/107, 16 Dec. 2009; Decision of the Council No. 2009/KH/R/2/029, 5 Jun. 2009, <http://www.antimon.gov.sk>.

346. Decision of the Council No. 2009/KH/R/2/029, 5 Jun. 2009, <http://www.antimon.gov.sk>, translation by author.

347. Decisions of the AMO and the Council on indirect price fixing in the Case *Association of bakers*, No. 2006/KH/1/1/143, 22 Dec. 2006 and No. 2007/KH/R/2/026, 27 Apr. 2007, <http://www.antimon.gov.sk>.

the competitor's pricing behaviour) as well as on a market controlled by undertakings linked by a price cartel.

It means that only finding the identity or similarity of prices and their development does not always have to be the proof of anticompetitive behaviour. It is then necessary to look for evidence proving that the respective behaviour was caused by an anticompetitive coordination. Proving the existence of a price cartel then will be sufficient for the AMO to state that the cartel is prohibited because already, from its very nature, it is obvious that it is detrimental to the competition.

170. The parties to the price cartel usually apply various control mechanisms which shall ensure that none of them deviates from the rules, possibly to reveal every deviation from the cartel that means they try to set up the model which enables the cartel to work effectively. A typical control mechanism can be the regular mutual reporting of the cartel's participants.

171. The AMO, in the Case *Hog raisers*[348] assessed the direct price-fixing agreement by which the hog raisers agreed on a minimum price for meat processors, concluded that the agreement between competitors concerning product price represented an 'agreement restricting competition by object' potential negative impact of which did not have to be reviewed.

Another decision concerning the price cartel concerns cartel of '*Laundry Detergents*'.[349] It was a cartel agreement among three groups of laundry detergent suppliers, Procter & Gamble (P&G), Henkel and Reckitt Benckiser ('RB'), while in relation to two of them, specifically, P&G and Henkel, the AMO stated that they had committed cartel acts in the relevant market of highly effective laundry detergents intended for household use. The cartel agreement was detected based on the submission of P&G´s Request for Leniency (Leniency Programme). The cartel acts had been taken since 1999 among participants from the Henkel and P&G Groups, specifically, within the Central European Region, where the participants had been negotiating, *inter alia*, a limitation of promotion actions and had been exchanging commercially sensitive information (mutual exchange of price lists). Within the framework of the limitation of promotion actions, they had been negotiating, for instance, an agreement not to mutually responding to certain bargain sale prices through sectoral measures. They had at the same time agreed that within the framework of standardization of volumes of packages, the prices would remain unchanged even in case of the application of a new standard (such mutual understanding of common procedure had allegedly been taking place since 1999–2001). The RB Group´s participation was not proved by the AMO. The AMO stated in relation to the cartel agreement that it had concerned a single continuous infringement, while relying upon the constant decision-making practice of European institutions and stating that:

A complex of several acts accepted within a certain time framework by several undertakings in order to reach a single anti-competitive aim may also be deemed as a single agreement restricting competition. The agreement itself may be changed over time and its mechanism may be developed, while taking into account, for instance, development in the given area, in a certain market, etc. Such understanding may not be doubted by the possibility that one or more practices within such complex creating

348. Decision of the Council No. 2005/KH/R/2/073, 1 Jun. 2005, <http://www.antimon.gov.sk>.
349. Decision of the AMO No. 2011/KH/1/1/055, 22 Dec. 2011, <http://www.antimon.gov.sk>.

an agreement restricting competition could in themselves represent a violation of law either.[350]

Another case reviewed by the AMO as a price cartel was an agreement restricting competition in the form of a decision of an association of undertakings. In the given case, the Association of Estate Agents determined the amount of commission for the estate activity as well as the amount of arranger fee. The price agreement was incorporated directly to the Code of Ethics and Professional Conduct. In case of cooperation of several agents, the commission should be divided among the total number of agents as per a key agreed among them in advance in writing. The AMO assessed the agreement in question as an agreement by object.[351]

172. A 'price-fixing agreement' will be treated by the AMO as always coming under the prohibition defined by the general clause (section 4(1) of the CA). The *ex lege* exemption can be applied only hypothetically due to the fact that four cumulative conditions[352] for the exemption can hardly be met.

B. Market/Client Allocation

173. The 'market-partitioning agreements' or 'agreements on customer allocation' are included in section 4(4) letter c) of the CA. These are constantly regarded by the AMO as hard-core agreements.

174. This agreement can have the form, for example, of an agreement on the division of the purchasing sources where more undertakings coordinate their demand towards a third person in the position of their supplier or towards the region where these suppliers operate.

175. Geographic market sharing may be combined with another type of a prohibited agreement, specifically, the price agreement, according to which all competitors will make supplies to their territories for the same price. If such territories are comparable in terms of the demand side, then such market sharing with a price agreement will provide for the certainty of profit for all cartel participants.

176. Accordingly, a horizontal market-sharing agreement may also be based on the fact that the competitors divide the sphere of influence by customers, i.e. they will supply to a certain group of customers only. For instance, competitors may agree that certain suppliers will supply to a retail network only or to services only; or, for example, that they will supply for a certain segment of customers only. Again, customer allocation may also be combined with an agreement on prices, when, in addition to the customer allocation, a price for which supplies will be made will also be agreed. As a result of such agreements, the customer's possibility to select a supplier of goods is eliminated and the price for which the customer is able to buy goods is increased. A customer allocation agreement may also be part of cartel agreements concerning collusion in public procurement. Here, particular competitors may agree that each of them will participate in procurement announced for certain customer segments only. The customer

350. Decision of the European Commission No, Comp/E-1/38.069 *CopperPlumbingTubes* (2006), OJ L 192/21, §§443–449.

351. Decision of the Council, No. 2010/KH/R/2/010, 26 Feb. 2010, <http://www.antimon.gov.sk>.

352. Section 6(3) of the CA.

allocation agreement may equally be accompanied by a measure according to which competitors will distribute profit among themselves according to a pre-defined key.

177. Agreements on market-partitioning on 'the suppliers' side' or on 'the buyers' side' or allocation of customers are characterized by the fact that suppliers or customers are limited by persons to whom they can supply products or by persons from whom they can buy products, or limitations concerning the territory to which products can be supplied or in which they can be purchased.

The market-partitioning agreement is not only linked to cooperation on a horizontal level but it may be concluded in a vertical relationship as well. The principles of operation of the agreement as described above are similar: the supplier divides 'its market' among several customers which are prohibited to make supplies to other territories. The vertical market-partitioning agreement can also be concluded in addition to a horizontal, and can thus raise the effectiveness of a horizontal cooperation.

178. These agreements are always treated by the AMO as prohibited according to the general clause (section 4(1) of the CA) and their 'approval' based on *ex lege* exemption (section 4(f) of the CA), is not very probable.

179. In 2009, the AMO, in the Case *Bank cartel,*[353] imposed a fine on three Slovak banks for an agreement on common procedures on the market of cashless foreign exchange operations provided to customers, regardless of the volume of transactions. The agreement focused against the Czech company (Akcenta CZ) which was a direct competitor of the respective banks on the defined relevant market. The Czech company, as a non-bank subject, may provide respective operations to its customers only if it has a bank account in a Slovak bank whereas the company can be effective if such an account is created in various banks. In the case in question, the issue of 'self-help' that could be applied by competitors in the market, provided that one of the competitors pursued business in conflict with generally binding legal regulations, has come to the fore. Here, the AMO reviewed the action of the Slovak banks specifically, Slovenská sporiteľňa (SLSP), Československá obchodná banka (ČSOB) and Všeobecná úverová banka (VÚB), which allegedly entered into a cartel agreement based on which they would terminate the already-existing contracts and would not again enter into current bank account agreements with Akcenta CZ. The AMO stated in its decision that the goal of the procedure of SLSP, ČSOB and VÚB had been to exclude Akcenta CZ as a competitor from the market of the provision of non-cash foreign exchange operations provided to customers regardless of the transaction volume. One of the chambers of the Regional Court in Bratislava decided within the framework of a judicial review of an administrative decision to cancel the AMO's decision. It adopted such decision also due to the fact that it took into account the fact that Akcenta CZ had been performing its activity in the Slovak market in conflict with generally binding legal regulations. At the time of the objected coordinated procedure of the Slovak banks, Akcenta CZ was operating in the market without holding the necessary foreign exchange license granted by the National Bank of Slovakia. In relation therewith, the Regional Court in Bratislava stated that the procedure of the said banks might not be deemed as a cartel agreement, if based on defence against an entity operating in the market illegally. The Regional Court decided that the banks'

353. Decision of the AMO No. 2009/KH/R/2/054, 19 Nov. 2009; Decision of the Council No. 2009/KH/1/1/030, 9 Jun. 2009, <http://www.antimon.gov.sk>.

action had been an acceptable action towards a risk client. The Supreme Court did not identify itself with this conclusion and considered the fact that Akcenta CZ had been operating in the Slovak market illegally to be irrelevant in terms of the assessment of the prohibition to enter into an agreement restricting competition pursuant to section 4(1) of the CA. In relation therewith, the Supreme Court referred to the Court of Justice with a preliminary question, which expressed its opinion in the given case that:

Article 101 of the TFEU is to be interpreted in the sense that the fact that an undertaking affected by a cartel agreement the target of which is to restrict economic competition is allegedly operating in a relevant market at the time of the conclusion of such cartel agreement illegally shall not affect the question whether such cartel represents a breach of this provision or not.[354]

The Court of Justice was at same time dealing within the framework of the prejudicial question with the issue whether the fact that at the time of the conclusion of the cartel agreement, the question of legality of the undertaking´s operation in the market was not doubted, was legally relevant for the interpretation of Article 101(1) of the TFEU (i.e., identically, section 4(1) of the CA). The above-quoted conclusion of the Court of Justice is applicable to this question too, while the Court of Justice relied in its justification upon the fact that the aim of the banks´ agreement to exclude Akcenta CZ had consisted particularly in a restriction of competition and that none of the banks had appealed and doubted legality of the performance of Akcenta´s business activity in the Slovak market. For this reason, the Court of Justice stated that Akcenta´s business in conflict with generally binding legal regulations had not affected the conclusion on violation of the cartel prohibition. In relation to the said conclusions, it is worth to mention that the Court of Justice did not individually deal at all with details of the issue whether defence against a competitor operating in a market illegally is capable of fulfilling the material condition of the general clause of the cartel prohibition, specifically, by the fulfilment of an anticompetitive aim or a potential of anticompetitive impact.

180. The AMO reviewed a horizontal agreement on market sharing in the *GIS* Cartel case.[355] In the case in question, the companies producing the so-called gas insulated switches agreed, *inter alia*, upon division of the sphere of their interest from the geographical aspect. In the proceedings, the Office had a document at its disposal submitted within the framework of the Leniency application, from which it resulted that the cartel participants had divided the market into the so-called available international markets, unavailable international markets, USA and Canada, Europe domestic market and Japan domestic market. Based on the concluded agreement, Japan companies had renounced the market in Europe, and European companies subsequently divided, in addition, the market within Europe, meaning that only companies with the allocated given territory were participating in tenders in particular European states. The cartel within Europe allegedly operated from 1987 to 2004. In relation to particular projects allocated to a certain cartel member, the so-called 'order meetings' were organized, where a procedure in a specific tender and participation of other cartel members was

354. Judgment of the Court of Justice, C-68/12 Slovenská sporiteľňa v the Antimonopoly Office of the Slovak Republic, 7 Feb. 2013.
355. 354. Decision of the Council No. 2009/KH/R/2/035, 14 Aug. 2009, <http://www.antimon.gov.sk.>.

being negotiated in order to minimize the suspicion of manipulating the tender. The member to which the tender was assigned within the framework of the market-sharing agreement notified other cartel members of its price for this case with which it wanted to tender, while a decision was thereafter made by which amount should the offer of other cartel members be higher, or they agreed on precise prices with which such members would participate in the tender. The goal of the cartel was to keep stable market shares of the cartel members, while the cartel was maintaining a list of all available projects. Free projects were being assigned based on a credit system designed in such a manner that the cartel members got projects in an approximately the same volume.

C. *Production/Innovation Limitation*

181. The next type of prohibited agreement assumed by the demonstrative list of section 4(4) of the CA is represented by agreements which control or restrict production, selling, research or innovation of products. These agreements are usually concluded on a horizontal level and involve, for example, situations where undertakings agree to limit their production in the case of a relatively stable decrease of demand for particular goods on the market; however, the production capacity needs to be maintained because of possible increase of demand, in the future. Moreover, a situation when two competitors, both supplying the market by two types of goods, make an agreement according to which one of these undertakings will keep supplying the market with one type of good and the latter with the second type of goods is also prohibited. A similar prohibited agreement can be made also in a vertical relationship when, for example, a supplier defines volumes and types of goods delivered to the market by its customers. The more of these vertical agreements that the supplier concludes with buyers, the higher is the possibility that these relations cause negative effects similar to the effects of a horizontal agreement.

182. These agreements are prohibited by the general clause and can be exempted according to section 4(5) of the CA (*ex lege* exemption) if all cumulative criteria are met, that is:

(i) the agreement contributes to the improvement of production or distribution of goods or to a promotion of technical or economic development whereby allows consumers an adequate share from the benefits resulting out of the agreement;[356]

(iii) the agreement does not impose on parties such restrictions that are not indispensable to the attainment of the claimed objectives of the agreement;[357]

(iv) the agreement does not afford the possibility to exclude competition on a substantial part of the relevant market[358] (see Part I, Chapter 3, §5).

356. Section 4(5) letter a) of the CA.
357. Section 4(5) letter b) of the CA.
358. Section 4(5) letter c) of the CA.

The character of agreements on limitation of production or innovation suggests that meeting such conditions would be difficult.

D. *Group Boycott*

183. Another type of prohibited agreements is a group boycott cartel. Even though they are not included in the demonstrative list of prohibited agreements, they come under the general clause on prohibition.

This type of cartel has similar characteristics to those that belong to the discriminatory cartels.[359] While in the case of discriminatory cartels, undertakings agree that they will cooperate with third persons under conditions that will not be profitable so that these third persons will subsequently lose interest in such cooperation, the boycott cartel focuses on an absolute refusal to cooperate with third parties. The negative impacts of these agreements on economic competition are in both cases the same. The discriminatory cartels as well as boycott cartels limit or eliminate the entry of potential competitors to the market and fix the market positions of those undertakings that have entered the cartel.

184. The group boycott cartel may appear in a horizontal relationship much like in a vertical relationship, however horizontal agreements are more effective. Competitors may fix their positions in a way that they agree on supplying their goods only to appointed customers or buying goods only from appointed suppliers (they may agree on the black list of customers or suppliers).

In a vertical boycott cartel, it can become impossible to get goods from certain distribution systems of respective suppliers, which means that potential customers will have to refer to other suppliers offering goods for higher prices, or even not be in a position to obtain these goods at all. If this situation concerns a customer for whom such goods are a necessary component, then this action (boycott) is capable of driving this customer out of the market. The combination of horizontal and vertical boycott agreements is very dangerous. If competitors agree on a group boycott on a horizontal level and at the same time keep the boycott's rules in their vertical relationships, the fixation of their position on the market is very effective.

The boycott agreement can be potentially exempted based on *ex lege* exemption according to the section 4(5) of the CA.

E. *Collusion on Other Objects*

185. The CA in its demonstrative list[360] further distinguishes agreements on 'other trade conditions', the object of which is coordination of business conditions other than price. In practice cooperation concerns, for example, conditions of providing loans, supply or purchasing deadlines and conditions. It is not crucial whether these trade conditions are agreed towards actual or potential competitors or exercised towards customers.

186. The AMO recently issued a decision against providers of meal vouchers claiming that they concluded a cartel agreement with the aim to limit number of

359. Section 4(4) letter c) of the CA.
360. Section 4(4) letter a) of the CA.

vouchers which can be used by the end-customers in supermarkets for one shopping.[361] The end-users in Slovakia are currently free to use the meal vouchers also in supermarkets for buying foods. The AMO claimed that the aim of the limitation was to force the end-customers to use the meal vouchers in restaurant in which the meal vouchers providers benefit from higher provision than in supermarkets. The AMO concluded that this is an agreement restricting competition by object from its very nature. The decision has been challenged by all suspected parties to the cartel mainly arguing that the discussion on limitation was connected to the protection from abuse of meal vouchers as secondary currency in supermarkets.

187. There are other types of agreements prohibited by the CA called tying contracts.[362] Tying refers to situations where customers that purchase one product, i.e. the tying product, are also required to purchase another distinct product, i.e. the tied product from the same supplier or a person designated by the supplier.[363]

Their substance lies in the tying of the conclusion of the contract to the fulfilment of other commitments that neither by their nature, nor according to the commercial usage, relate to the object of the contract. It follows from the relevant case law of the General Court that two products are distinct where, in the absence of tying, a substantial number of customers would purchase or would have purchased the tying product without also buying the tied product from the same supplier, thereby allowing a stand-alone production for both the tying and the tied product.[364]

By these agreements, parties to the agreement are mutually bound to proceed uniformly towards third persons and to accept concluding contracts with these third parties, only if they meet certain conditions, not related to the main object of the contract. Thus, the third party has in principle eliminated the possibility of concluding contract concerning only desired object and needs to accept even redundant commitments.

These kind of agreements can be assessed according the respective Vertical restrains block exemption or in line with *ex lege* exemption defined by section 4(5) of the CA.

188. The CA further distinguishes 'bid-rigging agreements' as it prohibits agreements that involve 'signs of collusive behaviour as a result of which undertakings coordinate their behaviour, especially in the process of a public procurement, in public tender or in other similar tender procedure'.[365]

189. The principle of bid-rigging means that all bidders or some of them, agree before submission of their bids that they will not compete in reality and make 'the most profitable' offers. The result of such agreements is that the contract is not assigned in reality to the best bidder as it would be assigned in cases when such an agreement would not exist. The bid-rigging can be realized on several principles such as:

(1) 'The principle of rotation' is a method when the undertakings take turns successively so that orders would be evenly divided among all the undertakings. Always one

361. Decesion of the AMO No. 2016/KH/1/1/004 11 Feb. 2016, Not Published, Pending.
362. Section 4(4) letter d) of the CA.
363. Paragraph 214 of the Vertical Guidelines.
364. Decision of the General Court in case T-201/04, *Microsoft*, 17 Sep. 2007, paras 917, 921 and 922.
365. Section 4(4) letter f) of the CA.

of the undertakings makes the most profitable offer in the tender, the rest of parties to the agreement then make only a 'formal', less profitable offer.

(2) 'The principle of market-partitioning' according to which each of parties to the cartel operates on 'his' territory where he is 'allowed' to win the tender. This approach can be agreed on a geographical basis and/or on the basis of the dividing of procurers or character of orders.
(3) 'The principle of compensation'; individual undertakings agree in advance on the winner of the tender, thus only one of the parties to the agreement submits a bid on the tender. The winner of the tender subsequently provides those undertakings not participating on the tender with the relevant fulfilment as a financial benefit, as a subcontracted conclusion.
(4) 'The principle of supplement offers'; this system binds some bidders to make offers with very high prices, thus the bidder selected as the winner of the tender can get the contract for a price which is above the level of competitive price.
(5) 'The principle of controlled offers' allows only those participants who are admitted to participate by the cartel to participate on the tender. The most efficient form of controlled offers is the payment of a so-called entry fee. Such fee then logically influences the offered price; a fund made from the entry fee income is divided on the basis of an agreed mechanism, among the cartel members.

190. To conclude that a bid-rigging agreement took place, the AMO has to prove the coordination between at least two participants of the tender concerning their offers; submission of the offers to the announced tender, and that the person who announced the selective procedure was neither conscious of the existence of any coordination before putting the offers forward nor required such coordination (e.g., for the purpose of fulfilling of specialized activities).

The existence of such agreement can be supposed because of the fact that only a limited number of interested undertakings participated on the tender whereas undertakings whose participation was expected did not. The main indicators of a collusive behaviour in tenders are:

– similarity of offers not only linked to prices;
– unacceptability of offers because of their flagrant inexpedience;
– repeating of unnecessary procedural mistakes by a tender participants;
– changing of winners on a regular basis;
– objectively non-justifiable difference between a winning offer and offers of other bidders;
– the same sub-suppliers of winning bidders as well as a regular participation of the same suppliers in tenders;
– the fact that tenders are won repeatedly by the same supplier;
– the fact that less bidders made an offer than is usual compared to other similar fulfilments;
– the fact that the winner intends to make sub-supplier contract/s with other tender participants;
– the fact that a certain supplier obviously submits the most non-profitable offers at certain intervals, than in other similar cases.

191. The model case concerning the bid-rigging cartel decided by the AMO is the cartel agreement of highway construction companies.[366] The cartel agreement was assessed by the AMO through an economic analysis – by comparison of individual prices of individual bidders which in respective items showed high level of conformity. The AMO came to the conclusion that this conformity could not be explained by other reasons then by collusive behaviour.[367] Furthermore, the Council justified the conclusion that the breach of competition rules took place by an explanation:

> The principal and key proof in these proceedings is represented by the relation among offers submitted by particular bidders… proofs together with this proof document that the parties to the tender have had a sufficient communication platform in order to coordinate their acting in submitting offers and they also prove that they have actually communicated to each other. The specific content of negotiations has not been found out, which has not been, however, necessary, since the Council considers the specific relation among particular submitted offers to be the sufficient proof of the coordination of the behaviour of the parties to the tender.[368]

The 'bid-rigging agreement' comes under hard-core cartels and its exemption from the prohibition defined by the general clause is only hypothetical.

192. Other agreements prohibited according to the general clause are so-called non-compete agreements. These are not of an individual type as included in the demonstrative list of section 4(4) of the CA whereas in practice are represented by exclusive provisions such as, for example, exclusivity on selling or purchase, exclusivity on performance of research and development or exclusivity following from a specialization. Non-compete obligations are tacitly included, for example, in the distribution agreements or the specialization agreements.

193. The AMO in its case concerning selective distribution of Electrolux products[369] assessed the obligation of the authorized distributors to exclusively reserve all its floor space for products delivered under the brands name of Electrolux group as the prohibited non-compete obligation.

The second group of these agreements is represented by those in which the non-compete obligation is expressed explicitly. These provisions can be found in sale-purchase agreements concerning the sale of a business of an undertaking or its parts and they are reviewed within a merger control proceedings as ancillary restraints.

---

366. Decision of the AMO No. 2005/KH/1/137, 23 Dec. 2005; Decision of the Council No. 2006/KH/R/2/116, 16 Oct. 2006, <http://www.antimon.gov.sk>.
367. Decision of the Council No. 2006/KH/R/2/116, 16 Oct. 2006, 26, <http://www.antimon.gov.sk>.
368. Decision of the Council No. 2006/KH/R/2/116, 16 Oct. 2006, 30, <http://www.antimon.gov.sk>, translation by author.
369. Decision of the Council No. 2004/KV/R/2/115, 5 May 2004, <http://www.antimon.gov.sk>; similar Decision in Case *Probugas* (LPG supplier) in which the obligation to buy LPG products only from the company Probugas was treated as non-compete obligation; Decision of the Council No. 2003/KV/R/2/279, 26 Nov. 2003, <http://www.antimon.gov.sk>.

194. Independent and specific types of agreements represent arrangements on the establishment of the association that should eliminate risks connected to otherwise independent activities of its members; so-called pools such as insurance and safety pools which are typical in practice.

II. Information Exchange Practices

195. As already mentioned above, each prohibited agreement needs to fulfil the criterion of materiality included in the general clause, that is, only agreements which are restrictive by their object or which potentially effect (the effect must be appreciable) restriction of competition, are prohibited.

An exchange of market sensitive information can be also treated by the AMO under certain circumstances as anticompetitive.

The evaluation of whether an exchange of information is prohibited results from the rule that each undertaking is obliged to determine its behaviour and activities on the market independently and that the general clause[370] pre-emptively excludes contracts between undertakings which aim at a restriction of competition or which can lead to a restriction of competition. The AMO will consider mainly the character of information that is exchanged, the frequency of the exchange and persons among whom the information exchange is made. Whether the exchanged information is in reality used in a business strategy of the respective undertaking is not relevant if, by its nature, it leads to an exclusion or a reduction of the undertakings' 'uncertainty' on the market and contributes to anticipation of other players' market behaviour.

According to the Horizontal Co-operation Guidelines,[371] anticompetitive exchange of information can have a form of an agreement restricting competition, a concerted practices and a decision of association of undertakings. Moreover, it can serve to support a cartel and to monitor compliance with the rules defined by the cartel members. In such case, the assessment of anticompetitive exchange of information forms part of the assessment of a cartel behaviour in any of the above-mentioned forms. The Council in its decision concerning price-fixing on the market of IT technologies distribution stated that also the mere exchange of information on prices could lead to price coordination and thus reduce the intensity of competition that would otherwise exist between undertakings. This occurs whether in the event when the exchange of information is directly linked to the prices or it concerns components of the price policy. The Council pointed out, that in the respective case the exchange of sensitive information led right to the coordination for the introduction of price components; on the other hand, the Council also stated that also the mere exchange of information may constitute in some cases a serious infringement of the competition rules, even in a form of an agreement by object.[372]

370. Section 4(1) of the CA.

371. Paragraph 59, Communication from the Commission – Guidelines on the applicability of Art. 101 of the Treaty on the Functioning of the European Union to Horizontal Co-operation Agreements, OJ C 11 14 Jan. 2011, pp. 1–72.

372. Decision of the Council of the AMO No. 2015/KH/R/2/010, 31 Mar 2015, §206, <http://www.antimon.gov.sk>.

196. Mainly the exchange of market sensitive and exact information on the highly concentrated market (low number of competitors – oligopolistic market) and the exchange of information in short and regular intervals can significantly negatively influence the quality of the competition. Commercially sensitive information under the Horizontal Co-operation Guidelines[373] is information that allows companies to be aware of market strategies of their competitors. The Court of Justice has in the case *John Deere*[374] said that as commercially sensitive information is considered the information that will remove uncertainty in the market to such an extent that undertakings based on the exchanged information can adjust their future behaviour on the market.

197. The case law of the AMO concerning the autonomous agreements on exchange of information is rather limited, but it can be presumed that the AMO will take into consideration present EU case law and recommendations of the European Commission, especially Horizontal Co-operation Guidelines[375] and will use similar criteria for the assessment as:[376]

(1) the market structure and the existing competition conditions on the market;
(2) the degree of confidentiality of exchanged information and the periodicity of the exchange; mainly the exchange of market sensitive information such as strategies of sale, prices for individual customers, cost structure, sale volumes, that is, the exchange of information usually protected by undertakings as a business secret would be treated as anticompetitive;
(3) whether the information exchange is provided on a regular basis in short intervals;
(4) the presence of the reduction of independent market behaviour; received information does not need to be even factually used, it is sufficient that via the exchange of sensitive information, the reduction of 'uncertainty' concerning other market players' behaviour is present. Neither the proof of a similar market strategy of individual market players is necessary.

198. It is not possible to suppose a priori that the main target of the horizontal agreements on the exchange of statistical information would be by the coordination of future competitive behaviour. Their impact on the economic competition has to be therefore examined by more careful analysis than is needed for the evaluation of hard-core cartels. The analysis has to include a comparison of the possible impacts of the agreement on the market; on the one hand, it is an additional increase of market transparency and on the other hand and to a real extent, the facilitation of the coordination of future market behaviour.

---

373. Communication from the Commission – Guidelines on the applicability of Art. 101 of the Treaty on the Functioning of the European Union to Horizontal Co-operation Agreements, OJ C 11 14 Jan. 2011, pp. 1–72.
374. Judgment of the Court of Justice C-7/95, Case *John Deere Ltd. v. Commission*, (1998), ECR I-03111.
375. Communication from the Commission – Guidelines on the applicability of Art. 101 of the Treaty on the Functioning of the European Union to Horizontal Co-operation Agreements, OJ C 11 14 Jan. 2011, pp. 1–72.
376. For example, Judgment of the Court of Justice C-7/95, Case *John Deere Ltd. v. Commission*, (1998), ECR I-03111.

199. The pure exchange of confidential data concerning a business strategy (e.g., price information, information concerning production capacities, information on selling conditions, etc.), from which it could be possible to infer a future business strategy, could have a potential to restrict competition, which is tolerated in cases when the exchange of information concerns aggregated and sufficiently historical data.

200. Due to the existence of the common historical trend of the Czech and Slovak antitrust laws, and relations between the AMO and the Czech competition office, it is worth mentioning the Czech case on an exchange of information agreement concerning *Building and loan associations.*[377] The Czech authority stated that individual building and loan associations, by their mutual agreement concerning a complex system of exchanging of actual statistical summaries on their business results on monthly bases, concluded a prohibited and invalid agreement on the exchange of information that could lead to a distortion of economic competition on the market for building saving. However, the Regional Court in Brno[378] dismissed the decision (its conclusion was supported also by the Supreme Administrative Court).[379] The Regional Court in Brno stated that only a consensus between market players that has a real influence on their future market behaviour, and therefore on their future autonomy in decision-making and a future competitive independency, is deemed to be anticompetitive from the antitrust legislation perspective. Furthermore, it stated that only a coordination that reduces the present extent of uncertainty concerning the future competitive behaviour of individual market players can meet the condition for a potential distortion of economic competition.

III. Cooperation Agreements

201. Cooperation agreements concern several areas of a horizontal cooperation and mainly involve cooperation concerning joint research and development, joint selling, joint production and distribution, specialization agreements or joint advertising, standardization and normalization agreements, and agreements aimed at protection of the environment.

202. This kind of agreement usually comes under the prohibition of the general clause even though they are not included in the demonstrative list of section 4(4) of the CA. However, the potential of their negative effect on competition needs to be appraised in each individual case. The AMO has not issued any guideline which would describe principles and rules for the assessment of cooperation agreements. Nevertheless, the AMO follows rules determined by EU regulations and guidelines, mainly by the Commission Notice – Guidelines on the applicability of Article 81 to Horizontal Co-operation Agreements[380] (Horizontal Co-operation Guidelines).

377. Decision of the Chairman of the Office for the Protection of Competition R161/2006/ 01,003,004,008,009,010/2007/ 01-07777/2007/310, 18 Apr. 2007.
378. Judgment of the Regional Court in Brno 62 Ca 15/2007, 8 Jan. 2008.
379. Judgment of the Supreme Administrative Court 1 Afs 78/2008, 25 Feb. 2009.
380. Communication from the Commission – Guidelines on the applicability of Art. 101 of the Treaty on the Functioning of the European Union to Horizontal Co-operation Agreements, OJ C 11 14 Jan. 2011, pp. 1–72.

203. The AMO considers the impact of each agreement on economic competition on the respective relevant market individually whereas it uses the economics-based approach that involves evaluation of relations between negative impacts on the competition and the economic (rationalization) gains that joint cooperation between the competitors brings; evaluation of the market share of the parties to the agreement, and the development of their market shares. The Herfindahl-Hirschmann's Index (HHI) is used for evaluation of the market concentration by the AMO in practice.[381] There are also other factors to be evaluated: stability of the market shares; the existence, character and extent of entry barriers, and the degree of homogeneity of products.

A. Research and Development

204. The horizontal research and development agreement (R&D agreement) may differ by its content and extent. Its object is mainly the improvement and development of already existing technologies, joint research and development, or the joint introduction of new products on the market.

R&D agreements are focused on a production sphere as well as on a business sphere. These agreements may have a form of cooperation agreement of established undertakings already on the market; however, they can also be realized via the establishment of a new company which will provide research and development for already existing undertakings. The establishment of such a new undertaking could come under the merger control rules. The main advantages of R&D agreements are particularly the reduction of double expenses and acceleration of the development of new products. This type of agreement can sometimes be used as a tool for a price-fixing cartel, cartel on restriction of production capacities or market-partitioning cartel. These are agreements which the AMO considers as prohibited under the general clause. Other agreements such as, for example, those which lead to the increase of quality of products, need to be reviewed in their economic context.

205. In assessing such agreements the AMO will follow the Horizontal Cooperation Guidelines thus the prohibition on concluding an agreement restricting competition does not apply to:[382]

(1) agreements related to the research and development that is only at the stage of a theory and a practical use of possible results cannot be supposed;
(2) the cooperation between undertakings who are not in a position of real or potential competitors;
(3) the cooperation made by specialized subjects such as research institutes and academic institutions, that are not active in the area of using the results of R&D;
(4) so-called pure R&D agreements; the prohibition of the general clause is not applied to agreements which relate exclusively to a stage precedent the business

381. HHI counts squares of single market shares of all market players, and it is supposed that HHI lower than 1,000 characterizes a low degree of the market concentration, and a high degree of the concentration can be supposed by HHI higher than 1,800.

382. Points 127–140, Communication from the Commission – Guidelines on the applicability of Art. 101 of the Treaty on the Functioning of the European Union to Horizontal Co-operation Agreements, OJ C 11 14 Jan. 2011, pp. 1–72.

usage of R&D, when the only aim of the cooperation is its joint performance; however, the competition problem can arise in the field of innovations, if the substantial restriction of competition on the innovations' market took place.

206. The general clause on prohibition is applied also to such agreements that restrict the parties' possibility to realize R&D independently outside the scope of a cooperation agreement, no matter whether this restriction follows explicitly from the R&D agreement or it is obvious from the factual behaviour of undertakings on the market.[383] Furthermore, the general clause will apply to R&D agreements according to which parties agree to restrict the independent usage of R&D results so they accept restriction concerning production and marketing.[384]

R&D agreements which do not show any obvious features for a restriction of competition however, their negative impact on the market can be inferred from their evaluation in a wider economic context also come under the prohibition of the general clause.[385] The evaluation will cover a cooperation to which existing competitors on the product/technologies market or on the innovations market enter at a stage close to the launch of the product to the market.

207. Negative effects on competition are present if the parties to the R&D agreement have a significant market power on existing markets or the substantial restriction of competition on the innovations market takes place. These negative effects are manifested as a restriction of innovations (e.g., the entry of strong players to the cooperation with the innovative competitor can lead to a control of the technological development),[386] coordination of behaviour on existing markets or market foreclosure on the level of using possible R&D results.

The R&D agreements which come under the general clause prohibition may be exempted under conditions of *ex lege* exemption,[387] after evaluation of all the factors against the CA specified criteria.

B. *Specialization*

208. The specialization agreements whereby the parties agree unilaterally or on a reciprocal basis to cease production of certain product and buy it from the other party represent one of the forms of so-called production agreements. Even though they are not listed in the demonstrative list of section 4(4) of the CA, they can be still prohibited under the general clause. When assessing these agreements, the AMO will proceed according to EU guidelines.[388]

383. Christopher Bellamy & Graham D. Child, *European Community Law of Competition* point 5-060 (5th ed., Sweet & Maxwell 2001).
384. *Ibid.*, point 5–062.
385. Article 3 of the Horizontal Co-operation Guidelines.
386. Christopher Bellamy & Graham D. Child, *European Community Law of Competition* point 5-065, (5th ed., Sweet & Maxwell 2001).
387. Section 6(3) of the CA.
388. Communication from the Commission – Guidelines on the applicability of Art. 101 of the Treaty on the Functioning of the European Union to Horizontal Co-operation Agreements, OJ Ç 11 14 Jan. 2011, pp. 1–72.

209. The production agreements is a general term, which covers specialization agreements and also joint production agreements as well (*see* section point iv below) and subcontracting agreements according to which the contractor entrusts the subcontractor with the production of a specific product; however, these are generally reviewed under the rules applicable to vertical agreements.

210. These agreements can be assessed based on the rules for *ex lege* exemption as well. The agreement will be prohibited if it includes restrictions such as price-fixing of the products which are the outcome of the joint production process, market-partitioning on a territorial principle or concerning allocation of customers; or other restrictions such as reduction of production capacities or investments, waiver of autonomous production.

C. *Standardization*

211. The principal aim of standardization agreements is to define technical or qualitative parameters of products (existing or future) or the production process or methods. The standardization agreements may contain several provisions concerning, for example, different ranks of products, size, technical specifications on the markets where the conformity or cohesion with another product or system is important. These agreements are concluded upon the undertakings' own activity or under the patronage of public institutions.

There is in principle the same situation as in the case of specializing agreements because the prohibition applies to agreements which include a price-fixing of products consequently delivered to the market or to market-partitioning (irrespective of whether it includes a territorial or a personal principle).

D. *Joint Production*

212. In the joint production agreement, parties agree to produce certain products jointly, whereby the agreement may be unilateral as well as reciprocal. This kind of cooperation is prohibited if the agreement includes also provisions/ agreements concerning hard-core restrictions as mentioned above, such as fixing of prices of the jointly produced products, market-partitioning – division of spheres of interests between parties. If the cooperation does not involve provisions which are deemed to be a hard-core cartel, the cooperation is evaluated on its economic and legal concepts and might be exempted based on the criteria defined by section 6(3) of the CA (*ex lege* exemption) as rules included in the EU guidelines are applied.

E. *Joint Purchasing*

213. The next type of horizontal cooperation agreement is the joint purchasing agreement. The joint purchasing agreement is agreed either by an undertaking acting under joint control, by individual undertakings participating on a cooperation agreement or by a new undertaking established by the parties to a cooperation, especially for the fulfilment of joint purchasing tasks. The cooperation may be formal (conclusion of a formal contract) as well as informal.

The cooperation agreements are usually concluded by Small and Medium Enterprises (SME), whose main purpose is receiving higher discounts which it would otherwise not get. These agreements are concluded mainly by companies operating on a retail market which usually create buyers' associations. Agreements concluded by SME are not usually anticompetitive due to the fact that they do not fulfil condition of materiality (aim to distort a competition or a potential of negative impact on the market).

214. It is necessary to mention that joint purchasing involves horizontal as well as vertical agreements. Usually the assessment of the cooperation comprises a 'two-step' test.[389] For example, the creation of a buyers' association of retailers needs to be assessed as a horizontal cooperation agreement and subsequently, if any restrictions of competition are present on the horizontal level, it would be necessary to also review an agreement concluded by the buyers' association with suppliers, according to vertical agreement rules.[390]

215. With regard to agreements which serve to 'disguise' a price cartel, or output restriction or market-partitioning, they always come under the cartel prohibition. On the other hand, the prohibition according to the general clause will not apply to joint purchasing agreements concluded between undertakings which are not competitors on the selling market (the market on which are delivered products used), and at the same time, parties do not have a strong position as buyers.

F. Joint Selling

216. This type of horizontal agreement covers a broad area of cooperation such as joint marketing and selling or even joint distribution and promotion of products. The joint selling represents one of the forms of commercialization agreements.

These agreements can have a lot of variations depending upon specific circumstances as well as intention of these agreements. If, for example, the undertakings agree on the distribution of their goods on a reciprocal basis, there is a risk that the agreement leads to market-partitioning.

When it comes to a prohibition defined by section 4(1) of the CA, the *ex lege* exemption can be applicable if the agreement does not cover any hard-core restrictions.

§2. Vertical Agreements

217. Vertical agreements are concluded between undertakings operating on the relevant market on different levels of the distribution chain, that is, between undertakings which are not in direct competitive relations.

Generally, differing price vertical agreements and other agreements are possible. The price vertical agreements include the obligation of the buyer to adhere to the seller-defined price for further sale to its customers (so-called RPM). Contrary to horizontal agreements, the prohibition is not related to agreements that only influence the prices. It is then possible to tolerate recommended prices or determination of

389. Article 5, Horizontal Co-operation Guidelines.
390. Article 5, Horizontal Co-operation Guidelines.

maximum prices. Regarding 'recommendation', it has to be made without any hint, or an indirect inclusion in an agreement, that the 'recommended price' is in fact fixed. Even the price recommendation can be considered as anticompetitive when the recommended price level is adhered to on the market, forcing distributors to respect the recommendation. Prohibited price-fixing in vertical agreements includes also the determination of a minimal price for a further sale. The exemption from the prohibition of the above-mentioned price-fixing agreements, which is basically treated as 'per se' illegal, is only hypothetical.

218. Besides the price vertical agreements, there are also non-price agreements that are reviewed in line with the 'legitimacy rule'. These non-price agreements cover various restrictions that often eliminate so-called intra-brand competition. If these agreements do not include provisions which are deemed to be per se illegal, the potential of their impact on the market is assessed in relation to specific circumstances. As the non-price vertical restriction could be treated agreements defining the exclusivity, vertical agreements by which a selective distribution system is established or various subcontracting agreements. Specifically, the prohibition may cover agreements containing restrictions concerning further supply or the restrictions of further supplies of products delivered for next processing.

219. The vertical agreements are deemed to be less harmful as horizontal agreements and basically can be exempted from the ban according to the rules of Commission Regulation No. 330/2010 of 20 April 2010 on the application of Article 101(3) of the TFEU to Categories of Vertical Agreements and Concerted practices (the Vertical Block Exemption), or after fulfilment of conditions of *ex lege* exemption.[391]

220. Vertical agreements which lead to price-fixing or market-partitioning are included in the demonstrative list of section 4(2) letter (a) and letter (c) of the CA. The assessment will follow rules specified by EU guidelines, particularly the Commission notice-Guidelines on Vertical Restraints (the Guidelines on Vertical Restraints).[392]

I. Distribution

221. There are several forms of arrangements between undertakings (some of them described in the text below) which fall under the term of distribution agreements:

(1) agency agreements;
(2) single branding agreements;
(3) exclusive distribution agreements;
(4) agreements on exclusive allocation of customers;
(5) selective distribution agreements;
(6) franchising agreements;
(7) exclusive supply agreements.

391. Commission Regulation No. 330/2010 of 20 Apr. 2010 on the application of Art. 101(3) of the TFEU to Categories of Vertical Agreements and Concerted Practices, OJ L 103, 29 Apr. 2010, 1–7.

392. Commission notice-Guidelines on Vertical Restraints, OJ C 130, 19 May 2010, 1.

222. As already mentioned above, assessment of possible restrictions of competition will follow rules defined by EU guidelines and EU case law. The evaluation of the impact of such agreement on competition is conducted in the respective economic and legal contexts of the reviewed agreement whereas the assessment is based on an economics-based approach.

The AMO has recently issued Guideline on the assessment of vertical agreements restricting competition by object[393] in which it presents approach towards the assessment of vertical agreements which are treated as 'per se' prohibited as their object is restriction of competition. The guideline also includes assessment of the RPM practices. The respective guideline follows the rules set by the Vertical Restraints Guidelines.[394]

Recent decisions of the AMO concerning vertical restraints are connected to automotive industry and cars distribution. In 2015, the AMO issued several decisions approving proposed commitments of cars importers concerning their after sales services. The commitments were proposed after conclusions of the AMO that an agreement on provision of the warranty to end-customers only if the maintenance services were carried out in a dealership represented a potential risk for competition on the market.[395]

223. The vertical agreements, hence also distribution agreements, may include RPM provisions by which the distributor is obliged to adhere to either a fixed price or to a minimum price for further supply of products.[396] Price-fixing agreements applied in vertical relationships are covered by section 4(4) letter a) of the CA.

An agreement enabling the supplier to define rules according to which a distributor has to determine prices for its customers would also be treated as prohibited. The result of such agreements would not be the 'same' price of products on the market; nevertheless, the different price would arise from the 'agreement' and thus would not be the result of individual pricing behaviour.

224. The price recommendation or maximum price determination is not prohibited as such. The principle of price recommendation works on an assumption that the supplier has at his disposal information about which product price would be suitable on the market, that is, which price level would be accepted by customers. However, if the supplier connects this price recommendation with some benefits for distributors (e.g., a possibility to receive discounts as an appreciation for adherence to the recommended price) the price recommendation would be also prohibited according to the general clause (section 4(1) of the CA). Such practice would factually motivate the dealer to keep recommended prices on the market and would lead to elimination of a price competition.

393. The AMO, 'Cieľové vertikálne dohody (pohľad PMÚ SR)', <http://www.antimon.gov.sk/data/files/422_cielove-vertikalne-dohody-pohlad-pmu-sr.pdf>.

394. Commission Regulation No. 330/2010 of 20 Apr. 2010 on the application of Art. 101(3) of the TFEU to Categories of Vertical Agreements and Concerted Practices, OJ L 103, 29 Apr. 2010, 1–7.

395. For example, Decision of the AMO No. 2016/KV/2/1/021, 25 May 2016 concerning commitments of Škoda Auto Slovensko; Decision of the AMO No. 2016/KV/2/1/027 concerning commitments of Mazda Motorst Logistics Europe NV, 7 Jun 2016; Decision of the AMO No. 2016/KV/2/1/026, 7 Jun 2016 concerning commitments of Honda Motor Europe Limited, <http://www.antimon.gov.sk>.

396. For example, RPM Case *OKTAN and OMV*, the decision of the AMO No. 2001/KV/1/1/187, 14 Jun. 2001, <http://www.antimon.gov.sk>.

Fixing of maximum prices in vertical agreements is not prohibited, provided that these prices are not followed by a substantial part of distributors.

Even though the CA does not treat RPM as 'per se' prohibited, it is very improbable that the AMO will accept application of *ex lege* exemption to such agreements.

The recent decision of the AMO on RPM practice concerns distribution of cars. The AMO assessed as contrary to section 4(1) of the CA conclusion of agreements with car dealers of ŠKODA whose object was fixing of minimum prices for resale of new passenger cars and defining a maximum discounts from recommended retail prices that authorized dealers could provide to individual end – customers and target groups of end – customers.[397]

A. Exclusive Distributorship

225. According to the obligation defined in the exclusive distribution agreement, the customer is required to buy all products from one supplier either directly or indirectly. The obligation factually means that the customer will not buy, process or sell the competitive goods.

The guiding principles for the assessment of these agreements followed by the AMO are included mainly in the Guidelines on Vertical Restraints and the AMO's Guideline on the assessment of vertical agreements restricting competition by object.[398] The AMO will consider mainly a supplier's position on the market, a factual extent and duration of the non-compete obligation and the position of other suppliers on the market. The important factor for evaluation is barriers to entry. The major anticompetitive effect would not be present if suppliers do not have a problem finding new (alternative) customers. In a market where sufficient power of customers is present, market foreclosure is less probable.

These agreements involve risk of distortion of the competition whereas they can lead to the same consequences as horizontal price-fixing agreements or market-partitioning agreements.

226. The AMO, for example, assessed as prohibited, an agreement concluded between Slovenské Aerolínie (the Slovak Airlines) and TIP TRAVEL (the travel agency),[399] according to which the travel agency was bound to cooperate exclusively with Slovenské Aerolínie concerning charter air transport. The Council stated that the application of several exclusive contracts may lead to a market foreclosure for other service providers.

B. Exclusive Dealing

227. The obligation of exclusive dealing restricts the number of customers in a certain territory, to whom the supplier can supply a particular final product. The CA does not comprise any special rules for the assessment of these agreements, thus, again the EU rules and guidelines are relevant.

---

397. Decesion of the AMO No. 2014/KV/2/1/029, 22 Oct. 2014, <http://www.antimon.gov.sk>.
398. The AMO, 'Cieľové vertikálne dohody (pohľad PMÚ SR)', <http://www.antimon.gov.sk/data/files/422_cielove-vertikalne-dohody-pohlad-pmu-sr.pdf>.
399. Decision of the Council No. 2004/KV/R/2/015, 6 Feb. 2006, <http://www.antimon.gov.sk>.

228. Whereas any exclusive arrangement can cause negative effects on competition, these agreements are also covered by the general clause, and their impact on the market must be properly assessed. The risk is mainly connected to a market foreclosure of other buyers. These agreements are either covered by the Vertical Agreements Block Exemption[400] or can be excluded based on *ex lege* exemption (section 4(5) of the CA). The analysis of the impact includes assessment of factors such as market position of the buyer benefiting from the exclusivity, scope and duration of the exclusivity, and position of buyer's competitors on the market.

C. Selective Distribution

229. The CA does not modify any special rules for this type of agreement. The selective distribution system restricts the number of distributors authorized to distribute a suppliers goods – it concerns brand products (e.g., perfumes or high quality electronics). The distributors are selected based on pre-defined qualitative conditions which relate to the nature of the distributed goods. However, distributors are restricted to make supplies to non-authorized distributors, that is, distributors outside the system.

230. Two types of selective distribution systems can be recognized. First of them is the qualitative selective distribution system, in which selection of distributors is based only on the qualitative criteria. The criteria are dependent on the nature of distributed products (e.g., requirements concerning points of sale or trained staff) as the number of distributors is not limited. On the other hand, the quantitative distribution system also includes additional quantitative criteria such as reaching a minimum turnover or a minimum number of sales agents.

231. The pure qualitative selective distribution system is not covered by the general clause if the following conditions are met:

(1) the nature of supplied products requires distribution via a selective distribution system; for example, quality preservation and the guarantee of appropriate usage require that goods are sold by professional and trained staff;
(2) the criteria for the selection of distributors are the same for all applicants, these are objective, in relation to a nature of distributed products, and are non-discriminatory;
(3) the criteria for a selection must be indispensably necessary.

232. All the above-mentioned criteria were acknowledged by the AMO in its decision concerning distribution of Husquarna's branded products. In its decision, the AMO stated:

> The system of a qualitative selective distribution usually represents no restriction of competition, that is, it is not a breach of section 4 of the Act, subject to the fulfilment of the following conditions:

400. Commission Regulation No. 330/2010 of 20 Apr. 2010 on the application of Art. 101(3) of the TFEU to Categories of Vertical Agreements and Concerted Practices, OJ L 103, 29 Apr. 2010, 1–7.

(1) the nature of a product requires this distribution manner;
(2) sellers are selected exclusively based on non-discriminatory, objective qualitative criteria;
(3) these criteria do not exceed the framework of necessity;
(4) the whole system finally has a pro-competitive effect.[401]

233. If the selective distributions system contains quantitative criteria, these have to be evaluated under the conditions of *ex lege* exemption, as the assessment of their impact on the market should take into consideration mainly the supplier's position on the market as well as the position of its competitors; the number of selective distributions systems on one market and the existence of cumulative effects of all similar networks; maturity of the market, and the existence of entry barriers.

The selective distribution system may reduce intra-brand competition, lead to an exclusion of competitors, or to collusive behaviour between suppliers or buyers.

D. *Franchising*

234. On the basis of the franchising agreement, the franchisor provides the franchisee with the license concerning IPR linked to the distribution of products and simultaneously provides it with business and technical assistance. At the same time, the franchisee pays a fee to the franchisor.[402] Even though this type of agreement may cause anticompetitive effects, for example, post term, non-compete obligations included in the franchising agreements are tolerated under conditions of the Vertical Block Exemption.[403] These agreements are usually exempted based on the Vertical Block Exemption or according to *ex lege* exemption.[404]

II. Technology Licensing

235. The subject of a technology licensing agreement is the provision of a license to the IPR which are related to a production of goods or provision of services, that is, not to a transfer of rights as such, as 'part of the risk associated with the exploitation of the technology remains with the assignor …'.[405] These agreements likewise fall under the general clause (section 4(1) of the CA) review. The evaluation of their impact on economic competition follows from the block exemption rules[406]

401. Decision of the Council No. 2003/KV/R/2/071, 16 Apr. 2003, <http://www.antimon.gov.sk>.
402. Guidelines on Vertical Restraints, §§189–191.
403. Guidelines on Vertical Restraints, §68.
404. Decision of the AMO No. 2009/KV/1/1/061, 16 Dec. 2009, <http://www.antimon.gov.sk>. The RPM was applied in franchise contracts concerning distribution of cosmetics; the case was closed by a settlement.
405. Jindřiška Munková & Pavel Svoboda & Jiří Kindl, *Soutěžní právo, Beckovy meziodborové učebnice* (C.H. Beck, 2006), 219.
406. Commission Regulation (EU) No. 316/2014 of 21 Mar. 2014 on the application of Art. 101(3) of the Treaty on the Functioning of the European Union to categories of technology transfer agreements Text with EEA relevance, OJ L 93, 28 Mar. 2014.

and application of *ex lege* exemption. The CA does not comprise any special rules for appraisal of technology licensing agreements, irrespective of whether they concern licensing of patents, trademarks and know-how or trade secrets.

The block exemption does not apply, for example, to such agreements that include features of price-fixing (restrictions concluded between competitors concerning the selling price),[407] market-partitioning[408] or the restriction of the licensee's ability to exploit its own technology rights.[409]

The *ex lege* exemption is granted only if the four cumulative criteria as defined in section 4(5) of the CA are met.

A. Patent Licensing

236. As the Slovak antitrust legislation does not comprise individual rules for the assessment of patent licensing agreements, the EC antitrust law and rules, mainly included in the Technology Transfer Block Exemption Regulation, will be followed by the AMO.

B. Trademark Licensing

237. The CA until its amendment in 2004 comprised a provision (section 5 of the CA valid till 2004) according to which license agreements concerning, *inter alia,* patents, industrial designs, trademarks and trade names were prohibited under the general clause (section 4(1) of the CA) provided that the restriction of competition included in this agreement was not indispensable for the protection of respective IPR.

The Slovak antitrust legislation currently does not comprise any special rules concerning the assessment of trademark licensing agreements or rules determining limits to the antitrust rules' application and application of intellectual property law.

C. Know-How Licensing

238. As the notion of 'technology' under the Technology Transfer Block Exemption Regulation covers also know-how and at the same time neither the CA nor any other document of the AMO (binding or non-binding) includes rules for know-how licensing, the AMO will accordingly apply the already-mentioned Technology Transfer Block Exemption Regulation as well as the Technology Transfer Agreements Guidelines for the assessment of know-how licensing agreements.

407. Article 4(1) letter a) of the Commission Regulation No. 316/2014.
408. Article 4(1) letter b) of the Commission Regulation No. 316/2014.
409. Article 4(1) letter d) of the Commission Regulation No. 316/2014.

Chapter 2. Dominant Undertakings' Prohibited Practices

239. The CA includes provisions on individual anticompetitive conduct of undertakings in section 8 under the heading 'Abuse of a dominant position'. An appraisal of the individual conduct of an undertaking as an abuse is necessarily, linked to the relevant market definition and determination of dominance. It is apparent from section 8(2) of the CA as well as from section 8(3) of the CA that the definition of dominance on the market is a basic precondition to the penalty proceedings' initiation. Section 8 of the CA, which includes a general clause of the prohibition, definition of a dominant position, and demonstrative list of most common abusive practices, is fully in line with Article 102 of the TFEU (ex Article 82 of the EC Treaty).

240. The section 8(2) of the CA comprises a demonstrative list of practices which come under abuse of a dominant position (details concerning individual abusive practices are described below in the text). The anticompetitive conduct which does not come under the individual subject matters included in section 8(2) of the CA is prohibited under a general clause.[410] A refusal to grant access to an essential facility was also treated as an individual subject matter of the abuse of a dominant position (until the amendment of the CA in July 2014. Currently, the practice of refusal to grant access to an essential facility is covered by the refusal to deal practices under section 8(2) letter b) of the CA (details are included in the §2, IV below).

241. As already mentioned (*see* Part I, Chapter 4, §2), the definition of a relevant market is included in section 3(2)–(4) of the CA. Equally, a definition of the dominant position is also directly involved in the CA[411] whereas the dominant position has an undertaking or several undertakings that are not subject to substantial competition or that can act independently as a result of their economic power. The definition of dominance is based on the concept of 'economic strength' and its determination is subject to assessment of several criteria which follow from the AMO's case law (*see* Part I, Chapter 4, §3). The dominant position can be held by one or several undertakings – a collective dominance even though no details of collective dominant position assessment are specified in the CA. The Supreme Court, in its judgment[412] by which it confirmed the AMO's negative decision on concentration in the Case *Südzucker AG,*[413] acknowledged that the AMO was entitled to follow the EU case law at assessing the existence of collective dominance on the market.

242. The dominance as such is not prohibited, however the dominant undertaking is responsible for its behaviour on the market (it has a 'special' responsibility) whereas it is responsible for an abuse even committed by negligence (*see* Part I, Chapter 3, §2).

243. The CA does not comprise any exemption (similar to exemptions concerning agreements restricting competition) from the prohibition to abuse a dominant position.

410. Section 8(3) of the CA: 'Abuse of a dominant position on the relevant market is prohibited.'
411. Section 8(1) of the CA.
412. Judgment of the Supreme Court of the Slovak Republic No. 4 Sž 122-123/03, 29 Apr. 2004, <http://www.antimon.gov.sk>.
413. Decision of the Council No. 2003/KH/R/2/121, 19 Jun. 2003, Decision of the AMO No. 2002/FH/3/1/272, 12 Dec. 2002, <http://www.antimon.gov.sk>.

Moreover, the CA does not distinguish between exploitative and exclusionary practices as it has done in the theory whereas the AMO stated 'the division of anticompetitive practices into exclusionary and exploitative…is unsupported by the Act and that no different legal consequences are contemplated for each such category …'.[414]

244. Neither the CA nor other documents of the AMO specify rules and principles of the assessment of an individual undertaking's conduct as an abuse of a dominant position, thus relevant national and EU case law as well as the EU guidelines will be followed by the AMO.[415]

§1. Exploitative Practices

245. The AMO in its 2007 Report on Activities[416] defined exploitative practices as practices which lead to a direct decrease of consumers' benefit, hence, to a collection of 'rent' at the expense of the customer, which a non-dominant undertaking could not gain. This means that the practices are aimed at contractual partners with the purpose of gaining extra profit or other benefits[417] and 'due to discrimination, the conditions are unequal for the dominant's business partners, whose input prices have been impacted by discriminatory practice, while such prices affect their competitive power on the market where their products or services are placed …'.[418]

I. Excessive/Unfair Pricing

246. The fist abusive practice included in the demonstrative list of section 8(2) letter a) of the CA is a prohibition to enforce excessive prices (it includes also prohibition to enforce unfair trade conditions).

247. The AMO acknowledged its competence concerning the assessment of excessive prices imposed by a dominant undertaking after the amendment of the CA in 2005.[419] Before its adoption, the AMO claimed that it was entitled to review only unfair trade conditions – excluding prices. The AMO in its statement from August

414. Decision of the Council No. 2007/DZ/R/2/102, 7 Dec. 2007, dismissed by the judgment of the Regional Court in Bratislava No. 3 S 9/2008-783, IČS 1008200074, 15 Dec. 2009, case pending, <http://www.antimon.gov.sk>.
415. Guidance on the Commission's enforcement priorities in applying Art. 82 of the EC Treaty to abusive exclusionary conduct by dominant undertakings, OJ C 45, 24 Feb. 2009, 7–20.
416. The Report in Slovak Language at: <http://www.rokovania.sk/appl/material.nsf/0/E3F893B7B5A83BEAC12574010047C44E/$FILE/vlastnymat.rtf>.
417. Radoslav Procházka & Juraj Čorba, *Právo Európskej únie, Vybrané otázky pre právnu prax* (Žilina, Slovak Republic: Poradca podnikateľa, 2006), 425.
418. Decision of the Council No. 2007/DZ/R/2/102, 7 Dec. 2007 dismissed by the Judgment of the Regional Court in Bratislava No. 3 S 9/2008-783, IČS 1008200074, 15 Dec. 2009. <http://www.antimon.gov.sk>.
419. Act No. 68/2005 Coll. On the Amendment and Supplementation of the Act on Prices, press release, <http://www.antimon.gov.sk/375/1712/nove-kompetencie-protimonopolneho-uradu-sr.axd>.

2004[420] (the statement was issued as a reaction to excessive retail prices of fuels) even declared that a problem with the excessive prices as a form of an abuse of a dominant position was linked to the fact that if the AMO determined the excessive price, it had to 'say' at the same time what price was appropriate. This means that the AMO would de facto regulate the price whereas it does not have such competence. Furthermore, it claimed that even though it treated the company Slovnaft (the Slovak refinery) as dominant on the fuelling retail market, it could not 'act' against its excessive prices whereas the AMO's competence was only to assess unfair trade conditions, discrimination or anticompetitive tying. Since then the AMO's position has changed.

248. The CA comprises neither the definition of excessive price (the price which is above the level of competition) nor detailed rules on how the excessiveness of prices has to be assessed. The AMO practice in the area of assessment of excessive prices is absent; however, from the AMO's case law concerning other abusive practices, it is apparent that it will follow the same approach as the European Commission or the European Courts. Thus, the assessment of the excessive price can be based on:

(1) the comparison with the price which would be otherwise present on a competitive market;
(2) benchmarking – comparison of the price with other relevant markets; or
(3) taking into account the 'economic value' of the product, which means that the amount of price needs to be assessed in relation to incurred costs and the 'economic value' of the product. Thus not only costs present in the accounting are taken into consideration but also non-costs factors which influence the final price of a product whereas increase the value of the product for customers.

249. Not even the European case law contains rules describing costs which would be taking into consideration – their amount and a structure or a 'threshold value' above which the difference between costs and the price would be regarded as excessive. The concept of excessive prices thus brings undertakings to a legal uncertainty in relation to its pricing behaviour. The lack of 'clear' rules might be also the reason for undeveloped case law in Slovak Republic.

250. The AMO in its only decision concerning pure excessive pricing required by the company *ZSE distribúcia*[421] noted:

The complexity of the taking of evidence of excessive prices has to be assessed in dependence on circumstances of an individual case, date and information available to the Office, together with the type or nature of a product or service. It may concern complex taking of evidence especially in cases of products with a complicated cost structure; in cases where it would be necessary to perform a price-cost text and where it is at the same time difficult to clearly affiliate all costs actually pertaining to the product (…), an inadequate price may be proved by comparing the price under review

420. 'Stanovisko Protimonopolného úradu Slovenskej republiky ku kompetenciám úradu v oblasti regulácie maloobchodných cien pohonných látok na čerpacích staniciach v SR.', 31 Aug. 2004, <http://www.antimon.gov.sk/312/1628/stanovisko-protimonopolneho-uradu-slovenskej-republiky-kukompetenciam-uradu-v-oblasti-regulacie-maloobchodnych.axd>.

421. Decision of the Council No. 2012/DZ/R/2/030, 29 Jun. 2012, points 46 and 49, <http://www.antimon.gov.sk>.

with various indicators: dominant undertaking's costs, dominant undertaking´s other prices or prices of other undertakings offering similar products in relation to the product the price of which is being reviewed.

The case *ZSE distribúcia* as already mentioned is the first case that can be considered to be a decision of the AMO exclusively on the question of an excessive pricing (as the issue of reviewing an excessive price is partially part of the analysis of the pricing practice of the so-called margin squeeze). In this case, the fee charged by ZSE Distribúcia for an above-standard reading of electrometers was deemed as an inadequate price. According to the electricity market rules valid at the time when the fee was charged, it was a fee determined for the provision of the so-called above-standard reading service, i.e. service of electrometer reading in case of a change of the electricity supplier, while according to the market rules, the competitor performing the reading could only include costs for the provision of the reading service in the fee. In this case, the AMO applied the benchmarking method to consolidate the excessive price practice, specifically, the time comparison (comparison of fees charged by ZSE Distribúcia in particular periods of the provision of the above-standard reading service) and, moreover, comparison of fees charges in other distribution territories (ZSE Distribúcia was designated as a dominant distributor in the territory of the West Slovak Region – the territory was designated on the basis of the distribution network coverage), i.e. the comparison was made with fees charged in other distribution territories, specifically, in the territories of the Central Slovak Region and East Slovak Region. In this case, the AMO stated that the issue of reviewing the inadequately high price was under the competence of the AMO; however, 'the Office is not a sector regulator and its role is not to determine a scope or a certain value of a difference that would be understood as acceptable, subject to which the price would be seen as adequate'.[422]

251. The AMO subsumes in its decision-making practice[423] also price squeeze practices under section 8(2) letter a) of the CA.

Anticompetitive behaviour by which a dominant undertaking directly or indirectly enforces unfair trade conditions is subsumed also under section 8(2) letter a) of the CA.

252. In the case *eustream*[424] (the Slovak company transporting natural gas in Slovak Republic), the AMO imposed the fine for abuse of a dominant position consisting of the enforcement of unfair trade conditions concerning a Gas Trading company's (the operator of a natural gas distribution network) connection to eustream's transport network. The unfair trade conditions consisted of an obligation to sell off the connecting device to the transport network to the company eustream. The company eustream argued that to ensure safe and reliable operation of the transport network, any of the connected operators could be owner of the connection device whereas eustream needed

422. Decision of the Council No. 2012/DZ/R/2/030, 29 Jun. 2012, <http://www.antimon.gov.sk>.
423. Decision of the Council No. 2009/DZ/R/2/017, 9 Apr. 2009; Decision of the AMO No. 2007/DZ/1/1/111, 21 Dec. 2007, <http://www.antimon.gov.sk>.
424. Decision of the AMO No. 2007/DZ/2/1/105, 14 Dec. 2007; Decision of the Council No. 2008/DZ/R/2/076, 26 Sep. 2008, <http://www.antimon.gov.sk>.

continual access to the device and control of it. The submitted reasons were treated as insufficient to justify enforcement of the above-mentioned trade condition.[425]

253. Another case in which the AMO assessed abuse by unfair trade conditions is the case *Slovenská správa letísk*[426] (Slovak Air Services (SAS), Slovak airport administration) established by the Ministry of Transport, as the organization whose role was to organize administration and operation of airports in Slovak Republic as well as the provision of ramp handling services. The essential for the provision of the ramp handling services is the access to the apron of the respective airport. The competing undertaking – the company SAS, a subsidiary of the company Czech Airlines (CSA), thus had to conclude a loan contract with SAS whereby it was forced to accept conditions according to which SAS could provide ramp handling services only to CSA.

II. Discrimination

254. The AMO will assess as an abuse of a dominant position also, a conduct by which the dominant undertaking applies different conditions for identical or comparable performance, to individual undertakings.[427] This approach thus leads to discrimination and to the disadvantage of some undertakings on the market.

255. The discrimination may have various forms (e.g., selection of customers to whom the dominant undertaking supplies its products, different conditions concerning the delivery) whereas the main form is the price discrimination (such as application of different prices, different discounts or commissions). The discrimination may have an exploitative as well as exclusionary effect.

256. Upon concluding that discriminatory behaviour under section 8(2) letter c) of the CA occurred, the following facts need to be proved:

(1) application of different conditions without objective reason for such approach;
(2) existence of identical or comparable fulfilment;
(3) existence of disadvantage or potential disadvantage of discriminated undertakings in competition.[428]

257. It must be borne in mind that the CA does not directly exclude the application of above-stated provision on tenders either in virtue of the Public Procurement Act or on the tender procedure under the CC. It is clear that conditions of tender represent a reflection of specific requirements of the individual awarding body, particularly in terms of price, price guarantee during a specified period, manner of deliveries, quality of deliveries and scope of provided services. In case of a tender under the Public Procurement Act, the respective legal conditions which the supplier has to meet are also applied. All these special requirements could represent a sufficient reason for the AMO to state that the tenders are different and not a comparable fulfilment in relation

425. Decision of the AMO No. 2007/DZ/2/1/105, 14 Dec. 2007, mainly §§61–62, <http://www.antimon.gov.sk>.
426. Decision of the Chairman No. 99/DZ/P/2/150, 28 Apr. 1999, <http://www.antimon.gov.sk>.
427. Section 8(2) of the CA.
428. Decision of the Council No. 2007/DZ/R/2/102, 7 Dec. 2007, <http://www.antimon.gov.sk>.

to the usual contracting of customers. Nevertheless, the potential of this conclusion must be reviewed under the circumstances of each individual case. The assessment of whether the fulfilment is identical or comparable is dependent mainly on the nature of the supplied products, quantities of deliveries, delivery conditions and special circumstances, and differences in logistics.

258. The open question in the AMO's decision-making practice remains as to the possibility of using 'meeting competition defence' which derives from a presumption that a dominant company must have as well, the possibility to defend its interests on the market against threatening attacks of its competitors, and protect these interests in an adequate manner. The boundaries for the use of such defence are given by the fact that a dominant player's primary aim cannot be for an increase of its market share and strengthening its market position whereas the defence has to be adequate. Possibility, to use a 'meeting competition defence' was accepted, for example, in relation to bidding process – specific market situations which are characterized by 'the winner takes all' situation.[429]

259. The AMO in the case *Slovnaft*[430] assessed the price discrimination against the main Slovnaft's competitors (companies Shell and OMV), and at the same time claimed the price discrimination of end-users caused by a non-transparent discount policy. The Council stated that non-objective and variable criteria and the fact that end-users were not familiar with the applied discounts enabled Slovnaft to set the end price ad hoc, on the basis of individual meetings, as applied price differences reflect neither a quantity or a quality of supplied products, nor any other factors justifying the difference. The Council in its decision stated:

> the undertaking Slovnaft ... set the terms of its discount policy in such a manner so as to be able to gain profit it would otherwise be unable to gain in terms of efficient competition. The discount system which was implemented on the basis of individual negotiations allowed it to become sufficiently familiar with its customers ... allowed it to charge them such a price as they were willing to accept.[431]

The company Slovnaft *inter alia* argued that even a dominant player had a right to attack competitive offer if there was a threat of losing a customer. Both decisions of the AMO were dismissed by the Regional Court in Bratislava[432] and the case was referred back to the AMO for a further proceedings. The court *inter alia* commented that the AMO did not sufficiently consider claims of Slovnaft concerning a possibility to react on competitive offer on the market.

429. OECD Roundtable, Loyalty and Fidelity Discounts and Rebates, 2003, DAFFE/COMP(2002)21, <http://www. oecd.org>, 197 and 215.
430. Decision of the AMO No. 2006/DZ/2/1/140, 22 Dec. 2006; Decision of the Council No. 2007/DZ/R/2/102, 7 Dec. 2007, <http://www.antimon.gov.sk>.
431. Decision of the AMO No. 2006/DZ/2/1/140, 22 Dec. 2006; Decision of the Council No. 2007/DZ/R/2/102, 7 Dec. 2007, <http://www.antimon.gov.sk>.
432. Judgment of the Regional Court in Bratislava No. 3 S 9/2008-783, IČS 1008200074, 15 Dec. 2009, <http://www.antimon.gov.sk>.

260. In the decision in the *Slovnaft II* case[433] where the AMO reviewed discrimination of customers not pursuant to the provision of section 8(2) letter c) of the CA but based on the general prohibition of abuse of a dominant position (section 8(6) of the CA) only, the AMO stated in its first instance decision[434] that section 8(2) letter c) of CA related only to the exclusionary form of discrimination where a dominant undertaking´s competitor or some of its customers was being pushed out of the market.[435]

As regards the discrimination practice, the AMO provided the following statements in this case:

Discrimination is one of the practices of abusing a dominant position. Its essence is that an undertaking in a dominant position sells the same products to various customers at various prices, while such differences in prices fail to reflect differences in selling costs; this means that with a comparable performance, different conditions are being applied towards undertakings.[436]

The practice of discrimination may have an exclusionary or exploitative nature. In case of discrimination as an exploitative practice, the dominant undertaking charges different prices to customers not based on the costs of goods (sale) but according to their willingness to pay and possibilities to go to competitors in such a manner that it is profitable for it. As a result of such practice, customers with higher willingness to pay and smaller possibility to go to competitors have unreasonably higher prices, whereby the dominant undertaking´s profit is being increased, while, however, nobody has to be excluded from the market. On the contrary, as a result of discrimination as an exclusionary practice, a competitor of the dominant undertaking or some of the dominant undertaking´s customers are pushed out of the market.[437]

In order that the discrimination practice (its exploitative form) could occur at all, two fundamental prerequisites have to be met. The first one consists in the fact that the dominant undertaking has to have a method for sorting, differentiating customers according to their willingness to pay, in such a manner that it could charge different prices to the customers in such a manner that it is profitable for it. The second prerequisite consists in the fact that no arbitration or re-sale – purchase and sale aimed at making profits from differences in prices may occur.[438]

If a company in a dominant position applies the practice of discrimination (exploitative form) and determines prices for each of the customers individually on a customized basis, according to each customer´s preferences and/or possibilities to go to competitors, then such practice results in the existence of difference prices for customers corresponding to the maximum of what they are willing to pay, while differences in prices among the customers may not be objectively (e.g. based on different costs) justified – those customers who, for instance, have fewer opportunities

433. Decision of the Council No. 2011/DZ/R/2/023, 8 Jul. 2011, Decision of the AMO No. 2010/DZ/2/1/068, 10 Dec. 2010, <http://www.antimon.gov.sk>.
434. Decision of the AMO No. 2010/DZ/2/1/068, 10 Dec. 2011, §317, <http://www.antimon.gov.sk>.
435. Decision of the AMO No. 2010/DZ/2/1/068, 10 Dec. 2011, §317, including, without limitation, §220, last sentence.
436. Decision of the AMO No. 2010/DZ/2/1/068, 10 Dec. 2011, §§317, 219.
437. Decision of the AMO of the SR No. 2010/DZ/2/1/068, 10 Dec. 2011, §220.
438. Decision of the AMO of the SR No. 2010/DZ/2/1/068, 10 Dec. 2011, §222.

to go to competitors, have unreasonably higher prices, as a result of which the consumer welfare is (surplus) is reduced and moved into the dominant undertaking´s profit.[439]

Thus, following from the last decision-making practice of the AMO of the SR, the pricing policy setting in relation to particular customer groups described is reviewed, on one side, pursuant to section 8(2) letter c) of the CA and, on the other side, pursuant to the general clause of the prohibition of abuse of a dominant position, i.e. pursuant to section 8(6) of the CA.

261. In the case *Slovenské Aerolínie* (Slovak Airlines),[440] the AMO reviewed discrimination related to seizing of the seats' capacity in the airplane. The Council came to the conclusion that a different distribution of the seats' capacity in the airplane followed from the requirements of individual travel companies presented during the selection of the carrier was not discriminatory. Moreover, it was not proven that the different seizing of the capacity would lead to a disadvantage of some travel companies on the market.

262. Concerning the third condition (existence at least of a potential disadvantage of discriminated undertakings on the market), it is necessary to mention the development of the AMO's decision-making practice. In some older cases, the AMO claimed that the discrimination might occur only against undertakings performing their activities on the same relevant market (product as well as geographic), that is, against competitors.

The AMO's recent practice is different whereas in already-mentioned case *Slovnaft,* it presented that 'the dominant undertaking's consumers subjected to discrimination do not have to be mutual competitors. This does not result from the legal definition of discrimination, as disadvantaging in the competition or its possibility does not reduce to merely mutual competitive interactions'.[441] Moreover, as already mentioned above the AMO changed its approach in case of *Slovnaft II* when it came to the conclusion that there are two types of discriminatory practices, one consist of a discrimination covered by section 8(2) letter c) of the CA (exclusionary practice) and the second of discrimination covered by the general clause of section 8(2) of the CA (exploitative practice).

263. In the case of *Cargo Slovakia*[442] (the Slovak railway carrier), a provision of commissions only to some undertakings was treated as discriminatory. At the same time, the discrimination occurred also between undertakings benefiting from provisions, as these were granted in different amounts. The claim of the dominant company that the AMO should respect the freedom of contract contained in the CC was not accepted. The Council quoted that interpretation of this principle cannot be made in a way that admits breach of other laws.

---

439. Decision of the AMO of the SR No. 2010/DZ/2/1/068, 10 Dec. 2011, §224.

440. Decision of the Council No. 2004/DZ/R/2/138, 4 Jun. 2004, <http://www.antimon.gov.sk>.

441. Decision of the AMO No. 2006/DZ/2/1/140, 22 Dec. 2006; Decision of the Council No. 2007/DZ/R/2/102, 7 Dec. 2007, <http://www.antimon.gov.sk>.

442. Decision of the AMO No. 2003/DZ/2/1/303, 18 Dec. 2003; Decision of the Council No. 2006/DZ/R/2/055, 12 May 2006, <http://www.antimonon.gov.sk>; imposed fined decreased by the Regional Court's in Bratislava, Judgment No. 2 S 258/06-69, IČS 1006201569, 7 Nov. 2007 confirmed by the Judgment of the Supreme Court No. 8 Sžhpu 1/2008, 14 Aug. 2008, <http://www.antimonon.gov.sk>.

In the case of the company 3H, the AMO assessed the behaviour of Slovnaft (Slovak refinery),[443] consisting of application of different payment conditions. The company 3H was discriminated against by Slovnaft whereas Slovnaft restricted the possibility of 3H buying products from the point of supply in Vlčie Hrdlo plant and transferred deliveries for this company, to the point of supply Horný Hričov plant. Both plants applied different supply prices, thus, 3H was discriminated against by suppliers who remained to buy products from Vlčie Hrdlo plant. Moreover, the AMO concluded that 3H was discriminated against also in relation to the payment conditions whereas Horný Hričov plant required cash payment when the Vlčie Hrdlo plant had invoice due date plus 14 plus three days from the date of the invoice issue.

§2. Exclusionary Practices

264. The exclusionary practices lead to a restriction or exclusion of competitors and to an indirect decrease of the consumer's benefit,[444] that is, the dominant undertaking's conduct is aimed at preservation of its market position. As already mentioned above, the CA does not include any special or detailed rules exclusively for the assessment of exclusionary practices.

I. Predation

265. The CA included predatory pricing in the demonstrative list of section 8(2) letter d) till its amendment in 2014 whereas predation was defined as 'temporary abuse of economic power with an intent to exclude competition'. At present, the predatory pricing could be assessed according to the general clause of the ban to abuse a dominant position defined in section 8(2) of the CA in connection with section 8(3) of the CA or pursuant to section 8(2) letter a) of the CA as unfair prices practice.

266. Whereas the AMO follows the EU case law in relation to other abusive practices, it can be assumed that it will do so also in the case of predatory pricing and the predatory pricing theory, mainly assessment of the level of average avoidable costs incurred in relation to supply of certain products. The price charged below average avoidable costs would indicate predatory behaviour. The competition law theory declares[445] that a dominant undertaking can recoup its loss by a subsequent price increase above the initial level after achievement of its aim to exclude competitors from the market. Nevertheless, the Commission in the case of *Wanadoo* stated that the compensation of the loss was not a condition for proving the predation.[446]

443. Decision of the Chairman No. 2001/DZ/P/2/003, 11 Jan. 2001; Judgment of the Supreme Court of the Slovak Republic No. 6 S6 36/01, 31 Oct. 2001, <http://www.antimonon.gov.sk>.

444. In Slovak at: <http://www.rokovania.sk/appl/material.nsf/0/E3F893B7B5A83BEAC12574010047C44E/$FILE/vlastnymat.rtf>.

445. David Raus & Robert Neruda, *Zákon o ochraně hospodářské soutěže, Komentář a souvisící české i komunitární předpisy*, 2nd edn (Prague, Czech Republic: Linde Praha, 2006).

446. Decision of the Commission, COMP/38.233, 13 Jul. 2003, §§333 and 334.

The above-mentioned theory could hardly be applicable in the telecom sector where the comparison based on Average Variable Costs (AVC) seems to be inappropriate due to the fact that the industry is characterized by high investment costs. According to the Commission's Access Notice[447] assessing the price, investment costs shall also be taken into account, particularly analysis based on 'average incremental costs' Long Run Incremental Costs (LRIC) methodology.

267. The AMO assessed the predatory practice of Slovenské Aerolínie[448] (Slovak Airlines) whereby the first-degree division stated that the company abused a dominant position by pricing charter flights at below the variable costs of the respective airplane used for provision of services to the respective travel agency. The relevant market was defined as the relevant market of charter air transport. In addition, the discriminatory approach of Slovenské Aerolínie consisting of application of non-transparent and discriminatory prices charged to the travel agencies was also treated as abusive. Nevertheless, the Council came to the conclusion that predation did not take place. It claimed that the AMO assessed properly that travel agencies were using various types of airplanes, thus the analysis should have taken into consideration not only AVC of one respective airplane, but also all the pricing models by the travel agencies using airplanes. The Council upheld the verdict concerning discriminatory behaviour.

II. Tying

268. Anticompetitive tying is included in section 8(2) letter d) of the CA as 'tying in the conclusion of a contract with the condition that the other party accepts supplementary obligations unrelated to the subject of the contract by their nature or according to the customary commercial practice'.

269. It follows from the soft-law of the European Commission that it will normally take action under Article 102 of the TFEU (section 8(2) of the CA) where: (a) the dominance is present in the tying market, but not necessarily in the tied market, (b) the tying and tied products are distinct products, and (c) the tying practice is likely to lead to anticompetitive foreclosure.[449] There are several general factors that are of importance when assessing the anticompetitive foreclosure such as the position of the dominant undertaking, conditions on the relevant market, position of the competitors, position of the customers, extent of the allegedly abusive conduct, possible evidence of actual foreclosure and direct evidence of any exclusionary strategies. There is also a specific factor within which it has to be examined which customers are being separated from the competitors of the dominant undertaking and subsequently assess whether or not these customers compose a sufficient part of the market.[450]

447. Notice on the application of the competition rules to access agreements in the telecommunications sector – framework, relevant markets and principles, OJ C 265, 22 Aug. 1998, 2–28, §§113–115.
448. Decision of the AMO No. 2003/DZ/2/1/239, 20 Oct. 2003; Decision of the Council 2004/DZ/R/2/138, 4 Jun. 2004, <http://www.antimon.gov.sk>.
449. The Guidance on the Commission's enforcement priorities in applying Art. 82 of the EC Treaty to abusive exclusionary conduct by dominant undertakings, 2009/C 45/02, §37.
450. The Guidance on the Commission's enforcement priorities in applying Art. 82 of the EC Treaty to abusive exclusionary conduct by dominant undertakings, 2009/C 45/02, §55.

There is also a fourth rather condition stemming from the *Microsoft* case,[451] according to which the dominant undertaking does not give customers a choice to obtain the tying product without the tied product.

The definition of tying under the CA supposes two main conditions which need to be fulfilled and these are:

(1) the existence of two independent products; nature and character of these products is appraised;
(2) the absence of such circumstances which would justify tying of both otherwise independent products; these circumstances are, for example, a technical conditionality of their joint supply, safety requirements, health protection, fulfilment of legal obligations, assurance of quality and functionality of products or customary commercial practice.

270. The case of the AMO concerns anticompetitive tying committed by the company *Slovak Telekom* (the so-called *Voice* case)[452] by which, according to the AMO's findings, this company excluded its competitors from the market. The AMO, in the respective case, determined several tying practices. The first tying practice concerned the tying of a provision of the connection to the fixed public telecommunication network with the provision (purchase) of telephone service. The AMO claimed that the customer was obliged to buy, apart from the instalment of a fixed line (connection to the network), also a telephone service – one of the calling programmes provided by Slovak Telekom. The AMO concluded that the customer thus could not choose another operator for the provision of telecommunications services as Slovak Telekom became a 'default' operator. Moreover, the AMO claimed that due to the fact that Slovak Telekom provided its customers with free of charge calling up to a certain volume of spent minutes, its competitors might attract customers (via carrier selection or carrier pre – selection) only after customers had spent those free minutes. Slovak Telekom, in its appeal against the first-degree decision, *inter alia,* claimed that it arose from the nature of the telephone service that it could be provided only if the respective facility was connected to the electronic communication network. Slovak Telekom therefore emphasized that the tying of the 'connection' and the 'telephone service' was justified by the nature of the provided service as well as by a customary commercial practice, as this conclusion was approved also by the Telecommunications Office of the Slovak Republic. It further claimed that the AMO did not prove whether the 'connection' and the 'telephone service' can also be provided independently. The second claimed anticompetitive practice was a tying of Internet services provided via a fixed line (it concerned a dial-up connection, ISDN, xDSL) with the telephone services, because a customer asking for the Internet instalment was obliged to buy at the same time, one of Slovak Telekom's calling programmes.

---

451. Decision of the General Court in case T-201/04, *Microsoft,* 17 Sept. 2007,§842.
452. Decision of the Council No. 2009/DZ/R/2/017, 9 Apr. 2009; Decision of the AMO No. 2007/DZ/1/1/111, 21 Dec. 2007, <http://www.antimon.gov.sk>. The decision of the Council has been challenged by the administrative complaint submitted to the Regional Court in Bratislava – pending.

271. In the case of *Ecopress*[453] (the Slovak publisher of newspaper 'Hosporárske noviny' – HN), the AMO concluded that Ecopress abused its dominant position on the market for the provision of HN data in electronic form, with the right to use them and to spread them through electronic means granted to third persons. Ecopress tied conclusion of the License agreement on provision of the HN data with the conclusion of the purchase contract concerning the purchase of printed versions of the newspaper. The License agreements should be concluded with the press monitoring companies not using newspaper's hard copies for provision of press monitoring to third parties.

III. Rebates

272. The provision of rebates with the anticompetitive effect is not expressly included in the CA as the independent subject matter of an abuse of dominant position practice. However, a dominant undertaking can only offer rebates under certain circumstances. In particular, any rebate that such an undertaking offers must be objectively justified; otherwise, there is a risk that the rebates will result in abusive price discrimination which follow from a non-transparent pricing and discounts system and/or provision of discounts not related to efficiency of the dominant undertaking but because they are provided to customers for their loyalty within the meaning of section 8(2) letter c) of the CA. The rebate scheme can also result in foreclosure effects within the meaning of section 8(2) letter b) of the CA.

Two groups of rebates can be distinguished: (i) conditional rebates; (ii) unconditional rebates. Conditional rebates are defined as rebates granted to customers to reward specific purchasing behaviour over a particular period of time.[454] These rebates can be in a form of volume rebates relating to objective amounts offered on equal terms to all customers without discrimination and are solely linked to the volume of purchases. The second form are loyalty/fidelity rebates that are conditional on customers obtaining all or most of their demands from the undertaking in a dominant position.[455] Loyalty rebates can be further subdivided into: (i) exclusivity rebates; (ii) target rebates. Target rebates are selective rebates granted on the basis of the customer having reached a specified sales target fixed individually between the dominant undertaking and its customer. Target rebates, may strongly encourage a customer to stay with the dominant supplier. In such a case, although there is no explicit exclusivity clause, the target rebates in fact have the same loyalty inducing and exclusionary effects. The main distinction between the volume rebates and both types of loyalty rebates is that the loyalty rebates do not depend on the distributor's ability to expand the volume of sales, as there is no efficiency/cost advantage, but in fact is a reward for distorting market conditions.[456] While exclusivity rebates are considered abuses of a dominant position

453. Decision of the Council No. 2006/DZ/R/2/062, 9 Jun. 2006; Decision of the AMO No. 2005/DZ/2/1/116, 11 Nov. 2005, <http://www.antimon.gov.sk>.
454. *See* the Guidance on the Commission's enforcement priorities in applying Art. 82 of the EC Treaty to abusive exclusionary conduct by dominant undertakings, §37.
455. *See* the decision of the European Union Court of Justice (CJEU) in case 85/76, *Hoffmann-La Roche,* 13 Feb. 1979, §§89–90.
456. Written observation of the Competition Authority in case P 809/2011, 8 Feb. 2012.

and are therefore always forbidden,[457] target rebates, because of their loyalty inducing characteristics, are subject to a strong presumption of illegality.[458] On the other hand, pure volume rebates do not generally lead to an infringement of Article 8 of the CA.

273. Fidelity rebates could lead to a market foreclosure, causing other suppliers to be unable to place their product on the market. According to the opinion of Advocate General in the *British Airways* case:

> The Court of First Instance was right to proceed on the basis that rebate schemes may infringe Article 82 EC even if they are not, as in Hoffmann-La Roche, linked to a condition of exclusivity, i.e. they do not require the contractual partner to obtain all or a specified part of its supplies exclusively from the dominant undertaking, or that it provides its own services exclusively, or as to a specified proportion, for the dominant undertaking. Even where there is no such conditionality, the foreclosure effect of a rebate or bonus scheme may arise from the other circumstances of the particular case.[459]

274. The AMO in 2001 reviewed pricing policy of the company *SLOVNAFTBENZINOL*[460] (the company active on the retail fuels market) applied in the City of Bytča. The review focused on the predatory pricing (retail prices sold in the filling stations within the defined territory of the City of Bytča) as well as on the appraisal of the so-called KLUB BONUS which represented a system of bonuses provided to customers. The first-degree body came to the conclusion that the bonus system applied by the dominant company involved conditional rebates whereas it allowed customers to collect 'points' for the purchase of fuel at the company's filling stations and to exchange these 'points' for products other than fuels. The AMO stated that undertakings operating filling stations in the respective territory could not attract customers by a similar bonus system. Nevertheless, the administrative proceeding was stopped because of the Chairman's conclusion (at that time in a position of an appellate body) that the subject to which the fine could be attributed ceased to exist. Even though the legal successor of SLOVNAFT – BENZINOL was the company Slovnaft (Slovak refinery), the AMO in this case did not apply the *Economic Continuity Test.*

IV. Refusal to Deal

275. Even though competition law respects freedom of contract, this principle is in relation to a dominant undertaking, if special circumstances occur, overturned. The dominant undertaking is obliged to supply products on the market if it does not

---

457. *See* the decision of the CJEU in case 40/73, *Suiker Unie*, 16 Dec. 1975, §513.

458. *See* the decision of the CJEU in case 322/81, *Michelin I*, 9 Nov. 1983; in case T-219/99, *British Airways*, 17 Dec. 2003; or the decision of the General Court in case T-286/09, *Intel*, 12 Jun. 2014, §§78 and 82.

459. Opinion of Advocate General delivered on 23 Feb. 2006 to the Case C-95/04 P, *British Airways plc. v. Commission*.

460. Decision of the Chairman No. 2001/DZ/P/2/283, 26 Sep. 2001; Decision of the AMO No. 2001/DZ/1/1/164, 23 May 2001, <http://www.antimon.gov.sk>.

have an objective reason for a refusal to supply. The anticompetitive practice of the refusal to supply/refusal to deal is formulated in section 8(2) letter b) of the CA as 'an actual restriction of the production, sale or technological development of goods to the detriment of users', that is, it arises from the definition that an actual refusal to deal does not need to be present, it is sufficient when the AMO proves only a threat of such refusal.

276. A refusal to supply is deemed to be anticompetitive if it is directly or indirectly aimed at consumers whereas it results in reduction of supplies to the market, insufficiency of products or a price increase to the disadvantage of the customers. Each refusal to deal must be assessed in relation to the individual circumstances of each case whereas the following must be taken into consideration, in particular:

(1) necessity of the interference to the freedom to choose a trading partner and to the freedom to treat ownership;
(2) balance between the will of the dominant company to invest to its infrastructure and to production capacities whereas this will can be reduced by a strict request to grand access to third parties.

277. The CA till its amendment in 2014 further distinguished a refusal to grant accesses to an essential facility (section 8(3) to (5) of the CA valid till 30 June 2014) as an individual abusive practice. At the moment, the refusal to grant access to the essential facility will be assessed under the section 8(2) letter b) of the CA as refusal to deal.

The notion of an essential facility under the CA valid till 30 June 2014 covered any facility, infrastructure, location or right which cannot be duplicated due either to enormous financial severity, technical complexity or regarding geographic or legal circumstances. At the same time, the CA required that the refusal to access the essential facility would or might lead to a restriction of competition on the respective relevant market. Under the notion of 'respective relevant market' comes any relevant market on which the restriction of competition may occur. The abuse of a dominant position could be committed only either by a possessor of the essential facility or by its administrator.[461]

278. The CA defined cumulative conditions that must be met to conclude that the abuse of a dominant position by refusal to grant access to an essential facility occurred. These were:

(1) According to the first condition,[462] the essential facility must at the time of a peak demand, satisfy at the same time the requirements of the applicant as well as of the owner/administrator of the essential facility. The obligation of the owner/administrator to fulfil long-term contracts had to be taken into consideration.
(2) Based on the second condition,[463] the applicant had to be able to ensure adherence to the respective qualitative and quantitative parameters of the essential facility resulting from its operational requirements or the applicant requiring access to a

461. Section 8(5) of the CA valid till 30 Jun. 2014.
462. Section 8(5) letter a) of the CA valid till 30 Jun. 2014.
463. Section 8(5) letter b) of the CA valid till 30 Jun. 2014.

right had to be capable of adhering to all requirements concerning the aforementioned right, as stipulated by special legislations.

(3) The last condition was the ability of the applicant to pay the appropriate/ adequate fee.

The AMO in its practice used the respective provisions on refusal to grant access to the essential facility in proceedings against the company *Slovak Telekom*.[464] It is possible to reasonably expect that if such a case occurs the AMO will proceed in line with the above-mentioned definition of the essential facility and take into consideration particularly above-mentioned criteria for the assessment.

279. Concerning 'refusal to deal' practices, it is necessary to mention the AMO's case in *Slovak Telekom*.[465] In its decision, the AMO stated that Slovak Telekom abused its dominant position through a refusal to grant access to the local lines system which represented the essential facility. Nevertheless, the verdict of the decision does not subsume the respective practice under the provision of section 8(2) letter b) of the CA (the refusal to deal practices) or under section 8(5) of the CA (the refusal to grant access to the essential facility). The AMO's conclusion was that the practice is anticompetitive and illegal based on the prohibition of the general clause (section 8(6) of the CA), thus it did not assess fulfilment of the above-mentioned conditions concerning the refusal to grant access to the essential facility. The Council concluded that it was not essential to assess each abuse of a dominant position concerning the essential facility pursuant to the rules defined by section 8(5) of the CA as claimed by Slovak Telekom. According to the Council's opinion, section 8(5) of the CA concerns only special cases of refusal of a respective request of other undertakings for access, and defines conditions that must be fulfilled so that behaviour is qualified as an abuse.

Assessing Slovak Telecom's behaviour, the AMO used so-called *No Economic Sense Test,* according to which the behaviour of the dominant undertaking constitutes an abuse if it makes an economic sense only in cases where its effect would be the elimination or restriction of competition. Moreover, the AMO claimed that the test could be used also as an offensive for proving that the behaviour was exclusionary because it had no other economic sense than exclusion of competitors as well as a defensive ploy to prove that the behaviour was not anticompetitive because this economic sense was present. The AMO concluded that in the case of Slovak Telekom, its behaviour was motivated only by the aim to hinder development of economic competition on the markets dependent on the access to the local line. The fact that Slovak Telekom gave up earnings from the local lines access, in terms of the *No Economic Sense Test,* was economically reasonless and the only economical explanation of its behaviour was the fact that exclusion of competitors was more beneficial than incomes from the provision of access.

The AMO further referred particularly to the EU case law according to which, as far as the dominant party refuses access to its facility, technology or network, this

464. Decision of the AMO No. 2008/DZ/2/1/066, 14 Aug. 2008; Decision of the Council No. 2009/DZ/R/2/026, 15 May 2009, <http://www.antimon.gov.sk>.

465. Decision of the AMO No. 2008/DZ/2/1/066, 14 Aug. 2008; Decision of the Council No. 2009/DZ/R/2/026, 15 May 2009, <http://www.antimon.gov.sk>.

behaviour is assessed as the abuse of a dominant position if the following conditions are met:

(1) refusal to grant assess prevents competition on the applicant's market;
(2) the access is indispensable for the applicant's activities on the market;
(3) the accessed is refused without any justified reason.

280. The AMO also fined *Bratislava Airport*[466] (Airport of M.R.Štefánika) for a refusal to grant access to an essential facility to the company Two Wings, even though this company fulfilled all the requirements. The apron of the Bratislava Airport was defined by the AMO as the essential facility. The company Two Wings tried to establish on the market provision of services of transport, loading and unloading of food and beverages to/from airplanes whereas Bratislava Airport provided the same services. The services could be provided only if the access to the apron would be granted.

In November 2014,[467] the Council upheld the fine imposed by the AMO on Railway Company Cargo Slovakia. The AMO imposed the fine in the amount of EUR 10,253,662 as a consequence of consideration of the conduct of the company Cargo consisting in restriction of sales and lease of electric locomotive for its customers. In the assessed period, Cargo held a dominant position in the freight rail transport market, where also other private carries operated. In order to provide their services in the Slovak market, they needed diesel or electric locomotives as an inevitable basic device. The electric locomotives were predominantly owned by Cargo. However, Cargo refused to sell or lease these locomotives to its rivals. Private carriers were forced to use less effective diesel locomotives which needed regular oil refuel. Also the network of fuel stations were owned by Cargo, which subsequently did not allow private carriers to refuel the oil into their diesel locomotives. According to the AMO's opinion, both restrictions were part of an overall strategy aimed at foreclosure of competitors from the market and maintaining the dominant position.

V. Price Squeeze

281. The price squeeze (margin squeeze) as the anticompetitive practice is not explicitly included in the demonstrative list of prohibited practices (section 8(2) of the CA) nevertheless the AMO in its decision (*Voice case*)[468] on the abuse of a dominant position by Slovak Telekom subsumed this practice under the subject matter of '*excessive prices and unfair trade conditions*' (section 8(2) letter a) of the CA).

282. Concluding that a price squeeze practice occurred it is necessary to prove a dominant position of the undertaking on the wholesale market (prove dependence on the inputs) and at the same time moderate prices on the retail market which could be even below prices charged for the wholesale product.

466. Decision of the Council No. 2006/DZ/R/2/048, 24 Apr. 2006, <http://www.antimon.gov.sk>.
467. Decition of the Council No. 2014/DZ/R/2/035, 5 Nov. 2014, <http://www.antimon.gov.sk>.
468. Decision of the Council No. 2009/DZ/R/2/017, 9 Apr. 2009; Decision of the AMO No. 2007/DZ/1/1/111, 21 Dec. 2007, <http://www.antimon.gov.sk>.

283. The AMO, in the already-mentioned *Voice case,* defined several individual practices of an abuse of a dominant position which according to the AMO led to a restriction of competition – exclusion of the dominant undertaking's competitors (alternative operators that entered the market after its liberalization). According to the AMO's decision, the practice of margin squeeze was connected, *inter alia,* to Slovak Telekom's calling programmes. The AMO concluded that before the signing of the wholesale access contracts with alternative operators in 2005, Slovak Telekom introduced end-users' individual calling programmes enabling customers to make thirty-minute calls for a very limited price or enabling customers to call free of charge at certain times. At the same time, Slovak Telekom required from the alternative operators to pay the wholesale access price, not enabling alternative operators to provide customers with similarly advantageous calling facilities. The practice of margin squeeze was based on the fact that if Slovak Telekom would be forced to pay the same wholesale price 'to itself', it would not be able to provide its customers with free of charge calls or with thirty-minute calls at a limited price. The AMO claimed that it used principles defined by the EU case law for the price squeeze assessment, that is, a regular margin squeeze test.[469] The AMO referred to Commission's *Telefonica* case according to which:

> Price squeezing may be said to take place when an undertaking which is in a dominant position on the market for an unprocessed product itself uses part of its production for the manufacture of more processed product, while at the same time selling off surplus unprocessed product on the market, sets the price at which it sells the unprocessed product at such a level that those who purchase it do not have sufficient profit margin on the processing to remain competitive on the market for the processed product…margin squeeze is a disproportion between an upstream and downstream price. Contrary to what Telefonica claims, there is no need to demonstrate that either the wholesale price is excessive in itself or that the retail price is predatory in itself.[470]

The AMO in this case made comparison between the price of the wholesale access – interconnection rate and the price of respective individual retail products. The AMO used methodology of comparison of two values namely: (i) the wholesale price of a dominant company (access price) and (ii) the retail price – tariff of the respective product, i.e. it did not consider average retail price of voice services. It is presumed that the price squeeze takes place if the dominant undertaking could not provide its services on the retail market with a profit if it would have to take into consideration the access price charged to its competitors.[471]

The AMO distinguished two circumstances which can occur. According to the first, the access price is higher than the retail price which automatically means that the practice of price squeeze is present because even the dominant undertaking could not

469. Decision of the Council No. 2009/DZ/R/2/017, 9 Apr. 2009, §§95–187 Decision No. 2007/DZ/2/1/111, 21 Dec. 2007, §§396–400, <http://www.antimon.gov.sk>.
470. Decision of the Commission, COMP/38.784, 4 Jul. 2007, Case *Wanadoo España v. Telefónica*, §§281 and 283.
471. Decision of the Council No. 2009/DZ/R/2/017, 9 Apr. 2009, §100, <http://www.antimon.gov.sk>.

be profitable on the retail market if it would base its retail services on the access price charge to its competitors. The second situation occurs when the retail price of a dominant company is higher than its access price. In this case, it is necessary to review whether the margin is sufficient. The AMO refers to following tests: (i) the *Equally Efficient Competitor Test* whereby the retail costs of a dominant undertaking are taken into consideration. These costs are added to the access price and the result is compared with the retail price. If the retail price is lower than the result, the margin squeeze is proved; (ii) the *Hypothetically Reasonable Efficient Competitor Test* in which retail costs of competitors are taken into consideration whereas this test is used only if the *Equally Efficient Competitor Test* does not prove margin squeeze.[472]

284. Another price squeeze case against *Slovak Telekom* concerned submission of the proposal to *Ľudová banka* (the Slovak bank) of a tender for a solution of 'Integrated communication platform'.[473] The communication platform consisted in the development of the data virtual private network allowing safe data transmission between several private networks via a public telecommunication network (interconnection of individual bank's branches and enabling their communication with a central office). The case was reinvestigated after the Regional Court in Bratislava dismissed the first penalty decision. Having reinvestigated the case, the AMO came repeatedly to the conclusion that Slovak Telekom abused a dominant position. The AMO concluded that the only possibility for other bidders to meet the technical conditions defined by the bank was to lease an access circuit from Slovak Telekom, which was indispensable in order for other bidders to make a bid (the AMO concluded that other technologies were not substitutable). Based on the investigation, the conclusion of the AMO was that the difference between the wholesale price (access price) and the retail price of the dominant undertaking (Slovak Telekom) did not enable to Slovak Telekom's competitors effectively compete on the retail market. The AMO used the margin squeeze test with reference to the Commission's case *Deutsche Telekom AG.*[474]

472. Decision of the Council No. 2009/DZ/R/2/017, 9 Apr. 2009, §100, <http://www.antimon.gov.sk>.
473. Decision of the Council No. 2009/DZ/R/2/011, 27 Mar. 2009, <http://www.antimon.gov.sk>.
474. Decision of the Commission COMP/C-1/37.451, 37.578, 37.579, Case *Deutsche Telekom AG*, 21 May 2005.

Chapter 3. Concentrations

285. The CA comprises merger control rules particularly under sections 9–13a. The term 'concentration' is defined as the 'process of economic combining of undertakings on the lasting bases'[475] and includes several forms of transactions, particularly:

(1) acquisition of direct or indirect control over another undertaking or a part thereof or over several undertakings or their parts gained by one undertaking (single control) or by several undertakings (joint control);[476]
(2) merger;[477]
(3) creation of a full-functioned joint venture.[478]

286. The merger is defined as a merger according to section 69(3) of the CC as well as a merger, whereby undertakings become only economically combined, even though they remain legally independent (the 'factual merger'). This is especially the case with the existence of joint economic management.[479] The CC distinguishes two forms of 'merger'. The first form represents the transaction, in which assets and liabilities of the undertaking/undertakings to be deleted are transferred to the other, already existing undertaking ('absorption', in Slovak *zlúčenie*). In the second form, the assets and liabilities of undertakings to be deleted are transferred to another newly established undertaking, which shall become a successor-in-law of the deleted undertakings ('amalgamation', in Slovak *splynutie*).

When proving the 'factual merger', it would be necessary to prove mainly the existence of permanent and single economic management as well as other factors adjusted by the Commission Consolidated Jurisdictional Notice under Council Regulation (EC) No. 139/2004 on the Control of Concentrations between Undertakings[480] (Commission Consolidated Jurisdictional Notice).

287. Control under the CA means any possibility of exercising a decisive influence on the undertaking's activities especially by means of:

(1) ownership rights or other rights to the undertaking, that is, control established by acquisition of shares and assets; or
(2) rights, contracts, or other facts that allow the exercise of a decisive influence on the composition, voting, or decisions of the undertaking's bodies (control on a contractual basis established by long-term contracts).[481]

---

475. Section 9(1) of the CA.
476. Section 9(1) letter b) of the CA.
477. Section 9(1) letter a) of the CA.
478. Section 9(5) of the CA.
479. Section 9(2) of the CA.
480. Commission Consolidated Jurisdictional Notice under Council Regulation (EC) No. 139/2004 on the Control of Concentrations between Undertakings, OJ C 95, 16 Apr. 2009, §10.
481. Section 9(4) letters a) and b) of the CA.

288. The control term covers sole control as well as joint control of several undertakings, whereby the person exercising control covers private entities, public bodies as well as a natural person, provided that they come under the term 'undertaking' defined by the CA.[482]

The AMO, in relation to the merger of two public health insurance companies ('*Všeobecná zdravotná poisťovňa*' and '*Spoločná zdravotná poisťovňa*'), after a deep analysis conducted outside a formal administrative proceedings, has come to the conclusion that these entities are not undertakings according to the CA thus the merger control does not apply.[483]

289. The joint control can be established by several means, whereas the purest one is the equity of voting rights of companies exercising the decisive influence. Another form is represented by the situation, when, even though the undertaking possesses a minority of shares, it can exercise control over the target because of the existence of veto rights. 'The most important rights of veto are, including, without limitation, those, which concern the decision-making on the appointment of management members and determination of budget and business policy of the undertaking. If the veto right concerns a business plan, in these situations, there is joint control even without the existence of any other veto right.'[484]

In case of an appraisal of veto rights (content thereof) as well as in other questions concerning the assessment of whether a change in the quality of control is present, the AMO shall also follow the Commission Consolidated Jurisdictional Notice.

290. Control can be acquired directly or indirectly. The AMO always reviews who shall execute the controlling influence in reality, that is, whether the real control is exercised by an undertaking, which is a direct holder of the rights or by another undertaking, who factually exercises the control via the direct holder. In such a situation, the control over an undertaking is deemed to be acquired indirectly. If it is assumed that the control is acquired indirectly, the AMO has to mainly prove relations (such as shareholder's links, financing or contractual relations) between the holder of the rights and company actually exercising the control.

291. Concentration may concern only a part of an undertaking. The 'part of the business of an undertaking' means all assets, based on which the turnover can be attained.[485]

292. Furthermore, the CA includes also a negative determination of transactions, which are not deemed to be concentration. Pursuant to section 9(8) of the CA, concentration is not established if:

(1) Companies (e.g., banks or other financial institutions), the normal activities of which include trading in securities on their own account or on the account of others, temporarily acquiring securities with the intention to resell them. These entities are prohibited from exercising voting and other rights with the intention to influence the competitive behaviour of the acquired undertaking or may exercise

482. Section 3(1) of the CA.
483. The press release of the AMO, in Slovak at: <http://www.antimon.gov.sk/491/tlacove-spravy-2009.axd>, 7 Dec. 2009.
484. Decision of the AMO No. 2001/ZK/4/1/250, 28 Aug. 2001, <http://www.antimon.gov.sk>.
485. Section 9(3) of the CA.

these rights only with the intention to prepare the sale of the acquired undertaking. The sale has to be effected within one year counted from the date of the acquisition of the securities and the banks or financial institutions will lose the control over the undertaking and part thereof. The time limit for the sale of securities can be extended by the AMO, if it is proved that the sale was impossible to execute within one year.

(2) The transaction concerns a temporary acquisition of control, which ensues from special legislation (e.g., the Act on Bankruptcy and Settlement).[486]

293. It is evident from the notion of 'undertaking' (even though that according to the CA, the term 'undertaking' does not cover non-subject, i.e. a 'single economic group'; (*see* Part I, Chapter 4, §1); that any transaction between undertakings under single economic control shall be treated as concentration. This was explicitly determined by the CA until its amendment in 2004. This accordingly applies to internal restructuring conducted within a group of companies, as the concentration, according to section 9(1) of the CA, can arise only if the transaction leads to a permanent change in the quality of control.

294. The merger control under the CA applies also to concentrations of state-owned companies. However, the conclusion on whether such transaction is a concentration depends on the assessment of whether the undertakings formed a part of the same economic unit, that is, were under the same control before the execution of the transaction.

A transaction, where control is acquired by a state administrative body, comes under the merger control review as well. This is, for example, the case of the acquisition of direct sole control over the company Transpetrol (Slovak transit and inland oil transportation company) by the Ministry of Economy of the Slovak Republic, as the Ministry is treated, due to the fact that it controls other undertakings, as an undertaking.[487]

295. The AMO follows the rules and principles applied by the Commission in merger control cases and included in its notices, guidelines or recommendations, mainly in the already-mentioned Commission Consolidated Jurisdictional Notice.

The CA does not comprise any distinction of concentrations based on mutual relations of the parties to the concentration or business sectors in which the concentration arises. All merger control rules, as stipulated by the CA, apply to all established concentrations equally (*see* Part III, Chapter 3 below).

§1. Horizontal Mergers

296. The term 'horizontal merger' covers concentrations which are established between competitors present on the same relevant market. As already mentioned, neither the CA, nor any non-binding recommendation or guideline of the AMO comprises a definition of a horizontal merger and principles of its assessment. Nevertheless, the AMO follows EC guidelines and recommendations concerning the

486. Sections 40–43 of the Act No. 7/2005 Coll., on Bankruptcy and Settlement and on amendment of further laws as amended.

487. Decision of the AMO No. 2009/FK/3/1/015, 7 Apr. 2009, <http://www.antimon.gov.sk>.

merger control such as, in case of horizontal concentrations, the Guidelines on the Assessment of Horizontal Mergers.[488]

297. In general, for the assessment of horizontal mergers, the AMO has to apply the merger test included in section 12(1) of the CA, that is, the AMO has to assess, whether the concentration does not significantly distort effective competition in the relevant market, mainly due to the creation or strengthening of dominant position. Test of dominance seems to be the leading test as it is presumed that if the dominant position is created or strengthened by the concentration, this automatically means that the concentration would significantly distort competition.

298. The competitive assessment of the merger covers the following: assessment of the market structure and the level of competition on the marker with the application of the HHI defining the level of concentration; market shares of merging firms, loss of competition between the merging firms and impact on the market behaviour of other competitors; likelihood of coordinated effects on the market (market-partitioning, customer allocation); impact of the merger on the possibility of other competitors to expand; possibility to keep prices above the level of competition; effects on vertically interconnected markets; impact on the entry of potential competitors by a merger gained efficiency including customers' benefits.

299. In 2003, the AMO prohibited gaining direct joint control of the companies, FIDES Zdravotnícke zásobovanie and BIAMA over VILLA PHARM.[489] The transaction was assessed as a horizontal merger, since all respective parties to the concentration had been present on the same relevant market, that is, the relevant market of the wholesale distribution of pharmaceuticals and medical aids. The Council concluded in its decision on appeal[490] that the transaction would cause the integration of financial, human, and organization resources via the elimination of independent wholesale distributors on the market. Having considered the existence of the dominant position, the Council stated:

> When considering the dominance, in addition to the market-share, other factors indicating the dominance, which have to be considered in this respect, play quite a significant role too. Such factors include also the economic and financial powers, vertical effects of the concentration under consideration, etc. In relation to the market-share, it is important to compare the aggregate share of the parties to the concentration by the remaining competitors, specifically, in relation to their real possibility to provide sufficient competitive pressure on concentrating business entities.[491]

The transaction (along with another acquisition of a wholesale distributor, which took place in the course of the administrative proceedings concerning FIDES/ BIAMA/ VILLA PHARM transaction) resulted in the creation of the economic group, FIDES/ BIAMA/VILLA PHARM/ DRUG – Impex with the market share above 38% on the

488. Guidelines on the Assessment of Horizontal Mergers under the Council Regulation on the Control of Concentrations between Undertakings, OJ C 31, 5 Feb. 2004, 5.
489. Decision of the AMO No. 2003/FH/3/1/112, 6 Jun. 2003, <http://www.antimon.gov.sk>.
490. Decision of the Council No. 2003/FH/R/2/294, 12 Dec. 2003, <http://www.antimon.gov.sk>.
491. Decision of the Council No. 2003/FH/R/2/294, 12 Dec. 2003, <http://www.antimon.gov.sk>.

relevant market for the wholesale distribution of pharmaceuticals and medical aids, whereby the second largest wholesale distributor has the market share a bit above 20% and others below 13%.

The Council concluded that based on the HHI index, the market had been highly concentrated. The Council in this case used the HHI test based on which a level of market concentration is measured. The HHI index is calculated by summing up the squares of individual market shares of all the firms present in the market.[492] The market is deemed to be not concentrated if the HHI index is from 0 to 1,000 points; the market indicates moderate concentration if the HHI is between 1,000 and 1,800 points; and the market is highly concentrated if the index is above 1,800 points.[493] Furthermore, the created economic group has the main number of distribution sheds, which represented a competitive advantage on the market. The Council at the same time concluded that the entry of a new distributor on the market was unlikely due to the high entry costs connected to mainly the establishment of a distribution network or marketing. The competitive advantage of the group was represented also by the fact that the economic group had extended its product portfolio. Moreover, the transaction would lead also to the cumulation of bonuses and discounts for buyers – pharmacies as the main trade partners. Subsequently, other distributors would have a limited possibility to create competitive pressure on the market. The transaction would lead also to an extension of the distribution network and would simplify the access to financial resources. All these factors would lead in the Council's opinion to the creation of a dominant position on the market of wholesale distribution of pharmaceuticals and medical aids. Furthermore:

> As a result of the concentration at issue, the position of FIDES, BIAMA, DRUG – Impex and VILLA PHARM shall be strengthened in relation to producers and suppliers of drugs and medical aids as well as the position in relation to subsequent customers, including, without limitation, pharmacies, while this fact shall necessarily be negatively demonstrated over time in the weakening of the current position of the remaining competitors on the relevant market.[494]

In addition, the Council observed that:

> The possibility to behave independently does not have to be demonstrated only in the provision of low-quality services for prices higher when compared to prices and quality generated in a competitive environment but even by a temporary provision of more advantageous conditions to own customers in order to push out competitors and gain control over the market. The ability of dominant companies to provide, when compared to competition, more significant advantages

492. For example, Commission Regulation (EC) No. 802/2004 of 7 Apr. 2004 implementing Council Regulation (EC) No. 139/2004 on the control of concentrations between undertakings, OJ L 133/1, 30 Apr. 2001.

493. For example, Decision of the AMO No. 2000/FH/1/1/038, 16 Feb. 2000, <http://www.antimon.gov.sk>.

494. Decision of the Council No. 2003/FH/R/2/294, 12 Dec. 2003, <http://www.antimon.gov.sk>.

> to other customer entities may represent a significant obstacle for effective competition with a subsequent negative impact on consumers.[495]

The Council took into consideration also the option to grant a conditional approval of concentration, whereby it stated the following:

> When proposing conditions for eliminating obstacles to effective competition, it is necessary that the parties prove the provision for a permanent recovery of conditions for effective competition on the relevant market... When considering the proposed conditions, it has been necessary for the Office to consider the type, scope, and coverage of the proposed conditions together with an acceptable, full, and time implementation thereof by relevant parties. These conditions have to be concurrently considered also with regard to the market structure and characteristics, including the development of the parties to the concentration and the remaining companies on the relevant market. The acceptability of conditions follows mainly from a realistic provision for an entry of a new competitive entity in the market or strengthening of the existing competitive companies by the transfer of an active business component of the concentrating entities to these companies. In case of a non-feasibility of these draft conditions, it is possible to consider also alternative conditions related to the existence of exclusive contracts, patents, etc.[496]

In this case, the Council did not accept the submitted conditions of the parties to the concentration related to the decrease of distribution sheds, number of products in product portfolio or market-share decrease as the submitted conditions did not meet the requirement for securing effective competition on the market. The Council acknowledged the first-degree decision and prohibited the transaction.

Even though the concentration had been prohibited, FIDES and BIAMA continued to exercise rights resulting from the transaction. The AMO fined these companies for their failure to adhere to the valid decision of the AMO (section 38(2) of the CA valid till 30 June 2014). The Council stated in its second-degree decision that:

> Statement of the decision on the prohibition of the concentration ... clearly provides for the prohibition of the concentration at issue, while it precisely specifies the said concentration – its parties, form, legal title, as well as the incurrence moment thereof ... Logically, by using the 'a minori ad maius' ... or 'a ratione legis' ... argument, it is also possible to deduce the prohibition to implement the concentration upon the validity and effectiveness of the decision also from the provision prohibiting the exercise of rights and obligations arising out of the concentration before the valid and effective decision on it ... since if the exercise of rights and obligations arising out of concentration is prohibited before the valid and effective decision on it, it is another reason why it is impossible

495. Decision of the Council No. 2003/FH/R/2/294, 12 Dec. 2003, <http://www.antimon.gov.sk>.
496. Decision of the Council No. 2003/FH/R/2/294, 12 Dec. 2003, <http://www.antimon.gov.sk>.

to implement the concentration in the period after the validity and effectiveness of the decision, by which it has been prohibited.[497]

300. In 2003, the AMO issued a conditional approval with the concentration[498] of the General Electric Company and AGFA-Gevaert (acquisition of AGFA-Gevaert) related to the relevant market of production and sale of equipment for non-destructive tests of materials – ultrasound NDT devices and NDT X-ray films and chemicals for their development. Both companies were European leaders on the market and nearly exclusive suppliers to the Slovak market. The AMO came to the conclusion that because of the General Electric Company's high market share after the transaction, the structure of the market and high entry barriers and non-existence of potential competitors not only in Slovak Republic but also in Europe, its dominant position on the market would be created or strengthened. The AMO conditioned the approval by the obligation to transfer the business of the General Electric Company concerning activities of ultrasound non-destructive business in Slovak Republic (the transferred business consisted of all assets related to the respective business, IPR, agreements, documentation, employees or other assets) to another undertaking not connected to the General Electric Company. During the transitional period, the General Electric Company was obliged to maintain the economic value and competitiveness of the transferred business and its effective business activities.

In the case *Holcim / VSH,*[499] the AMO approved the concentration consisting of the acquisition of the sole control of the company Holcim over the company VSH (Východoslovenské stavebné hmoty) with conditions. The company Holcim was obliged to sale part of its business which could be able to survive on the market as an independent competing entity. The part of the business thus had to involve: all tangible and intangible assets including IPR necessary to safeguard viability and competitiveness of the sold business; all licenses, permits and authorizations issued by any public authority in favour of the sold part of the business; all contracts and all customers' records, credit and other records of the sold part of the business; all personnel necessary to maintain the viability and competitiveness. The part of the business had to be sold to an undertaking approved by the AMO which should be independent from the company Holcim; it should have financial resources, proven expertise and incentive to maintain and develop as viable and active competition of the companies Holcim and VCM.

§2. Vertical Mergers

301. The vertical merger is established if the parties to the transaction, that is, the parties to the concentration are undertakings operating in supplier-buyer relations; it means undertakings with activities at different levels of the supply chain.

As neither the CA, nor any other document of the AMO includes principles and guidelines for the assessment of vertical merges, the AMO follows the Guidelines on

497. Decision of the Council No. 2005/FH/R/2/090, 25 Aug. 2005, <http://www.antimon.gov.sk>.
498. Decision of the AMO No. 2003/FH/3/1/241, 23 Oct. 2003, <http://www.antimon.gov.sk>.
499. Decision of the AMO No. 2011/FH/3/1/018, 16 May 2011, <http://www.antimon.gov.sk>.

the Assessment of Non-horizontal Mergers under the Council Regulation on the Control of Concentrations between Undertakings[500] (Commission Guideline on the Assessment of Non-horizontal Mergers).

302. The Commission in its Guideline on the Assessment of Non-horizontal Mergers stated that vertical mergers (as well as conglomerate mergers) are less likely to significantly impede effective competition as they do not entail the loss of direct competition and they can at the same time provide substantial efficiencies.

The Commission Guideline on the Assessment of Non-horizontal Mergers described two main ways of how a non-horizontal merger can negatively effect the competition. These are non-coordinated effects (mainly a foreclosure of actual or potential competitors) and coordinated effects (such as the likelihood of coordination of the behaviour on the market, for example, by a coordinated price increase). Both are subject to a merger analysis, which includes especially, the following:

- market-shares analysis as the concentration, where post-merger market shares of the parties to the concentration are below 30% in each of the reviewed markets, shall be unlikely treated as harmful;
- foreclosure effects in the form of 'input foreclosure' (restriction of competitors to access important inputs) or 'customer foreclosure' (restriction of the access to a customer base) including incentives to foreclose the market;
- likely impact on effective competition such as an increase of barriers to the entry;
- efficiency brought by the merger such as better coordination of distribution;
- possible coordination effects.

303. The AMO is obliged to adhere to the merger test included in section 12(1) of the CA also in the case of vertical mergers and to approve the merger only if it does not significantly impedes effective competition (significant impediment of effective competition (SIEC) test), mainly by creation or strengthening of a dominant position.

304. In 2003, when the test of dominance had been the leading merger test under the CA, the Council[501] acknowledged the first-degree decision of the AMO,[502] by which it prohibited vertical concentration of the companies, Heineken Slovensko (beer producer) and Ledos Nápoje (beer distributor), as the AMO came to the conclusion that the concentration would create barriers to effective competition on both assessed relevant markets – the relevant market of production and sale of beer and the relevant market of wholesale distribution of beer to HORECA in the region of the Cities of Levice, Zlaté Moravce, and Nové Zámky.

The AMO stated that the wholesale distribution market, before the establishment of concentration, has been the market with effective competition. However, the biggest number of beer supply contracts with HORECA on the market was concluded just by Heineken Slovensko, that is, it was the main supplier of beer in the specified region. The analysis proved that beer distributors in the respective region had to also have

500. Guidelines on the Assessment of Non-horizontal Mergers under the Council Regulation on the Control of Concentrations between Undertakings, OJ C 265, 18 Oct. 2008, 6.
501. Decision of the Council No. 2003/FV/R/2/082, 7 May 2003, <http://www.antimon.gov.sk>.
502. Decision of the AMO No. 2002/FV/3/1/231, 28 Oct. 2002, <http://www.antimon.gov.sk>.

Heineken's beer in their product portfolio; otherwise, they would not be able to compete effectively on the market.

The Council concluded that Heineken would, by the acquisition of Ledos Nápoje (beer distributor operated in the respective region), extend its market power to another level of the distribution chain and would acquire control over the already existing distribution and logistics system.

The Council further commented that it was probable that Heineken Slovensko would transfer all its supplies to the distribution network of Ledos Nápoje after the acquisition, which would cause a reduction of beer supplies to other distributors. Consequently, because of the strong market position of Heineken Slovensko in the HORECA market (existence of long-term contracts with HORECA, which led nearly to 80% bindingness of the market) other distributors would be eliminated in competition.

Moreover, the Council concluded that for Heineken Slovensko competitors (other beer producers), it would be impossible to effectively create their own distribution network, which would subsequently lead to a strengthening of the Heineken Slovensko position on the market. Finally, the Council, based on the fact that Heineken Slovensko had the leading position on the relevant market of beer production (market share above 40%); the existence of long-term contracts with HORECA and the high level of bindingness of the HORECA market; creation of vertical integration of the beer producer with the well-established wholesale distributor; supposed transfer of supplies to the gained distribution network; strong presence of Heineken's beer in the respective region; acknowledged prohibition of the respective transaction as a concentration creating the dominant position of Heineken Slovensko on the wholesale distribution market with a negative effect on competition.

§3. Market/Product Extension Mergers

305. Market extension mergers cover companies which are not in a relation of mutual competitors and not even in supplier-buyer relations. However, it covers parties, which operate in the same product line but in geographically different relevant markets; thus, the transaction enables an undertaking or undertakings to extend their business activities in different geographical markets.

This accordingly applies to product extension mergers, as the concentration enables the extension of activities of an undertaking to a different product line, which have some technical, marketing or production process relations with the already existing products in its product portfolio.

306. Both of the above-mentioned types of transactions are deemed to be sub-types of conglomerate mergers. The AMO has not issued any separate document which includes the principles of market extension or product extension mergers assessment. Moreover, the AMO does not distinguish these types of transactions explicitly or separately in its case law. The Commission Guideline on the Assessment of Non-horizontal Mergers is supposed to be used by the AMO also for the assessment of product/market extension mergers whereby the following factors are to be considered:

- position of parties on respective markets;

- market foreclosure effects and the possibility to leverage market power from one market to another market, for example, by tying products or exclusionary practices;
- efficiencies such as costs savings related to distribution or joint sale of products (sale in bundles);
- possibility of tacit cooperation.

§4. Pure Conglomerate Mergers

307. Conglomerate mergers are defined in the Commission Guideline on the Assessment of Non-horizontal Mergers as 'mergers between firms that are in a relationship, which is neither horizontal (as competitors in the same relevant market), nor vertical (as suppliers or customers) ...'.[503]

The assessment of their impact on the market shall follow the same rules as described above (*see* §3 above); however, pure conglomerate merges generally do not induce any negative impact on effective competition on the market.

308. The AMO assessed, as a conglomerate merger,[504] the acquisition of Carrefour Slovensko by the ECM Group. Carrefour Slovensko had been the company operating hypermarkets in Slovak Republic and filling stations linked to hypermarkets. The ECM Group as a financial company had been active in real estate and securities investment activities. The AMO defined the concentration as a conglomerate merger due to the fact that the ECM Group had not entered the market of hypermarkets despite the acquisition of Carrefour Slovensko; thus, the activities of parties to the concentration had not led to an overlapping of their activities in Slovak Republic.

§5. Joint Ventures

309. The CA explicitly deals with joint ventures under the merger control provisions. The law does not define any specific rules for the assessment of partially functioning joint ventures (cooperative joint ventures); however, it is indubitable that cooperative joint ventures come under rules concerning the assessment of agreements restricting competition.

310. An establishment of a joint venture represents concentration under the Slovak law, provided that the joint venture is under the joint control of two or more undertakings and performs all functions of an independent economic entity on a lasting basis.

311. The factors which the AMO takes into consideration to decide on whether a notified transaction fulfils the criteria to be declared as a full-function joint venture, that is, the concentration, can be derived from its case law. The joint venture must perform all functions which are normally executed by undertakings acting on the same relevant market, that is, it:

503. Guidelines on the Assessment of Non-horizontal Mergers under the Council Regulation on the Control of Concentrations Between Undertakings, OJ C 265, 18 Oct. 2008, 6, §5.

504. Decision of the AMO No. 2008/FK/3/1/007, 29 Jan. 2008, <http://www.antimon.gov.sk>.

(1) must have independent and sufficient access to financial and personal resources or raw materials;
(2) must have necessary tangible and intangible assets, which on a lasting basis enable it to be active on the relevant market;
(3) must act as an independent market participant – as independent seller or buyer – separately from mother companies. The AMO in its decision concerning the creation of full-function joint venture of companies Ramirent Plc. and Zeppelin Rental GmbH & Co. KG[505] came to the conclusion that even though the joint venture was established for the purpose of joint construction works of the tunnel, it needs to be treated as full-function joint venture as it will not be present on the market only for the duration of the construction of the tunnel but also during the construction of additional infrastructure and provision of related services and the duration of all liabilities in respect of guarantees for all construction works;
(4) must have an independent commercial policy aimed at achieving its own economic objectives.[506] The AMO in the case of notified cooperation of Hella KGaA Hueck & Co. and SL CORPORATION[507] further declared that if the purpose of the joint venture creation is defined narrowly – only as purchase and selling of some components for a single undertaking, necessary for the production of only a specific type of motorcar, including provision of services related to warranties; the joint venture will not have access to the supply market for other actual or potential buyers and its activity will be aimed only at deliveries made to one buyer; marketing activities of the joint venture are not aimed at other motorcar producers; the number of employees is limited to administrative staff – not exceeding five to ten persons, the joint venture is not full-functioned. In this case, the AMO further stated that the joint venture is not full-functioned if it takes over only a specific part of business activities of one or several mother companies without an access to the market.[508]

The AMO will also assess a change of non-functioned joint venture to full-functioned joint venture as an concentration if the criteria for the notification of the concentration are met. This situation occurred in case BULK TRANSSHIPMENT SLOVAKIA (BTS).[509] The joint venture BTS after its creation in 2008 has not acted as an independent company on the market. However, after subsequent evaluating activities of BTS by its mother companies during the period 2009–2011, both shareholders came to the conclusion that BTS could operate on the market of rail freight transport and forwarding services and to provide services to final customers (shipping) or other existing suppliers (railway transport). In the notification, the mother companies indicated that BTS will act as an independent market participant separately from its mother companies and will perform all the functions normally carried out by companies operating in the same market; it will have management dedicated to its day-to-day operations and access to sufficient resources including finance, staff and assets. The aim of mother companies

505. Decision of the AMO No. 2014/FH/3/1/034, 24 Nov. 2014, <http://www.antimon.gov.sk>.
506. Decision of the AMO No. 2006/ZK/3/1/018, 8 Mar. 8 2006, <http://www.antimon.gov.sk>.
507. Decision of the AMO No. 2006/ZK/3/1/059, 25 May 2006, <http://www.antimon.gov.sk>.
508. For example, Decision No. 2003/FH/3/1/171, 23 Jul. 2003, <http://www.antimon.gov.sk>.
509. Decision of the AMO No. 2013/FH/3/1/004, 22 Feb. 2013, <http://www.antimon.gov.sk>.

was to have BTS operating on a lasting basis particularly in the Czech Republic and Poland in the area of rail transporting and Hungary in the field of freight forwarding. The AMO assessed the change of BTS activities as separate concentration.

312. The assessment of a joint venture under merger control includes not only the appraisal, whether the transaction is a concentrative joint venture, but the coordination of the business behaviour of undertakings controlling the joint venture is at the same time assessed under the prohibition to conclude agreements restricting competition (section 4(1) of the CA). Concentration is approved, only if this coordination is not prohibited as an agreement restricting competition.[510]

510. Section 12(2) of the CA.

Part III. Administrative Procedure

Chapter 1. Administrative Investigation Before the Antitrust Authority

313. The administrative proceedings before the AMO are regulated by the CA as well as by the APC. The CA adopted in 2001 and further amended, specifies some aspects of the administrative proceedings before the AMO differently from the APC which remains applicable as a supporting regulation.[511]

314. The CA contains autonomous legal regulation of some institutes of the administrative proceedings concerning mainly the initiation of the administrative proceedings and its termination, the delivery, the time limits for issuing a decision or it contains specific provisions concerning statement of facts[512] ('Statement of objections'). The CA, for example, comprises procedural institutes not included in the APC, that is, the possibility of connecting matters, third parties' rights, the delivery of documents or right to consult administrative files. Nevertheless, general principles of administrative proceedings (e.g., principle of material truth or principle of legality) and procedural rights connected to the right of defence or the right to request oral hearing as well as regulations on essentials of administrative decisions, remain applicable according to the APC.

Authorizations provided to the AMO may be used by it *when performing tasks under law* and only to the extent *necessary for activity*. Such requirement for proportionality of the AMO´s procedure is fully in compliance with the principle of *avoiding unnecessary burdening of parties to proceedings and third parties*, set forth in section 3(4) of the APC, as well as with other principles applicable especially in cases where unannounced inspections are carried out in undertakings´ business premises. It must not be forgotten that the principle of proportionality is a core principle of the EU law, which also results from the decision-making practice by which undesired intervention in the freedom of such entities is prohibited, in such a manner that executive´s acting does not represent a disproportionate and illegal interference. As regards the arbitrary and illegal procedure of the AMO in collecting data, information and taking of evidence, it is accordingly possible to state the opinion of the Constitutional Court, according to which:

it is the role of a legally consistent state to prepare legitimate conditions that would guarantee fair hearing of a case before a competent public authority. The creation

511. Section 37(1) of the CA.
512. In Slovak: '*Výzva pred vydaním rozhodnutia*'.

of such conditions consists in a legal regulation of particular proceedings within the framework of which substantive relations are protected and thereby fundamental rights and freedoms are actually exercised. There is no doubt that only by following an objective procedure, self-will is excluded in a decision-making process, as well as the completely unfounded possibility of a public authority´s consideration without any objective limits defined in legal ways of ascertaining the factual basis to make a decision...[513]

§1. Initiative

I. General Sector Inquiries

315. The AMO is empowered[514] to conduct a so-called investigation in particular sectors of the economy in order to obtain information on state of competition in the respective sector which is a form of a general inquiry into a particular business sector ('investigation on the relevant market '). The AMO is also empowered to perform investigation concerning an individual undertaking.[515]

316. Despite this fact, the CA does not comprise any particular provisions concerning the AMO's activities related to this investigation on the relevant market. The AMO usually uses the same investigatory techniques as used within formal administrative proceedings. These mainly include submission of questionnaires or requests for information addressed to undertakings. The AMO is also entitled to request any trade documents, data or information from undertakings as well as to make inspections in business premises or/and in any vehicles related to business activities,[516] to make copies of, or make notes from required documents, to require certified translations of documents into the Slovak language. Moreover, the AMO is entitled to request, and an undertaking is obliged to provide oral or written explanations. The investigatory powers of the AMO are further described, in the text below, in detail.

317. The CA does not determine any obligation or a manner by which the undertaking has to be informed of the initiation of the general investigation on the market. The AMO usually sends the information at the beginning of the general investigation along with the written request addressed to the undertaking concerned which includes a description of the relevant market which is subject to investigation and if the general investigation refers to a specific undertaking (investigation concerning the conduct of the respective undertaking on the relevant market); the AMO provides information on the business name as well.

318. The general sector inquiries are not conducted by the AMO frequently. For example, in 2008, the AMO made an analysis of the water sector aimed at the position and functioning of companies in this business sector,[517] in 2009, analyses on

513. Judgment of the Constitutional Court, No. III. ÚS 283/2010, 27 Oct. 2010.
514. Section 22(1) letter a) of the CA.
515. Section 22(1) letter b) of the CA.
516. Section 22a of the CA.
517. The Annual Report, 2008, <http://www.antimon.gov.sk>.

the functioning of the electricity and natural gas markets amended in 2015,[518] in 2014, it conducted marked analysis concerning financial services provided for natural persons and SME segment.[519]

More often, the AMO conducts investigations related to a specific claim of an undertaking concerning an alleged anticompetitive practice on the market of a respective undertaking or it begins an investigation towards respective undertaking based on general information from the press or gained in the course of its activities. The investigation concerning a conduct of a particular undertaking is limited to assessing any potentially anticompetitive behaviour of this undertaking and usually precedes the official administrative proceedings. More often, especially when the AMO has a suspicion of existence of the hard-core cartel, it conducts the investigation against the respective undertaking by beginning a so-called down-raid (unannounced inspection in business premises).

II. Ex officio Investigations

319. The administrative proceedings before the AMO may commence following a complaint or a notification of a party to the proceedings or following the AMO's own initiative.

The administrative proceedings concerning agreements restricting competition and abuse of a dominant position begins only ex officio. This means that according to the CA, not each complaint of a party to the proceedings initiates the formal administrative proceedings. Consequently, undertakings can submit a complaint to the AMO at any time, but only the AMO is authorized to begin the administrative proceedings related to the alleged breach of both antitrust prohibitions. The aim of the AMO while preparing the CA and taking the decision to incorporate rules deviating from the APC in this respect was to minimize the number of formal administrative proceedings initiated upon ungrounded submissions.

320. However, a claim of an undertaking and/or a party to the administrative proceedings usually launches an investigation pursuant to section 22(1) letter b) of the CA (investigation concerning the conduct of respective undertaking on the market). The AMO will initiate the formal administrative proceedings only if there is a real suspicion of the breach of competition rules. The AMO may further initiate the administrative proceedings (ex officio) also upon a written complaint of a natural or a legal person which is not an undertaking.

321. The AMO is obliged to initiate the administrative proceedings whenever it detects a breach of competition rules (antitrust prohibitions) or a violation of the CA (mainly failure to notify concentration, violation of the prohibition to exercise rights and obligations arising from the concentration before an approval of the concentration) or a violation of obligations and commitments imposed on an undertaking by an individual decision. However, the AMO in January 2015 implemented its Prioritization

518. In Slovak language at: <http://www.antimon.gov.sk/sektorove-studie-a-analyzy/>.
519. In Slovak language at: <http://www.antimon.gov.sk/sektorove-studie-a-analyzy/>.

policy[520] according to which the highest priority for the investigation is given to hard-core cartels cases and abuse of a dominant position exclusionary practices.

322. The administrative proceedings initiated ex officio by the AMO commences on the day the AMO makes its first action towards a party to the proceedings.[521] This 'first action' is usually a formal letter addressed to the party to the administrative proceedings. The commencement of the administrative proceedings must be announced by the AMO to all parties. Neither the CA nor the APC defines the essentials of the letter on commencement of the administrative proceedings. The announcement of the initiation of the formal administrative proceedings shall mainly include 'the legal reason justifying the commencement of the administrative proceedings ex officio (reference to the specific rule of the statute which was infringed according to the administrative authority's view and which empowers it to decide in the matter), the case being the object of the administrative proceedings (i.e., Revocation of a license), description of facts that are a basis for initiating the administrative proceedings ...'.[522] In general, the announcement must be sufficiently explicit and comprehensive, for the right to a fair trial to be safeguarded. At the beginning of the formal process, the AMO is further obliged to inform the party to the administrative proceedings that it has the right to indicate which of the submitted information and data is to be considered as a business secret, or confidential.[523]

III. Complaints

323. The CA does not include a limitation on the number of subjects that can submit a complaint to the AMO. The complaint can be filed by the undertaking as well as by any natural or legal person[524] – by a third party[525] and, as mentioned above, it can instigate either a general investigation or a formal administrative proceeding. Complaints submitted by undertakings which are not a party to the administrative proceedings, complaints concerning agreements restricting competition and abuse of a dominant position and complaints of third parties or non-undertakings, serve as the bases for initiation of an investigation concerning the review of a conduct of respective undertaking in the relevant market pursuant to section 22(1) letter b) of the CA. Subsequently, the formal administrative proceeding is commenced, ex officio, providing that the general investigation provides hints about possible breaches of competition rules.

520. In Slovak: 'Prioritizačná politika PMÚ SR' <http://www.antimon.gov.sk/data/att/1635.pdf>.
521. Section 18(2) of the APC.
522. Soňa Košičiarová,*Správny poriadok, Komentár* (Šamorin, Slovak Republic: Heuréka, 2004), 7.
523. Section 28(1) of the CA.
524. Section 25(2) of the CA.
525. According to s. 27(1) of the CA 'a third party shall be a natural or a legal person that is not a party to the proceedings, in particular a consumer, supplier, purchaser, or competitor of a party to the proceedings'.

324. The CA specifies the notion of a 'party to the proceedings' based on the subject of the administrative proceedings. The party to the proceedings is in the case of:

(1) an agreement restricting competition, the party to this agreement restricting competition;
(2) a dominant position, the undertaking activities or conduct of which may constitute an abuse of a dominant position;
(3) a concentration established in a form of a merger, the undertakings being parties to the merger;
(4) a concentration by acquisition of direct or indirect control, the undertaking or undertakings which acquire direct or indirect control over another undertaking or part of another undertaking or undertakings;
(5) a restriction of competition caused by administrative bodies,[526] the state administration authority, the territorial self-government authority or the special interest body.

A party to the proceedings (other than specified in the points (i)–(v) above) is also the person the rights, interests or obligations of whom are to be decided on by the AMO according to the CA. The CA excludes from the definition of the party to the administrative proceedings those who are only affected by the restrictive behaviour on the market. For example, the dominant undertaking the behaviour of which is under the review is a party to the administrative proceedings concerning an abuse of a dominant position with no exception, but the undertaking or other persons affected by the abusive conduct (e.g., end-users) are not a party to it.

325. The essentials of a complaint or any submission referred to the AMO are regulated by the APC.[527] The complaint is always assessed according to its content which means that the complainant does not need to specify exactly which provisions of the CA are allegedly breached. The complaint must provide: (i) information on the complainant – name and address of the complainant, (ii) a description of the matter, (iii) what the complainant proposes. The different approach is applied by the leniency applications (section 38d of the CA). In addition, it is not unusual submitting any compliant via attorney at law and thus not disclosing an identity of a de facto complainant.

The description of the matter depends on the specific situation which is subject to the complaint. It is advisable that the complainant submits a clear description of the situation or alleged violation of the CA along with specification and characterization of products and services affected by the alleged infringement, description of the situation on the market or specification of business relations and market players. Even though it is not required to support the complaint by relevant documents or potential evidence, it is useful to do so. From the beginning of the communication with the AMO, it is advisable to indicate all information which is treated as confidential or a business secret by the undertaking. The definition of a business secret is included in

526. Proceedings of the AMO according to s. 39 of the CA.
527. Section 19 of the APC.

the CC,[528] and the AMO usually treats as a business secret only information fulfilling conditions of this definition, thus a written justification of indicated information is not only useful but required. Moreover, the AMO issued Guideline on assessment of business secrecy by the AMO[529] which provides detailed rules observed by AMO when assessing the business secrecy and confidentiality of information.

326. Other essentials of the complaint can be specified by respective legal regulations (e.g., notification of a concentration must include not only the essentials of the submission but also other information required by the CA).

327. The submission can be made in written form or orally to the minutes or by electronic means (e.g., by email or fax). Submission made by electronic means (email submission) must be accompanied by a secure electronic signature[530] or needs to be confirmed also in writing or orally to the minutes[531] within three days. Submissions made by a non-undertaking must be in written form. A non-undertaking can request the AMO to inform it on further proceedings whereby the AMO is obliged to provide this information within two months from the day of the receipt of the request.[532]

If the complaint of the undertaking which directly initiates the formal administrative proceedings (submissions not related to agreements restricting competition and abuse of a dominant position) contains any deficiencies, the AMO is obliged to ask the party to the administrative proceedings to amend these deficiencies within a determined time limit. Within this period, the time limit for the issuing of a decision is not in effect. Providing that the deficiencies are not amended within the stipulated time-period, the AMO can decide on the termination of the administrative proceedings.[533]

328. It is worth to mention that concerning the merger control proceedings, the essential of the notification are defined by the CA and by the Decree on Notification. The AMO begins the merger control proceedings only if the notification is completed.[534]

§2. Powers

329. The investigatory powers of the AMO in investigation (both regarding the sector inquiries as well as the investigation concerning the respective undertaking's conduct) and in the formal administrative proceedings are specified directly by the

528. Section 17 of the CC: 'Business secrets shall consist of all the facts of trading, manufacturing and technological nature related to the enterprise, which have actual, or at least potential, tangible or intangible value, are normally not available in the respective industry and the entrepreneur wishes that the same are not disclosed, provided that the entrepreneur adequately provides for the confidentiality thereof.'
529. The AMO, in Slovak: 'Usmernenie k posudzovaniu Protimonopolného úradu SR k posudzovaniu ochrany obchodného tajomstva, dôverných informácií a osobných údajov', <http://www.antimon.gov.sk/data/files/454_usmernenie-protimonopolneho-uradu-sr-k-posudzovaniu-ochrany-obchodneho-tajomstva-dovernych-informacii-a-osobnych-udajov-pdf.pdf>.
530. Act No. 215/2002 Coll. on Electronic Signature and on amendment and supplement of some acts as further amended.
531. Section 19(1) of the APC.
532. Section 25(2) of the CA.
533. Section 25(7) of the CA.
534. Section 11(3) of the CA.

CA. These are the same, for both types of the AMO's procedural activities. In general, the AMO can obtain all information necessary for the detection of the CA violation[535] from undertakings. The selection of investigatory tools is dependent on the circumstances of an individual case.

One of the most significant powers of the AMOM which falls outside common authorizations of state administration bodies is the AMO´s possibility to perform an inspection in business premises of an undertaking, both announced as well unannounced, in accordance with the authorizations and procedure provided for in section 22a of the CA. In the case of unannounced inspections, it concerns the so-called *dawn raids*.

330. For the sector inquiries preparation, the AMO uses mainly questionnaires or written requests for information. The scope of information requested within the general investigation is in no manner limited by the CA; thus, the AMO is entitled to request necessary information of the same depth and quality as within the formal administrative proceedings.

I. Request for Information

331. The AMO (employees as well as persons entrusted with the fulfilment of tasks falling within AMO's jurisdiction) is entitled to request all information and documents necessary for the AMO's activities from: (i) undertakings, (ii) senior employees, (iii) statutory and control bodies and their members. The range of requested information is very broad and requested documents include all legal, trade and accounting documents regardless of the medium on which they are recorded. The AMO is entitled to also request for officially certified translations of documents into the Slovak language and make copies of, or notes from, the submitted documents.[536] The AMO is entitled to also request oral or written explanations and is authorized to make audio recordings of oral explanations.[537]

332. The request for information is usually in written form, sent to the undertaking by a formal letter. Sometimes the AMO requests information also informally by an email. This mainly concerns requests for clarification of already submitted data or documents.

333. The CA limits the authorization of the AMO to request information by the fact that the request must concern only data, documents and information which are necessary for the proceedings of the AMO. This means that the link between the subject of the proceedings (irrespective of whether this is a general investigation on the market or a formal administrative proceeding) and the requested information is required. Nevertheless, it might be difficult for the undertaking or for the party to the administrative proceedings to claim that the information required by the AMO is not connected to the investigation, as it is on the discretion of the AMO to decide which information is necessary. The refusal to submit required information because the undertaking claims the lack of its 'necessity' for the AMO's investigation will be, in general, the reason for an individual penalty proceeding concerning the non-submission of information

535. Section 22(2) of the CA.
536. Section 22(2) of the CA.
537. Section 22(2) of the CA.

in which the party to the proceedings would have to justify its position. Evenly, the APC stipulates that the administrative decision is based mainly on submissions, proposals and explanations of the parties to the proceedings, evidence and declarations on word of honour. The scope and the manner of finding evidence for the decision is determined by the AMO.[538]

334. The undertakings are obliged to submit the required information within the provided time limit. The time-periods for submission differ according to the scope and the amount of requested data. If the undertaking is not able to submit the requested information before this deadline, it can ask the AMO for its prolongation. This right is not directly stipulated by the applicable procedural rules, but it is the standard practice recognized by the AMO. The prolongation of the deadline is granted if well-founded reasons justify it. In case the undertaking fails to provide required information to the AMO within a time limit or within an extended period, it is fairly common for the AMO to address to the undertaking, though it is not obliged to do so, an additional request for information.

335. Providing that the AMO's request for information is not clear, it is advisable to contact the AMO and clarify the uncertainty before sending any answer which could be used further in the investigation or the administrative proceedings.

336. The undertaking that fails to comply with the request is likely to be fined by a penalty up to 1% of its turnover achieved in the previous closed accounting period.[539] The AMO starts a formal administrative proceeding in which it assesses the circumstances and the argumentation of the undertaking underlying the failure to submit the requested information. After issuing a penalty decision, the undertaking is obliged to submit the requested information unless it is no longer necessary for the investigation. The penalty can be imposed repeatedly. The penalty for failure to submit information is imposed on the undertaking or legal person directly; thus, senior employees or members of statutory bodies cannot be fined for obstructions individually. Submission of incomplete or untrue information is also fined by the AMO irrespective of whether the incorrect information was submitted intentionally or not.

337. The AMO is also entitled to request information from persons other than undertakings. Natural or legal persons are obliged to submit requested information and documents concerning an undertaking, without any delay, if this is not contrary to a special legislation such as the Act on Banks[540] or the Act on Tax and Fee Administration.[541] As the AMO is entitled to request information also from a natural person – non-undertaking, refusal to provide the information by this person can be fined up to EUR 1,650,[542] also repeatedly.

538. Section 32(2) of the APC.
539. Section 38a(1) of the CA. According to s. 38c(1) of the CA, the preceding accounting period is the year preceding the year in which the AMO issues a decision, or the year preceding that year if the data for that year is not available.
540. Act No. 483/2001 Coll. on Banks and on Amendments and Supplements to Certain Laws as amended.
541. Act No. 563/2009 Coll. on Tax Administration (Tax Code) and on amendments and supplements to other acts.
542. Section 38a(2) of the CA.

338. The AMO may appoint a specialized expert (sworn expert) for preparation of the expert's opinion if the case requires appraisal of specific facts and circumstances. The expert is appointed by an authoritative decision which is subject to an appeal.[543]

339. According to the APC as well as in line with section 40(1) of the CA, the parties to the proceedings have access to administrative files. Moreover, according to the Freedom of Information Act,[544] any person (natural or legal) has access to the administrative file or to the file concerning the investigation without the necessity to justify the request. Taking into consideration the rights of access to files, it is advisable to mark all confidential information as business secrets beforehand, in order to avoid any undesirable disclosure of information.

II. Investigating and Search Powers

340. Investigative and searching powers of the AMO include its possibility to search business premises (section 22a (1)–(7) of the CA) as well as private premises (section 22a(8)–(10) of the CA).

341. The AMO – its employees and entrusted persons empowered by a written authorization – are entitled to search and to make investigations in all premises, buildings and all means of transport of the undertaking, that are used for business purposes.[545] The investigation may be announced to the undertaking prior to its performance, or can be executed even without a prior notification.

342. The written authorization for the inspection on business premises has the form of a formal letter and is issued by the Deputy chairperson of the AMO if the inspection takes place during the investigation or the first-degree proceedings. The inspection can be conducted also during the second-degree proceedings of the Council, and in this case, the Chairperson of the AMO issues the authorization. The CA includes formal essentials for the written authorization in section 22a(2) of the CA which cannot be omitted; otherwise, the authorization would be treated as unlawful and insufficient basis to perform the inspection. In particular, the authorization contains the full name of the person who issues the authorization and its signature along with the stamp of the AMO, number of the authorization and the date of its issue the names of the AMO's employees entitled to make the inspection, the business name of the undertaking concerned, the scope of the inspection and the time limit within which the inspection can be performed, subject and purpose of the inspection as well as a general description of the reason of the inspection. The authorization further includes information on the investigating powers of the AMO along with the wording of relevant provisions of the CA and description of rights and obligations of an undertaking under investigation.

The omission to fulfil the formal prerequisites of the authorization represents the first opportunity to file objections or a complaint against the AMO´s procedure or thereafter an action for illegal interference pursuant to section 252 of the CPAC. In relation therewith, it is worth referring to the Judgment of the Supreme Court in the

543. Section 36 of the APC.

544. Act No. 211/2000 Z.z. Free Access to Information (Freedom of Information Act) as further amended.

545. Section 22a(1)of the CA.

undertaking *Ševt* case. In the given case, the Supreme Court decided on an illegal interference and imposed the obligation on the AMO to refrain from further illegal interferences with rights of Ševt, specifically, not to subsequently view the data carrier that had been copied by the Antimonopoly Office (AMO) during an announced inspection. In this case, the Supreme Court stated an illegitimate interference of the AMO with rights of the undertaking Ševt due to the fact that the authorization to carry out the inspection had failed to contain all prerequisites prescribed by law, specifically, the authorization had failed to bear a round stamp of the AMO. In this specific case, the Supreme Court linked the way in which the authorization was formulated also with the scope in which employees of the AMO might thereafter carry out an inspection in business premises, specifically, in relation to carriers that could be expected to contain private data. Here, the Supreme Court stated that:

When carrying out an inspection, it is necessary to differentiate invasive and non-invasive acts. Invasive acts interfere with fundamental rights and freedoms. There is a difference if the defendant claims within the framework of investigation business and accounting records and documents in case of which it is unambiguous that they contain no private data, and there is difference if it concerns copying data carriers of employees of an undertaking in case of which it may not be excluded and it may reasonably be assumed that they also contain private correspondence (e.g. PC hard disk, notebook, USB keys, etc.). In such cases, the authorisation has to be justified as well.[546]

The authorization to carry out an inspection thus has to be seen as a primary document authorizing the AMO to carry out an inspection in business premises and as a document from which legality of the inspection carried out is, *inter alia*, derived.

Clear definition of the purpose of an inspection is necessarily affected by reasons for which the AMO has commenced the inspection. The AMO should have sufficient information available, at least in the form of actual indications that it is probable that there are underlying documentation, documents and information in the premises of undertaking concerned, which may prove a breach of the prohibition to enter into a cartel agreement. In case of an absence of such reasonable suspicion before the inspection is carried out and the inspection goal itself potentially consists only in ascertaining, finding out any potential anticompetitive practices, we are referring to the so-called fishing expedition.

343. The power for execution of the investigation on business premises is linked to the authorization of the AMO to request all business documents and data from undertakings. Therefore, the AMO's employees are entitled to search all documents, business records, meeting minutes, accounting documents and to search for information on all means of information storage (discs, tapes, fax machines). The undertakings concerned are obliged to permit such inspection. Any destruction of documents during the inspection is subject to a fine up to 5% of the turnover achieved within the previous closed accounting period.[547] Even though the CA does not directly explain what the obligation 'to submit all required documents' means, it must be interpreted in such a way that it designates obligation to provide the AMO with all documents that the undertaking has at its disposal and also the obligation to find them. Any explanation

546. Judgment of the Supreme Court, No. 3 Sžz 1/ 2011, 5 Apr. 2011.
547. Section 38a(2) of the CA.

why some documents are not at the disposal of the undertaking must be well justified (e.g., if retention policy stipulates specific time limits for the retention of documents after which all documents are destroyed). Due to the fact that non-cooperation with the authority is subject to a penalty, the active approach of the undertaking is required. It must be still kept in mind that the inspection can be conducted only to the extent necessary for the respective investigation.

344. Powers of the AMO may be used by it when performing tasks under law and only to the extent 'necessary for activity'. This specifically concerns the non-announced inspections in business premises. Such requirement for proportionality of the AMO´s procedure is fully in compliance with the principle of 'avoiding' unnecessary burdening of parties to proceedings and third parties', set forth in section 3(4) of the APC, as well as with other principles applicable especially in cases where unannounced inspections are carried out in undertakings′ business premises. It must not be forgotten that the principle of proportionality is a core principle of the EU law, which also results from the decision-making practice by which undesired intervention in the freedom of such entities is prohibited, in such a manner that executive´s acting does not represent a disproportionate and illegal interference. As regards the arbitrary and illegal procedure of the AMO in collecting data, information, and taking of evidence, it is accordingly possible to state the opinion of the Constitutional Court of the SR:

it is the role of a legally consistent state to prepare legitimate conditions that would guarantee fair hearing of a case before a competent public authority. The creation of such conditions consists in a legal regulation of particular proceedings within the framework of which substantive relations are protected and thereby fundamental rights and freedoms are actually exercised. There is no doubt that only by following an objective procedure, self-will is excluded in a decision-making process, as well as the completely unfounded possibility of a public authority´s consideration without any objective limits defined in legal ways of ascertaining the factual basis to make a decision.[548]

345. It is worth to mention that the AMO has issued guideline in which it clarifies the process and all steps conducted during the inspection (Inspection Guideline).[549] Already in the first provisions of the document, the AMO emphasizes that an undertaking with which an inspection is being performed is obliged to submit itself to the performance thereof. This is also proved by another case reviewed by the AMO concerning the undertaking AUTOMAX, which hindered the AMO from conducting the inspection in its business premises. The AMO imposed a sanction on the undertaking in the amount of EUR 44,358, representing 0.6% of its total turnover achieved in 2013.[550] The Executive of the company in question was not in the undertaking´s premises at the time of the performance of the inspection and, after being contacted by phone, refused to grant its consent with the performance of the inspection and at the same

548. Judgment of the Constitutional Court, No. III. ÚS 283/2010, 27 Oct. 2010, as well as Judgment of the BA Regional Court, No. 2S/305/2012, 6 Feb. 2013.

549. The AMO, Guidence on the Power of the AMO to Carry Out Inspections (in Slovak: *Usmrnenie Protimonopolného úradu Slovenskej republiky vykonávat' inšpekcie*), <http://www.antimon.gov.sk/data/files/489_usmernenie-k-pravomoci-protimonopolneho-uradu-slovenskej-republiky-vykonavat-inspekcie.pdf>.

550. Decision of the AMO, No. 2014/SP/2/2/026, 12 Sept. 2014, <http://www.antimon.gov.sk>.

time refused to authorize other employees to represent it in the performance of the inspection. The undertaking´s defence was based, *inter alia*, on the argumentation according to which the AMO had insufficiently identified and clarified which information was to be submitted during the inspection, had failed to explain the subject matter and reason of the inspection even at the time of the phone call between the Executive and the AMO´s authorized employees, while it had been impossible to secure the access to email accounts of the company´s Executive in a manner other than with the on-site cooperation of the Executive and, in addition, the AMO had had the possibility to provide for the documents in another manner, e.g. by sealing the premises. The AMO justified its procedure in imposing the sanction by powers held by the AMO during the performance of an inspection as well as by an explanation of the procedure that is commonly followed in case of an unannounced inspection in business premises. During an inspection, the AMO obtains 'information and underlying documents allowing the course of the inspection itself, including information about the undertaking´s organizational structure, description of the undertaking´s premises, information about the employment status of particular persons, information where such persons are staying at the given time, about the responsibility for the performance of certain tasks falling under the competence of the undertaking, information about the working equipment of employees and other persons with the undertaking, including, without limitation, about computing equipment (computers, notebooks, telephones, etc.) and related passwords to access the same, explanations to the documents being searched, etc.'[551] The AMO relied in the justification of the decision in question on the fact that active cooperation from an undertaking´s side is required by the AMO mainly when providing for access to computing equipment and data stored with the undertaking in the e-form, i.e. active cooperation of employees responsible for information technologies is required above all. The scope of the obligation to submit oneself to the performance of the inspection was explained in the decision in question in such a manner that the undertaking was obliged to provide oral information but at the same time provide employees of the AMO with the possibility to actually verify the oral information provided. The AMO´s employees have to be allowed during the inspection to enter all business premises and means of transport for the entire period during which they are authorized to carry out the inspection. The undertaking is obliged to set aside premises where the employees may work, while allowing them, at the same time, to move in the business premises without restricting them in doing so and making no other obstructions that would hinder a smooth course of the inspection. It is also the undertaking´s obligation to provide for the documents not being disguised or concealed in any manner, while in this regard, the CA requires active cooperation from the undertakings. If an undertaking fails to voluntarily submit itself to acts which the AMO is authorized to take in the undertaking´s premises, the AMO may enforce the performance of an inspection by referring to the possibility of imposing a sanction or by overcoming the resistance. Right these authorizations, as described and justified by the AMO in the decision in question, support the need for a strict observance of the principle of proportionality from the AMO´s side, as it is impossible to accept the Office´s attitude pursued many times that since it concerns the exercise of a power in the public interest, this prevails over the undertaking´s private interest. The above-stated jurisprudence clearly proves

551. Decision of the AMO, No. 2014/SP/2/2/026, 12 Sept. 2014, <http://www.antimon.gov.sk>.

that the authorization entrusted on the AMO by law may not be seen at extreme level without any restrictions.

As regards the need for the presence of a statutory authority in the performance of an inspection, the AMO provided its statement in this specific case that it was not necessary and its presence had to be seen in terms of law only, while it was fully at the undertaking´s discretion whether it would provide for the performance of its activities in the absence of a statutory authority by authorizing another person to represent it. In addition, the AMO states in the given decision that it is fully at its discretion to decide upon the scope in which it will exercise its powers pursuant to the CA during an inspection, i.e. whether it decides to violently enter the premises by overcoming an obstacle (for instance, by calling a locksmith) or whether it decides to seal the premises where the inspection is to be carried out for a certain, necessary time, while taking into account what kind of premises or facilities it concerns and considering the scope of the interference of such procedure in the undertaking´s rights.

As already mentioned, powers of the AMO´s employees are specified in detail right in the provision of section 22a of the CA, while it is necessary to refer in relation therewith to the restrictions resulting from the right of protection against self-incrimination pursuant to Article 6 of the European Convention of Human Rights as well as from the right to privacy and protection against unauthorized interference with secrecy of correspondence pursuant to the already-mentioned Article 8 of the Convention. The decision of the Supreme Court in the '*AT Computer*' case[552] is also related with the requirement for the right of protection against self-incrimination. The proponent stated in the case in question that its rights had been infringed even by the manner in which the Office had been asking questions and requiring explanations during the inspection and by requiring information that had led to an explanation of the undertaking´s acting in such a manner that the undertaking had been forced to testify in a manner leading to self-incrimination. The Supreme Court stated in this case that the obligation to 'provide explanations during the course of an inspection had its limits. The provision of explanations prior to the commencement of administrative proceedings has to be strictly limited to the provision for the course of the inspection, i.e. questions are to be aimed at the defendant´s being able to obtain the required underlying documentation, documents or information to perform the inspection and fulfil the purpose thereof consisting, above all, in taking evidence. By using the institute of explanations during an inspection, it is, however, impossible to accede to ascertaining grounds for the decision in administrative proceedings by clarifying an undertaking´s acting in the context of a suspicion of an infringement of competition rules, specifically, by hearing a party (hearing an Executive) or employees.'[553] In accordance with this conclusion, the Supreme Court prohibited the application of the parts of minutes having the nature of a clarification of the undertaking´s acting in further investigation, since the scope of the questions exceeded the condition that these had to be necessary for the performance of the inspection.

346. Neither the CA nor the AMO's legal regulation or explanatory documents stipulate whether legally privileged documents have to be submitted to the AMO during the inspection. It is not provided in any normative text whether the lawyer-client

552. Judgment of the Supreme Court, No. 4Sžz/1/2013 of 17 Oct. 2013.
553. Judgment of the Supreme Court, No. 4Sžz/1/2013 of 17 Oct. 013.

privilege concerns only communication with an external legal advisor, or also communication with internal lawyers. There is no clear rule how the AMO will treat internal analytical or advisory legal documents and use their contents in its investigation. It is in general up to the undertaking to prove and justify that specific documents are protected by lawyer-client privilege and up to the external lawyer to insist on the confidentiality of its communication with the client. Due to the fact that the CA does not comprise provisions which would regulate the AMO's approach towards documents marked as legally privileged and moreover, due to the eventuality that the undertaking can be fined for the refusal to provide requested documents, it is probable that the position of the undertaking and the AMO towards this type of document will be clarified only during the penalty proceedings concerning the non-submission of information. The recent experience from the inspection of the documents and data during the inspection in business premises or subsequent review of documents of the AMO shows, that the AMO usually accepts the lawyer-client privilege.

347. The AMO is entitled to make copies and extracts from all required documents. The AMO's employees (including entrusted persons) have a right to seal all documents, information as well as buildings and premises for a specified time-period and to the extent necessary for the execution of the investigation (as discussed above, this is basically at the AMO's discretion). All information and documents may be taken away with the aim of making copies or gaining access to information (especially access to computers, databases, electronic mail) when the AMO is not able to make copies directly during the inspection or gain relevant data due to the technical reasons.[554]

348. The AMO is also authorized to ask for oral explanations from senior employees or members of statutory or controlling bodies during the inspection. The CA is not clear whether the requested oral explanation must be provided on the spot and whether the request for explanation must be limited only to documents, data and information provided to the AMO during the inspection. Due to the fact that the investigatory powers can be executed only to the extent necessary for the investigation, it is reasonable to believe that during the inspection, the AMO is authorized to ask for explanations connected only with the inspected documents, ask questions to safeguard smooth process of the inspection and is obliged to avoid self-incriminating questions as mentioned above. Other explanations, data and information can be further required by the AMO through a written request.

349. The AMO is also entitled to conduct inspections on private premises which include private buildings, premises or means of transport mainly of senior employees, or members of controlling and statutory bodies of the undertaking. The four basic preconditions must be met for carrying out such an inspection. These are:[555]

(1) Reasonable suspicion that the information or documents can be found in the private premises (the grounds and facts concerning the inspection are specified in the explanatory part of the decision on the inspection).
(2) The decision on the inspection of private premises must be issued by the AMO, in which the AMO defines the purpose of the inspection, specifies buildings, premises or means of transport, states the date and the time-period within which

554. Section 22a(5) of the CA.
555. Section 22a(8)–(10) of the CA.

the inspection will be performed. This decision must also contain the specification of persons who will perform the inspection, including their investigatory powers. The decision on the inspection of private premises can be appealed, however, such appeal does not have any dilatory effect.

(3) The court's approval of the inspection must be issued. The court's approval is based on the AMO's proposal issued by the competent court.[556] This approval has to be delivered to the person being inspected at the beginning of the investigations.

(4) The presence of a custodian appointed by the court in its approval during the inspection.

The AMO is also entitled to conduct investigations of private premises if the person is not present during the inspection. In this case, the AMO delivers the court's approval with a copy of the record from the performed inspection to this person by mail within twenty-four hours after the performance of the inspection along with the minutes from the inspection.

The AMO is entitled to enforce the entry on the premises or means of transport, whether business or private, providing that its request for entry is unsuccessful. Enforcement of the entry also includes the possibility of using all means by which created obstacles could be overcome, including the possibility of inviting other persons who can help the AMO to overcome all obstacles.[557] The AMO is also entitled to ask the police for cooperation and protection during the execution of the inspection.[558]

350. In the 2014 amendment to the CA, the institute of the reward for the provision of evidence of an agreement restricting competition (the informant institute, whistle blower reward) has been introduced, specifically, in section 38g of the CA, aimed at supporting the AMO´s investigative powers and thereby increase the rate of the detected cartels. The AMO has presented the introduction of the informant institute in an explanatory report as follows:

The possibility to receive an reward for a natural person – informant who submits evidence of the existence of a cartel, representing one of the most serious breaches of economic competition rules with a negative impact on the consumer, represents a completely new provision in the Act. It seeks, in addition to a more effective detection of such prohibited and concealed practices, also stimulation of the use of the so-called 'leniency programme'. Such reward may only be obtained by one, the first informant. The payment thereof is, however, conditioned by the use of the evidence provided as the main evidence decisive for a decision of the office, by the finality and enforceability of the decision as well as by a confirmation thereof by a court, if decided by it.[559]

The provision of section 38g of the CA through which the informant institute has been introduced represents rather substantive conditions of the application of the institute without revealing the AMO´s procedural practice in negotiations with an informant. A notifier is being created a claim by this provision to require a reward; however, the AMO´s obligation to provide the reward to the notifier does not correspond

556. Sections 430–437of CPAC.
557. Section 22a(5) letter d) of the CA.
558. Section 22(11) of the CA.
559. Explanatory Report available at: http://www.rokovania.sk/file.aspx/ViewDocumentHtml/Mater-Dokum-162515?prefixFile=m_, link available as of 07 Jun. 2014.

thereto; this means that it is fully in the AMO's discretion to decide whether conditions for the provision of the reward have been met or not.

The obtainment of the reward requires the provision of evidence by an informant concerning exclusively an agreement concluded among competitors, since the proposed wording directly states that it concerns an agreement restricting competition pursuant to section 4(1) of the CA or Article 101 of the TFEU concluded among undertakings at the same level of a production or distribution chain.

It results from the provision of section 38g(1) letters a) and b) of the CA that a natural person who is at the same time not an undertaking pursuant to the definition of the undertaking given by section 3(2) of the CA may only be an informant. Such natural person may not at the same time be an employee of such undertaking who is applying for not imposing or for reducing a sanction within the framework of a Leniency Programme and a Request for Leniency has been filed before the informant has provided evidence to the AMO. Thus, a natural person that would be an undertaking defined under the CA or a natural person – employee employed with an undertaking that has already applied, before a notice of an employee of the AMO, for the Request for Leniency may not be an informant either. Any other natural person having information about cartel acts of any undertaking may be an informant. Thus, it is not necessary that only an 'insider' is an informant, i.e. an employee of a cartel participant, member of statutory or supervisory bodies, or a manager or a person cooperating in another manner with the affected undertaking.

III. Cooperation with Other State Institutions

351. The cooperation of the AMO with other state institutions is primarily related to the regulated industries such as electronic communications and the energy sector. The AMO thus closely cooperates mainly with the Regulatory Authority for Electronic Communications and Postal Services of the Slovak Republic (mainly the cooperation in defining of relevant markets which are subject to *ex-ante* regulation or related to market analyses)[560] and with the Regulatory Office for Network Industries (the cooperation refers mainly to the exchange of general market information or the preparation of reports on functioning of the regulated markets).[561] The AMO also cooperates with the Ministry of Finance of the Slovak Republic in relation to price regulation.[562]

All legal and natural persons are obliged to submit to the AMO all required information or documents without delay, which also means that all state institutions are obliged to cooperate fully with the AMO. Furthermore, as already mentioned

560. Sections 8(1) letter c) and 8(2) of the ECA.
561. For example, according to s. 19a(8) of the NIRO, the AMO cooperated with the NIO SR on the preparation of the report on functioning of the electricity and gas market.
562. According to s. 4(3) letter b) of the Act No. 18/1996 Coll. on Prices as amended, the AMO issues a statement on the state of the competition environment on the market prior to the adoption of the price regulation.

above, the AMO is entitled to ask the police for cooperation during the execution of the inspection of private or business premises.[563]

§3. Right of Defence

I. Content and Notification of Opening Decisions

352. The administrative proceedings related to agreements restricting competition and to an abuse of a dominant position can be initiated only by the AMO ex officio (details are mentioned above in the text). In this case, the proceeding is initiated on the day of the delivery of the notification on the administrative proceedings opening to the party to the proceedings ('the announcement of the commencement of the proceedings'). This notification is made by a formal letter of the AMO, and no additional decision concerning the opening of the formal administrative process is required. The same applies if the administrative proceeding is initiated upon the submission of a party to the administrative proceedings whereby the administrative proceeding is commenced on the day of the delivery of the submission to the AMO. In this case, the AMO is obliged to inform all other parties to the administrative proceedings on its commencement by a formal letter.

II. The Proceedings: Hearings, Access to Files, Briefs

353. The right of the party to the administrative proceedings to be heard is secured by several procedural instruments, and it can be executed in writing or orally. The administrative process before the AMO is basically a process in which the parties to the administrative proceedings can execute their rights by submission of written statements, comments and replies to arguments and accusations presented by the AMO, that is, the right to be heard is basically executed in writing. The same is applicable to third parties since according to the CA, any third party (it is the natural or legal person which is not deemed to be a party to the administrative proceedings, especially end customer, supplier, buyer or competitor) can request the AMO in writing to be heard in relation to the case being the subject of proceedings. The AMO sets the date by which this third party may submit its statement.[564]

354. The possibility of executing the oral hearing is regulated by the APC.[565] The AMO orders the oral hearing if it is necessary in respect of the character of the matter in issue, especially if the oral hearing can contribute to the clarification of the case or if a special regulation requires ordering it. The AMO also order the oral hearing if parties to the administrative proceedings file such request as a reaction on the Statement of objections.[566] The CA does not include an obligation for the AMO to

563. Section 22a (1) of the Competition Act.
564. Section 27(2) of the CA.
565. Section 21 of the APC.
566. Section 33 of the CA.

order the oral hearing, thus, it is upon the discretion of the AMO to decide whether the oral hearing has added value for the proceedings. If the AMO orders the oral hearing, it is obliged to call in all parties to the administrative proceedings and ask them to submit their comments and opinions during such oral hearing. The oral hearing before the AMO is not public, and it can be executed in first-degree as well as in second-degree proceedings.

355. The CA further stipulates that if any third-party requests participation on the oral hearing and it shows interest in the matter at the same time, the AMO may allow it to participate as well as express its statements.[567]

356. Apart from the legal regulation of the oral hearing included in the APC, the AMO usually also provides the party of the administrative proceedings with the possibility of explaining its position, argumentation and opinion orally without a formalized process defined by the APC. The oral hearing is conducted by an employee or employees of the AMO (usually by case handlers and lawyers of the respective AMO's department), special position of a Hearing Officer is not created by the CA.

357. If it is necessary for the investigation (e.g., for gathering the information on the respective relevant market) and for the collection of evidence (such as the information on the behaviour of the parties to the administrative proceedings on the market), the AMO may hear also other persons (any natural or legal person)[568] as witnesses. The AMO cannot hear as a witness the person that is obliged to observe confidentiality of information (e.g., the bank or business secrecy), if this person has not been relieved of confidentiality by the respective authority or person for which the confidentiality had to be observed. The APC further stipulates that the testimony can also be refused by the person who can cause a threat of criminal prosecution to himself or to persons close to him, by this testimony.

358. Neither the APC nor the CA defines the proceedings of the oral hearing. Usually the competent employee of the AMO opens the oral hearing, introduces participants and informs participants on the subject matter and summarizes the facts gathered by the AMO. At the oral hearing, the parties have an opportunity to express their statements, opinions, clarifications and views on the presented subject matter. The parties may present their legal argumentation as well as economic analyses. If parties plan to discuss and/or clarify some information or economic analyses, it is recommended to submit it to the AMO before the oral hearing and thereby avoid the risk of the AMO refusing to deal with it during the oral hearing. The aim of the oral hearing is to clarify open questions concerning the subject matter, and so the parties focus on the clarification and do not only repeat information submitted to the AMO in writing. The questions concerning the subject matter can be raised by the AMO's employees as well as by the participants. The AMO's questions are usually linked to the oral presentation submitted at the beginning of the oral hearing by the parties. The obligation to answer these questions during the oral hearing is not directly stipulated by the law. A party may propose to the AMO to send the reply to the submitted questions after the oral hearing, especially in cases where the person that is the most competent to reply is not present or the party does not have relevant information at their disposal at the hearing. Nevertheless, it must be borne in mind that the aim of the oral hearing

567. Section 27(3) of the CA.
568. Section 35 of the APC.

is basically to clarify open issues and to provide additional argumentation to the AMO, thus the parties have to be prepared also for unexpected questions from the AMO. At the end of the hearing, the parties may usually provide their final observations.

359. The AMO is obliged to take down minutes from all oral submissions of the parties to the administrative proceedings and other important actions executed during the proceedings, such as the oral hearing.[569] The minutes must include mainly the specification on who, where and when the proceedings were executed, the subject of the proceedings, the persons that were present, the course of the proceedings, the submissions that were presented and the measures that were adopted. The minutes are signed by all the parties concerned and by the competent employees of the AMO. If any party refuses to sign the minutes, the reason of this refusal and objections against the content of the minutes are included in the minutes.

360. Furthermore, the right to be heard is executed also by the right of the party to the administrative proceedings to inspect administrative files. The right to access administrative files enables the undertaking to be informed on the facts and evidence collected by the AMO as a means to proving the violation of competition rules. This right is granted by section 40(1) of the Competition act and the APC.[570] The right to inspect administrative files provides the party to the administrative proceedings, its representatives and the party concerned with the possibility of inspecting administrative files, to make extracts and copies from it (this means from all the documentary evidence gathered by the AMO in connection with a specific case). The records of final votes in the proceedings are excluded from the execution of this right. Also, documents marked as business secrecy or confidential are excluded from possibility to inspect them. However, if such documents need to be disclosed to parties to the administrative proceedings due to execution of the right of defence, the CA provides a possibility for lawyers of the parties to the administrative proceedings to inspect the files.[571] The AMO always prepares minutes from the inspection of administrative files.

361. The AMO is obliged to take all necessary steps for protecting the confidentiality of the information such as the business, tax or bank secrecy or confidential information. Even though it is not explicitly stipulated by the legal regulation, it indirectly follows from the constitutional principle of the right for a fair trial (including the right of the defence) that the protection of confidential information cannot prevent the party to the administrative proceedings to be informed on facts and evidence which support the AMO's findings concerning the violation of the CA. However, some information remains undisclosed to the parties of the administrative proceedings. This concerns, for example, communication between the AMO and the Commission concerning the application of Article 101 or/and Article 102 of the TFEU (ex Article 81 or/and Article 82 of the EC Treaty) which is, according to the Regulation 1/2003, confidential, and the parties do not have access to it. Moreover, all internal documents, draft documents or notes of the case handlers are not disclosed to any party to the administrative proceedings. Documents and evidences submitted within the leniency application (section 38d of the CA) are disclosed to other parties to the proceedings at the moment of submission of the Statement of Objections.

---

569. Section 22 of the APC.
570. Section 23 of the APC.
571. Section 40(9) of the CA.

362. According to the APC, the AMO can also provide access to administrative files to other persons that prove justification of their requirement.

The parties can inspect the administrative files at any time during the formal administrative proceedings and their access is neither limited by the time nor by the number of entries.

It needs to be noted that the AMO disposes with the administrative files also during the investigation pursuant section 22(1) letter b) of the CA, i.e. concerning the conduct of the respective undertaking on the relevant market. Provision of access to administrative files during the investigation when it is conducted because of questionable behaviour of a particular undertaking is a specific problem. The CA does not include rules regulating the possibility of undertakings to make inspections of administrative files and to have access to information gathered during the investigation. Even though there is an understanding, confirmed by the Supreme Court, that undertakings under investigation shall benefit from the same rights as they possess during the formal administrative proceedings, the current practice of the AMO shows that this is not the case. The possibility to inspect administrative files during the investigation is limited only to documents of respective undertaking requesting the access to documents. The AMO does not provide access to other evidence gathered in files during the inspection, neither the access to documents which deemed to be a basis for the inspection in business premises of an undertaking. The access to such files is provided only after beginning of the formal administrative proceedings in line with the section 40 of the CA. The access to evidence which was the basis for issuing of the written authorization to conduct the inspection[572] is granted at the moment of the Statement of Objections issue.

According to the Freedom of Information Act,[573] even undertakings and third persons that are not parties to the formal administrative proceedings can receive information from the administrative files of a case. This is the insufficiency of the Freedom of Information Act as it does not exclude administrative files of the AMO from the right of free access to information. Moreover, it is usual practice of the AMO to provide third parties, based on the provision of the Freedom of Information Act, with the full access to the first-degree decision even not valid.

Refusal to grant access to administrative files can be challenged in the appeal against the first-degree decision as well as in the administrative complaint against the Council (the appellate body) addressed to the Regional Court in Bratislava. The decision can be reversed if it is proven that the refusal to provide access to administrative files breached the right of defence of the party to the administrative proceedings (detailed information is included in Part III, Chapter 4).

III. Statement of Objections

363. The constitutional right of fair trial and the *audi alteram partem* principle is demonstrated also by the possibility of the party to the administrative proceedings

572. Section 22a(2) of the Competition Act.

573. Act No. 211/2000 Z.z. Free Access to Information (Freedom of Information Act) as further amended.

to have an opportunity to challenge the outcome of the administrative proceedings and to be informed about the evidence on which the decision is to be based before issuing its final decision.

364. The CA stipulates that the AMO is obliged to provide the parties of the administrative proceedings with a possibility to submit their statements and observations and addresses them as a Statement of Objections (in the CA defined as a 'Call Before Issuing the Decision') ahead of issuing the final decision. In the Statement of Objections, the AMO informs the parties about the grounds for the decision and the method of establishing it and presents the conclusions of its investigation. The party to the proceedings can express, orally or in writing, its views on the submitted information.[574]

The right of the undertaking to express its views includes also the possibility to inspect administrative files in question before the submission of the reply to the AMO. The access to administrative files (as discussed above) includes access to all documentary evidence which supports the AMO's conclusions in the respective case.

The Statement of Objections usually includes information on the undertakings, description of applicable legal regulations, relevant market definitions as well as a determination of the position of undertakings on the defined relevant market, description of the alleged anticompetitive behaviour and the facts of *delictum*, description of circumstances influencing the basic amount of fines along with the description of aggravating and mitigating factors and in the recent decision also exact calculation of the fine. Recently the AMO is issuing the Statement of Objections usually with the same wording as the final first-degree decision and it is very detailed.

365. This is probably due to the fact that the AMO was attacked by undertakings due to submission of insufficient Statement of Objections, in their view, contrary to the right of defence. The fact that the CA stipulates the content of the Statement of Objections only in a general manner caused many disputes in practice over the extent to which the AMO should inform the party to the proceedings on its conclusions and findings. For example, the AMO in its decision concerning the *GIS cartel* stated as follows:

> It should also be noted that a Statement of Objections [it means the Call Before Issuing the Decision, in Slovak: Výzva pred vydaním rozhodnutia] the purpose of which is to inform the party to the proceedings about the preliminary outcome, cannot be (mis)taken for a duly substantiated decision that must be more precisely reasoned, while the former bears less strict legal requirements than the latter.[575]

366. The CA does not define the time limit (neither the minimum time limit nor the maximum time-period) within which the parties to the administrative proceedings can submit their statements to the Statement of Objections. This time limit is defined by the AMO on a case-by-case basis and is fixed in the Statement of Objections. The time limit depends on the difficulty and complexity of the case, the quantum and the types of evidence, and the number of the parties to the proceedings, the necessity to make translations of the Statement of Objections (the AMO issues it in the Slovak

574. Section 33 of the CA.

575. Decision of the Council No. 2009/KH/R/2/035, 14 Aug. 2009, §773, <http://www.antimon.gov.sk>, translation by Mgr. Bc. Daniel Uherek, Ph.D.

language). In practice, the time limit is usually fifteen working days from the delivery of the Statement of Objections, but it is not unusual for the undertaking to be granted a thirty-day period for the submission of the reply. The deadline can be extended by the AMO, but the AMO is not obliged to do it. It is not unusual that the parties to the proceedings raise objections of the time limit being insufficient to provide the reply to the Statement of Objections, which should constitute a violation of the right for defence.

IV. Final Hearing and Decision

367. The CA provides the party to the administrative proceedings with a possibility to submit its opinion on the AMO's conclusions expressed in the Statement of Objections orally or in writing. Final statements of undertakings are usually submitted to the AMO in written form (this is in accordance with the character of the administrative proceedings) as the oral hearing takes place only if it can help to clarify some problematic facts. The AMO is not obliged by the CA nor by the APC to hear the party to the administrative proceedings before the decision is issued. It is at the sole discretion of the AMO to decide whether the oral hearing is ordered.

368. The formal administrative proceeding of the AMO is always finished by a formal decision. The AMO's decisions can be basically divided as: (i) decisions by which the administrative proceedings in the respective subject matter ends; (ii) the procedural decisions by which the formal process is stopped; (iii) procedural decisions by which the administrative proceedings is guarded; and (iv) interim measures.

A. The Decision on the Merits

369. The decision on the merits is the decision by which the AMO decides on the violation of the CA. In the decision, even though it is not explicitly stated by the law, the AMO can require the undertaking to bring respective infringements to an end within a defined time-period.[576] The verdict on the fine and, eventually, the verdict on other obligations/measures imposed on the undertaking in relation to the breach of competition rules such as, for example, obligation to deal, obligation to provide access to an essential facility or obligation to provide transparent information on contractual conditions are also contained in the decision. If the decision on the breach concerns the conclusion the bid-rigging cartel, the AMO is obliged, when imposing the fine, to impose on participants of the cartel, the ban to participate in public tenders within three year period.[577]

370. The decision on the merits is also the decision issued in a merger control proceeding, that is: (i) the decision on approval of the concentration; (ii) the decision on conditional approval; (iii) the decision on disapproval with the concentration as well as; (iv) the decision by which the AMO enables the parties to the concentration

576. Decision of the Council No. 2009/DZ/R/2/017, 9 Apr. 2009; Decision of the AMO No. 2008/DZ/2/1/052, 6 Jun. 2009, <http://www.antimon.gov.sk>.

577. Section 38h of the CA.

to execute rights and obligation ensuing from the concentration prior to the validity of the final decision.

371. This category of decision includes also the decisions by which the administrative proceeding is stopped due to the fact that the AMO was not able to prove the alleged violation of the CA or because the alleged behaviour does not restrict competition.[578] This decision has also an effect of res judicata.

Furthermore, the decisions issued in the Settlement procedure[579] or within the proceedings on commitments submitted by the undertakings[580] are also decisions on the merits.

372. Even though the aim of the decisions by which the AMO imposes penalties for a failure to submit requested documents or information or for submission of false or incomplete data is to secure the smooth progress of the proceedings, these decisions are treated as decisions on the merits. They can be appealed, and they are also subject to judicial review under the CPAC.

373. The decision on the merits is also the decision by which the AMO imposes fines on undertakings that fail to fulfil conditions, violate obligations or commitments imposed by a decision, fail to execute a decision, or exercise rights and obligation ensuing from a concentration.

B. Procedural Decisions by Which the Administrative Proceeding is Stopped[581]

374. Termination of the administrative proceedings is either obligatory or dependent on the AMO's discretion. The obligatory termination of the proceedings includes several reasons such as:[582]

(1) termination of the proceedings because the only party to the proceedings dies or ceases to exist without a legal successor;[583]
(2) termination of the proceedings because the party to the proceedings has withdrawn his/her appeal or a petition for reopening of the proceedings;[584]
(3) termination of the proceedings because the reason for proceedings has not been provided or ceased to exist;[585]
(4) termination of the proceedings because during the commenced proceedings it has been established that the undertaking is not a party to the proceedings while so far having been the only party of the proceedings in question;[586]

578. Section 32(2) letter c), g), h) of the CA.
579. Section 38e of the CA.
580. Section 8a of the CA.
581. Section 32(1) and (2) of the CA includes circumstances based on which the AMO can or is obliged to terminate its administrative proceedings.
582. Section 32(1) and (2) of the CA includes circumstances based on which the AMO can or is obliged to terminate its administrative proceedings.
583. Section 32(2) letter a) of the CA.
584. Section 32(2) letter b) of the CA.
585. Section 32(2) letter c) of the CA.
586. Section 32(2) letter d) of the CA.

(5) termination of the proceedings because the AMO is already dealing with or has decided on the same matter;[587]
(6) termination of the proceedings because the proceedings involves such a restriction of competition the effects of which are exclusively manifested on a foreign market, unless an international treaty published in the Collection of Laws of the Slovak Republic and binding the Slovak Republic provides otherwise;[588]
(7) termination of the proceedings because during the commenced proceedings it has been established that activities or other conduct performed by undertakings abroad do not, and cannot, lead to a restriction of competition on the Slovak market;[589]
(8) termination of the proceedings because the Commission is already dealing with or has decided on the same matter according to Articles 101 and 102 of the TFEU;[590]
(9) termination of the proceedings because the Commission is already dealing with or has decided on the same concentration.[591]

375. The AMO may decide on the termination of the administrative proceedings by a decision if:

(1) one of the parties to the administrative proceedings dies or has ceased to exist without a legal successor;[592]
(2) a petitioner does not comply with the AMO's request to remove deficiencies from the petition within a specified time limit;[593]
(3) another national competition authority is already dealing with or has decided on the same matter concerning the violation of Articles 101 and 102 of the TFEU (ex Articles 81 and 82 of the EC Treaty).[594]

C. Procedural Decisions by Which the Administrative Proceeding Is Suspended

376. The AMO is also empowered to issue decisions by which the administrative proceeding is suspended. This decision is not subject to judicial review according to the CPAC.[595]

The AMO is authorized to suspend the proceedings under the conditions stipulated by the APC[596] as well as by the CA.[597] The AMO issues the decision on the suspension

587. Section 32(2) letter e) of the CA.
588. Section 32(2) letter f) of the CA.
589. Section 32(2) letter h) of the CA.
590. Section 32(2) letter i) of the CA.
591. Section 32(2) letter j) of the CA.
592. Section 32(1) letter a) of the CA.
593. Section 32(1) letter b) of the CA.
594. Section 32(1) letter c) of the CA.
595. Section 248 letter a) of the CPAC.
596. Section 29 of the APC.
597. Section 31 of the CA.

of the proceedings if the proceeding, on a preliminary question was initiated, or the party to the proceedings is requested to remove deficiencies of the submission or does not have a legal representative or appointed custodian required by the special legal regulations.

Furthermore, the proceedings can be suspended by the AMO based on the joint request of the parties to the proceedings if there is an important reason for such measure. In this case, the proceedings can be suspended only for thirty days. Additionally, the AMO can suspend the proceedings if another national competition authority is already dealing with the same matter or until it is determined which authority will deal with the concentration. These decisions cannot be appealed.

D. *Interim Measures*

377. According to the APC,[598] the AMO has powers to grant interim measures concerning violation of the competition rules. The interim measure can be granted if it is essential to secure the progress of the administrative proceedings, that is, there is a need to arrange legal relations prior to issuing the final decision. By the interim measure, the AMO is entitled to impose, to a necessary extent, on the parties to the proceedings to perform something (e.g., to continue to supply customers) or to cease some operations (to refrain from dissolution) or to endure something. In the decision, the AMO can also order the party to provide material proof necessary for the presentation of evidence. The interim measure should be treated only as a temporary measure and should not go beyond necessity, which means that it must be reversed if the reason for which it was issued ceases to exist. Due to the fact that the interim measure represents serious intervention with the freedom of the undertaking to behave on the market, the decision of the AMO on interim measures must be supported by sufficient evidence and the need to issue the interim measure must be linked to the respective administrative proceedings in the subject matter (e.g., necessity to avoid irreparable damage of other parties or safeguard the state of competition on the market until the decision in the subject matter is issued).[599] The Council, in relation to the review of the first-degree decision by which company *UPC* was imposed the obligation to refrain from the switching off of contractual customers, stated:

> As for the substantiation of the need to grant the interim measure, the AMO only stated that the behaviour of the UPC ltd threatened the rights of customers of the UPC ltd and it was necessary to preserve the factual state of the matter in order to protect the customers from switch-offs. According to the legal opinion

598. Section 43 of the APC.
599. In Decision No. 2002/PO/R/2/196 (18 Sep. 2002) the Council confirmed the interim measure imposed on Slovenské Telekomunikácie in relation to launching its ADSL technology offer on the market. The Council reasoned necessity to issue the interim measure so that: ‘the aim of this interim measure is to maintain the existing state of the determined relevant market in telecommunication services ... ensuring that during the proceedings, no strengthening of the ... dominant position on the relevant market occurs, which is questionable without granting the interim measure in question.’, <http://www.antimon.gov.sk>, translation by Mgr.Bc. Daniel Uherek, Ph.D.

of the Council of the AMO the reasons substantiating the first-degree decision is not sufficient and it lacks the assessment of the inevitability or the need to grant the interim measure as well as the specification in what ways the proceedings on the abuse of a dominant position are at peril in case it had not been granted. The first instance authority in its decision failed to provide reasons for the extent of the obligation imposed to UPC ltd and also for the fact that the interim measure granted was adequate to secure the purpose of the proceedings on the abuse of a dominant position.[600]

378. The decision on interim measures can be appealed against, but the appeal does not have a dilatory effect. The decision on interim measures cannot be subject to judicial review due to the fact that it is only a preliminary decision.[601] The interim measure ceases to be effective, at the latest, on the day the decision on the merits becomes valid.

379. The essentials of the AMO's decision (irrespective of the fact whether this is a decision on the merits or a procedural decision or an interim measure) are defined by the APC.[602] The decision must contain the verdict, reasoning and the instruction on the possibility of appeal against the decision. The lack of these defined essentials is one of the reasons for the revocation of the decision by the court.

380. The operative part of the decision (*le dispositif*) must include primarily the specification of the provisions of legal regulations on which the AMO's decision is based. If the decision imposes an obligation to fulfil 'something' to the undertaking, the AMO is obliged to define the time-period within which this obligation has to be met.[603] The Supreme Court stated that:

> The essentials of the verdict in the decision are stated in section 47 subsection 2 of the Administrative Procedure Code. From this regulation does not explicitly ensue that the verdict must contain specifications on material, time and place aspects of the action by which the offence was committed. On the other hand, it is unimpugnable that only the verdict part of the decision is capable of affecting the rights and obligations of the parties to the proceedings and only this part can become valid. A verdict formulated with no fault is an unsubstitutable part of any decision; only the verdict is the part where it is possible to find out what obligation is being imposed; only by comparing two verdicts the use of the principle of res judicata can be decided, as well as the exclusion of the principle of litispendence or double punishment for the same offence; the verdict is important for the extent of presentation of evidence to be determined as much as for the provision of the right of defence; only the verdict of the decision (and not the reasons of the decision) may be enforced by administrative execution and so on.[604]

600. Decision of the Council, No. 2002/PO/R/2/236, 11 Nov. 2002, <http://www.antimon.gov.sk>, translation by Mgr.Bc. Daniel Uherek, Ph.D.
601. Section 248 letter a) of the CPAC.
602. Section 47 of the APC.
603. Section 47(2) of the APC.
604. Judgment of the Supreme Court No. 2 Sžo 106/2007.

381. The reasoning of the decision (*les motifs*) must present all relevant legal regulations which were applied by the AMO, the manner of their application, all principles, considerations and facts upon which the decision is based and must also describe all reflections which led to the conclusion specified in the verdict of the decision. The APC specifies that the reasoning of the decision must contain facts which are the basis for the decision; the AMO must inform the parties on leading considerations in assessing evidence, on how it used its discretion in using legal regulations and how it handled submissions, proposals and objections of the parties to the proceedings. If the AMO rejects proposals and objections of a party to the administrative proceedings, it should provide a clear and sufficient justification of this approach. According to the decisions of the Regional Court in Bratislava:

> The reasoning sums up all facts found that sustain the verdict of the decision. In the reasoning of the decision the conclusions on the facts considered proved with no doubt must be stated, the legal weight of these facts is assessed and the account of the matter of the proceedings given. The basic right of judicial protection in the administrative judiciary presupposes not only a formal access of a person to judicial protection, but at the same time such kind of access that represents an effective attempt of protecting individual interests of this person.[605]

382. Moreover if a penalty is imposed by the decision, the reasoning of the decision must contain proper substantiation of the amount of the penalty and information on all circumstances defined by the law that influence the final amount of the fine whereas the Supreme Court concluded that:

> A decision imposing a fine for an administrative offence substantiated only by a statement that in imposing the fine the degree of guilt was considered, that the amount of the fine was set within the limits imposed by the law, but not containing clarification on deliberations about all the conditions that the law requires to be taken into account in the process of imposing a fine, such a decision is irreviewable in this part because of absence of reasons.[606]

383. Consequently, the reasoning of the decision must contain information, facts, principles and justifications that support the operative part of the decision. The factual and logical contradictions between the operative part of the decision and its reasoning induce that the decision is irreviewable for its incoherency.[607]

384. The inevitable part of the decision is the notice on the right to appeal the decision which must contain information whether the decision is final or whether it may be reviewed. Furthermore, the notice must contain information on the time-period within which the appeal should be submitted, to which authority, and where the appeal has to be submitted. The notice must contain also specification on whether the decision is subject to judicial review.

---

605. Judgment of the Regional Court in Bratislava No. 1 S 424/06-161, 21 Jun. 2007, <http://www.antimon.gov.sk>, translation by Mgr.Bc. Daniel Uherek, Ph.D.
606. Judgment of the Supreme Court No. 4 Sž 24/96, 30 May 1996, <http://www.antimon.gov.sk>.
607. Judgment of the Supreme Court No. 7 Sž 177/03, 24 Sep. 2004, <http://www.antimon.gov.sk>.

385. The decision needs to be notified to all the parties to the administrative proceedings. The notification is made by the delivery of a record of the decision, if the law does not provide otherwise. The day of the delivery of the decision is deemed to be the day of its notification.[608] The decision is valid if there is no possibility of filing an appeal against it and it is enforceable if it cannot be appealed or the appeal does not have a dilatory effect.[609]

386. The decision needs to be issued within six months following the beginning of the proceedings. In complicated cases, the chairperson of the AMO may repeatedly extend the period, prior to its expiration. The time limit for the issuing of a decision cannot exceed twenty-four months in total. The AMO is required to notify the party to the proceedings on the prolongation of the period and indicate the reasons.[610] This time limit does not apply to merger control proceedings in which the time limit is shorter[611] (detailed information in Part III, Chapter 3, §2, II).

608. Section 51(1) of the APC.
609. Section 52(1) of the APC.
610. Section 30 of the CA.
611. Section 11 of the CA.

Chapter 2. Voluntary Notifications and Clearance Decision

387. The currently valid CA does not provide undertakings with a possibility of requesting a clearance decision from the AMO concerning agreements restricting competition. Neither the previous legal regulations nor the CA empower the AMO to issue a clearance decision concerning the unilateral conduct – the abuse of a dominant position.

388. The possibility of submitting voluntary notification and to ask for a clearance decision existed in Slovak Republic before the accession of the Slovak Republic to the European Union. According to the CA valid until April 2004, the undertakings could ask the AMO to issue a so-called 'individual exemption' from the prohibition to conclude an agreement restricting competition. The 'individual exemption' was issued only if the agreement restricting competition in question fulfilled the criteria defined by the CA (these criteria are the same as currently valid criteria for *ex lege* exemption,[612] that is, criteria similar to Article 101(3) of the TFEU). Moreover, the individual exemption was limited in time. Additionally, the Protection of Economic CA No. 188/1994 valid until 2001 comprised a so-called negative attest, that is, the decision in which, based on the request of undertaking, the AMO decided whether or not the actions stated constituted an agreement restricting competition.

389. Even though the currently valid CA does not contain an option for undertakings to ask for a clearance decision (either in a form of an 'individual exemption' or a 'negative attest') undertakings may ask the AMO for an opinion[613] on a draft agreement or a draft decision of an association of undertakings. The AMO issues the opinion, in which it states whether the submitted draft agreement or the draft decision constitutes an agreement restricting competition. Nevertheless, the assessment of the AMO does not include the review of the criteria for '*de mininis* exemption',[614] '*ex lege* exemption'[615] or 'block exemption'.[616] The opinion is issued within thirty working days following the day of the request's delivery or within sixty working days, in complicated cases. The opinion is issued by a formal letter and cannot be appealed.

390. Despite the fact that the CA does not include any rules on discussions outside formal administrative proceedings or general investigations between the AMO and undertakings, concerning their conduct on the market,[617] it is possible to approach the AMO and to informally discuss some open issues related to behaviour of undertakings on the market. The AMO usually does not issue its opinion in writing. It must be borne in mind that the AMO provides only informal views which do not preclude the AMO's authority to open a general investigation or a formal administrative procedure in the

612. Currently s. 4(5) of the CA.
613. Section 6(3) of the CA.
614. Section 4(2) of the CA.
615. Section 4(5) of the CA.
616. Section 5 of the CA.
617. Neither the Competition Act nor the secondary binding legislation or not even non-binding recommendation of the AMO includes rules similar to the Commission Notice on informal guidance relating to novel questions concerning Arts 81 and 82 of the EC Treaty that arise in individual cases (guidance letters), OJ C 101, 27 Apr. 2004, 78.

future, if the discussed conduct constitutes a breach of antitrust rules. This discussion can be conducted within the competition advocacy of the AMO as well.

Chapter 3. Merger Control

391. Merger control rules are primarily contained in the CA as well as in the implementary regulations. The AMO used its secondary legislation empowerment to issue the Decree on Details of Concentration Notification.[618] In addition to this binding regulation, the AMO has issued explanatory documents that do not have the power of a binding legal regulation but provide undertakings with a broad range of information relevant for the assessment of their transactions or for the submission of a notification. These explanatory documents arise from the EU recommendations and guidelines concerning merger control and consist of:

(1) the Guideline on exception from the ban to implement concentration;[619]
(2) the Guideline on Simplified procedure;[620]
(3) the Guideline on Turnover calculation;[621]
(4) the Ancillary Restraints Guideline;[622]
(5) the Pre-notification Guideline.[623]

§1. Preliminary Filing Obligations

I. Criteria and Thresholds

392. The concentration (acquisition, merger or creation of a full-functioned joint venture) is subject to merger control, provided that threshold criteria stipulated directly by the CA are met.[624] The preceding statutory text of the CA contained combination of two criteria – a turnover and a market share. After the change of the CA[625] in 2004, the market-share criterion was abandoned.

618. Decree of the Antimonopoly Office SR No. 170/2014 Coll. Laying down details of essentials of Concentration Notification.
619. The AMO, 'Usmernenie o podrobnostiach udelenia výnimky zo zákazu implementácie koncentrácie, <http://www.antimon.gov.sk/87-sk/legislativa/>.
620. The AMO, 'Usmernenie o podrobnostiach pri zjednodušenom oznámení koncentrácie' <http://www.antimon.gov.sk/87-sk/legislativa/>.
621. The AMO, <'Usmernenie k výpočtu obratu' http://www.antimon.gov.sk/87-sk/legislativa/>.
622. The AMO, 'Usmernenie o obmedzeniach hospodárskej súťaže, ktoré s koncentráciou priamo súvisia a sú nevyhnutné na jej uskutočnenie', <http://www.antimon.gov.sk/87-sk/legislativa/>.
623. The AMO, 'Usmernenie úradu o prednotifikačných kontaktoch v procese posudzovania koncentrácií', <http://www.antimon.gov.sk/87-sk/legislativa/>.
624. Section 10(1) of the CA.
625. Act No. 204/2004 Coll. Amendment of the Act No. 136/2001 Coll. on Protection of Economic Competition and on Amendments and Supplements to the Act of the Slovak National Council No. 347/1990 Coll. on Organization of Ministries and Other Central Bodies of State Administration of the Slovak Republic as amended.

393. Currently, the CA stipulates only one criterion for the assessment of the necessity to notify concentration, which is the relevant turnover of the parties to the concentration, achieved worldwide and on the Slovak territory.

394. According to the CA, the concentration is subject to merger control if one of the below-described turnover criteria is met. The conditions arise from the combination of a worldwide total turnover and a turnover achieved in Slovak Republic by the parties to the concentration. The aim of the AMO when preparing the amendment of the CA in 2014 was to define the criteria thus the parties to the concentration are in reality present on the Slovak market with their supplies.

The threshold criteria are defined based on the form of established concentration. The concentration shall be subject to control by the AMO if:

(a) the combined aggregate turnover of the undertakings concerned is at least EUR 46,000 attained for the accounting period preceding the establishment of the concentration in the Slovak Republic and at least two of the undertakings concerned each attain the aggregate turnover of at least EUR 14,000,000 in the Slovak Republic for the accounting period preceding the establishment of the concentration; or

(b) aggregate turnover attained for the accounting period preceding the establishment of the concentration in the Slovak Republic:

(1) if it is a matter of concentration pursuant to section 9(1) letter a) of the CA (a merger) at least by one of the undertakings concerned is EUR 14,000,000 and simultaneously the worldwide aggregate turnover for the accounting period preceding the establishment of the concentration attained by another undertaking concerned is at least EUR 46,000,000;
(2) if it is a matter of concentration pursuant to section 9(1) letter a) of the CA (an acquisition of direct or indirect control) at least by one undertaking concerned which is acquired or part of it is acquired is at least EUR 14,000,000 and simultaneously the worldwide aggregate turnover for the accounting period preceding the establishment of the concentration attained by any undertaking concerned is at least EUR 46,000,000;
(3) if it is a matter of concentration pursuant section 9(5) of the CA (the establishment of a joint venture) at least by one of the undertakings concerned creating jointly controlled enterprise is at least EUR 14,000,000 and simultaneously the worldwide aggregate turnover for the accounting period preceding the establishment of the concentration attained by another undertaking concerned is at least EUR 46,000,000.[626]

395. The combined aggregate turnover of a party to the concentration contains not only the turnover of this party but also the turnovers of undertakings belonging to the same economic group, specifically of:[627]

626. Section 10(1) letter a) of the CA.
627. Section 10(2) of the CA.

(1) undertakings in which a party to the concentration directly or indirectly:

(a) holds more than a half of the share capital; or
(b) is entitled to exercise more than a half of the voting rights; or
(c) has the right to appoint more than a half of the members of the undertaking's bodies; or
(d) has the right to manage the undertaking concerned.

(2) undertakings which have rights referred to in point (i) in an undertaking of a party to the concentration;
(3) undertakings in which an undertaking referred to in point (ii) has rights mentioned in point (i);
(4) undertakings in which two or more undertakings referred to in points (i) to (iii), including the party to the concentration, have joint rights referred to in point (i).

II. Turnover Calculation

396. The calculation of the turnover is determined directly by the CA[628] and further specified in the Guideline on Turnover Calculation.[629]

397. Under the CA, the turnover means a total of revenues, yields or incomes from the sale of goods excluding indirect taxes, to which financial assistance[630] granted to the undertaking shall be added.[631]

It must be borne in mind that the combined turnover of undertakings does not include revenues, yields or incomes from the sale of goods between individual undertakings belonging to the same economic group.[632] The special rules concerning turnover calculation apply if the concentration consists of gaining of a direct or indirect control over only one undertaking or a part of one or several undertakings. In these situations, the relevant turnover includes turnover of the undertaking or its part that is the subject of the concentration.[633] Where the parties to the concentration jointly, directly or indirectly, control another undertaking (hold more than a half of the share capital, are entitled to exercise more than a half of the voting rights, have the right to appoint more than a half of the members of the undertaking's bodies or have the right to manage the undertaking concerned), the calculation of the combined turnover will not include the turnover resulting from the sale of goods between the joint venture and each of the parties to the concentration or any other undertaking associated with

628. Sections 10(3)–10(6) of the CA.
629. The AMO, <'Usmernenie k výpočtu obratu' http://www.antimon.gov.sk/87-sk/legislativa/>.
630. Section 3(6) of the Competition Act. Financiàl assistance means any financial aid granted to an undertaking from public resources related to an activity performed by an undertaking that is reflected in the price of goods.
631. Section 3(5) of the CA. F.
632. Section 10(3) of the CA.
633. Section 10(3) of the CA.

any of them.[634] The turnover from the sale of goods between the joint venture and other undertakings has to be equally apportioned among the parties to the concentration.[635]

398. The turnover achieved in the closed accounting period preceding the establishment of the concentration is relevant for the calculation.

The Guideline on Turnover Calculation further stipulates, in more detail, principles of turnover calculation.[636]

III. Market-Share Calculation

399. After the change of the CA[637] in 2004, the market-share criterion was abandoned.

IV. Other Relevant Notions

400. If two or more concentrations established between the same undertakings, which are not independently subject to merger control, are established within two years and are jointly subject to merger control, they must be notified to the AMO. These transactions are deemed to be one concentration that arose on the day of the last transaction.[638]

401. The CA stipulates that the turnover expressed in a foreign currency needs to be converted to Euro according to the exchange reference rates set and announced by the European Central Bank or by the National Bank of Slovakia, valid for the relevant account period.[639]

§2. Structure of Proceedings

I. Preliminary Assessment and Full Investigation

402. Only the concentration which fulfils threshold criteria specified by the CA is subject to a full investigation of the AMO within a formal administrative procedure. This concentration has to be notified to the AMO after its establishment ('notification')[640]

634. Section 10(8) of the CA and s. 10(2) of the CA.
635. Section 10(8) of the CA.
636. The AMO, 'Usmernenie k výpočtu obratu', <http://www.antimon.gov.sk/87-sk/legislativa/>.
637. Act No. 204/2004 Coll. Amendment of the Act No. 136/2001 Coll. on Protection of Economic Competition and on Amendments and Supplements to the Act of the Slovak National Council No. 347/1990 Coll. on Organization of Ministries and Other Central Bodies of State Administration of the Slovak Republic as amended.
638. Section 10(5) of the CA.
639. Section 3(5) of the CA.
640. Section 10(7) of the CA.

or prior to its establishment ('pre-notification').[641] The notification has to be submitted to the AMO before the rights and obligations resulting from the concentration are executed and after:

(1) the conclusion of the contract;
(2) the announcement of the acceptance of a bid in a public tender;[642]
(3) the delivery of the decision of the state authority to the undertaking;[643]
(4) the announcement of an acquisition bid;[644]
(5) the day the Commission informed the undertaking that the case would be handled by the AMO;
(6) the day of occurrence of another fact based on which concentration has arisen.

403. The pre-notification of concentration is submitted before its establishment and is subject to merger control if the turnover criteria, as specified above, are met.[645]

404. It must be borne in mind that the submission of a notification or a pre-notification directly initiates a formal administrative proceeding,[646] and thus all steps concerning the assessment of a concentration are performed within a formal administrative process.

405. The CA, along with the Commission Consolidated Jurisdictional Notice,[647] determines subjects that a notification of concentration is obligation to contain (this is relevant also for a pre-notification). Primarily, the notification has to be submitted by the undertaking or undertakings that acquire sole or a joint control. The notification of a concentration established in a form of a merger has to be jointly notified by the parties to the concentration in question.[648] Further, the CA stipulates that the obligation to notify arises:

(1) in case of a public tender to the selected bidder;
(2) in case of a decision on a merger issued by a state authority jointly to the parties to this concentration;
(3) in case of an acquisition bid to the proposer of this bid.[649]

406. The correct definition of the notifying party is also necessary for the determination of the party to the administrative proceedings.[650] The fact that the undertaking is a party to the concentration does not necessarily mean that this undertaking

641. Section 10(10) of the CA.
642. Sections 281–288 of the CC.
643. Article 14 of the Act No. 111/1990 Coll. on State Enterprises as amended by the Act of the National Council of the Slovak Republic No. 317/1996 Coll.
644. For example, Art. 114 and following of the Act No. 566/2001 Coll. on Securities and Investment Facilities and on Amendments and Supplements to Certain Acts (Act on Securities) as amended.
645. Decision of the AMO No. 2009/FH/3/1/053, 25 Nov. 2009, <http://www.antimon.gov.sk>.
646. Section 25(1) of the CA.
647. Commission Consolidated Jurisdictional Notice under Council Regulation (EC) No 139/2004 on the control of concentrations between undertakings.
648. Section 10(8) of the Competition Act.
649. Section 10(11) of the CA.
650. Section 25(3) of the CA.

is also a party to the administrative proceedings (this applies, for example, to a target company, which is a party to the concentration but which is not a party to the administrative proceedings).[651]

407. The notification of a concentration as well as the pre-notification must contain the essentials stipulated by the Decree on Notification. The notification shall include information required in questionnaires included in the Decree on Notification. The submission has to be supported by relevant documents.

The extent of information can be reduced by the AMO on the basis of a reasoned request of the notifying undertaking. However, if the reduced extent of information is not sufficient for issuing a decision, the undertaking can be asked to complete its notification. From the time of the delivery of the Call for Information to the undertaking until the submission of additional data or/and documents, the time limit for issuing a decision on concentration is not in effect.[652]

Moreover, the pre-notification must, except the information required by the Decree on Details of Notification, contain written reasoning and documents that certify facts relevant for a future concentration.[653]

408. The notification (pre-notification) is subject to an administrative fee according to the special legislation[654] which is currently EUR 5,000.

409. Within the formal administrative proceedings the AMO, primarily reviews whether: (a) the transaction falls under the jurisdiction of the AMO (*see* §4 below); (b) the transaction is a concentration according to the relevant provisions of the CA; and (c) the essentials of the notification are fulfilled. In case the AMO comes to the conclusion that the notified transaction does not fall under the merger control review, it will stop the administrative proceedings by a formal decision.[655] If the concentration is subject to its merger control, the AMO will review all relevant factors and issue a final decision (an approval, a conditional approval or a prohibition of the concentration) within a stipulated time limit. Moreover, the AMO reviews whether the submission is made by the undertaking or undertakings having an obligation to do so. If the submission is made by an undertaking that is not a party to the proceedings or it has to be made also by the other party to the concentration, the AMO informs the undertakings – the notifying parties to this fact, and asks them to change or to amend their notification. The AMO usually asks for the change of the submission in the course of the initiated administrative proceedings.

410. The CA directly imposes an obligation on undertakings under which they are prohibited to exercise the rights and obligations resulting from their concentration, before the decision on the concentration becomes legally valid.[656] The CA stipulates several exemptions from this prohibition. According to the first exemption, the

651. Section 25(3) of the CA.
652. Section 10(13) of the CA.
653. Section 10(10) of the CA.
654. Item No. 212 of the Administrative Fees Tariff of the Act of the National Council of the Slovak Republic No. 145/1995 Coll. on Administrative Fees as amended.
655. According to s. 32(2) letter c) of the Competition Act, the AMO shall stop the proceedings due to the fact that the reason for the proceedings has not been provided or ceased to exist.
656. Section 10(11) of the CA.

prohibition does not apply to the right of the selected bidder in a public tender[657] to execute their bid provided the voting rights arising in connection with the implementation of the bid are not exercised by the acquirer. The ban to exercise rights arising from the concentration is not further applicable to trading in publicly marketable securities[658] under the conditions that: (i) such concentration is immediately notified to the AMO; and (ii) an acquirer of the control does not exercise its voting rights connected with these securities or it only does so only for the purpose to maintain the full value of these investments based on the exemption granted by the AMO pursuant to section 10(14) of the CA.[659]

Besides the legal exemptions from the prohibition, an exemption can be granted also by the AMO, upon a request of the respective undertaking,[660] provided that serious reasons for the exception exist[661] or that its purpose is to allow obtaining ownership of necessary assets, or announcing and/or executing a tender.[662]

Parties to the concentration usually ask the AMO for exemptions concerning the execution of a transfer of shares, the possibility of exercising shareholder's rights or the appointment of new members of statutory or controlling bodies.

411. When deciding on the exemption, the AMO at the same time considers the effects of such an exemption on the parties to the concentration and third parties. The exception granted by the AMO can be subject to conditions which should ensure effective competition. In its exemption decision concerning the request of the Imperial Tabacco Group Plc., the AMO stated:

> The situations when the acquired undertaking is in bankruptcy or this state is imminent ... and the sole existence of the acquired undertaking is endangered without allowing investors to intervene after the implementation of the concentration with the effect of producing a threat of domestic or foreign market deficiencies, losing a license necessary for conducting business of the acquired undertaking, terminating contractual relations with suppliers and consumers may be considered reasons serious enough for granting an exception while, at the same time, the possibility of exercising the rights and obligations arising from the concentration is unable to impede effective competition on the relevant markets concerned.[663]

412. If the AMO finds out that the prohibition to exercise rights and obligations arising from the concentration was breached, a decision in which it imposes the obligation to restore the status and the level of economic competition that existed prior

657. Section 10(12) of the CA along with Arts 281–288 of the CC.
658. Sections 71–78 of the Act No. 566/2001 Coll. on Securities and investment services as amended; ss 25–40 of the Act No. 429/2002 Coll. on the Stock Exchange.
659. Section 10(13) of the CA.
660. Section 10(14) of the CA.
661. For example, Decision of the AMO No. 2002/FH/3/1/256, 29 Nov. 2002, <http://www.antimon.gov.sk>.
662. For example, Decision of the AMO No. 2003/FH/3/1/022, 14 Feb. 2002, <http://www.antimon.gov.sk>.
663. Decision of the AMO No. 2002/FH/3/1/068, 18 Apr. 2002, <http://www.antimon.gov.sk>, translation by Mgr.Bc. Daniel Uherek, Ph.D.

to the establishment of the concentration can be issued. The obligation may consist of the necessity to split the undertaking or to cede rights or any other obligations.[664] The same approach applies if the parties to the concentration executed rights and obligations contrary to the decision on the prohibition to execute the concentration pursuant section 12 of the CA or the rights and obligations were executed in contrary to the commitments defined by the conditional approval of the concentration. Moreover, the AMO is obliged to impose a fine for the breach, of up to 10% of the total turnover achieved in the preceding accounting period. This fine can be imposed repeatedly.[665]

II. Time Framework

413. Before the adoption of the amendment of the CA in 2009,[666] the legal regulation stipulated that the notification of a concentration[667] needed to be submitted to the AMO within thirty days from the day of its establishment. The CA currently does not define the time limit for filing a notification and only stipulates that the party to the concentration has to file the notification before the rights and obligations resulting from the concentration are exercised and after its establishment.

414. The CA stipulates a shorter period for issue of a decision on concentration as applicable to other antitrust proceedings (the proceedings on agreements restricting competition and on the abuse of a dominant position).[668] The AMO shall issue its decision on concentration within twenty-five working days in a simplified procedure. In this case, the decision includes only a short reasoning and the AMO does not submits the Statement of Objections to the party to the administrative proceedings.[669]

If the analysis of the effects of concentration requires more time, the AMO issues a decision within ninety working days following the date of the delivery of the notification.[670] The time-period for issuing a decision on concentration starts on the day after the delivery of a complete notification.[671] If, during the proceedings, the AMO comes to the conclusion that the notification has been filed incomplete, a new time limit begins on the day following the date of the delivery of the complete notification.[672]

Based on the reasoned request of notifying party or with its consent, the AMO may extend the time limit for issue of a decision before its expiration, even repeatedly by a total of thirty working days at a maximum.[673]

664. Section 13a of the Competition Act.
665. Section 38(1) letter d) of the CA in connection with s. 38c(3) of the CA.
666. Act No. 165/2009 Coll. Amending the Competition Act.
667. The Competition Act before its amendment in 2009 did not include a possibility to submit a pre-notification.
668. The time limits for issuing a decision by the AMO are defined in s. 30 of the CA.
669. Section 11(1) of the CA.
670. Section 11(2) of the CA.
671. Section 11(3) of the CA.
672. Section 11(4) of the CA.
673. Section 11(6) of the CA.

415. The exemption from the prohibition to exercise the rights and obligations arising from a concentration is issued by the AMO within twenty working days following the delivery of the request.[674]

III. Right of Defence

416. The notifying parties, that is, the parties to the administrative proceedings, have the same right of defence as applies in other administrative proceedings before the AMO. These rights are described in detail in the Part III. Chapter 1, §3, and include primarily the right of the party to the administrative proceedings to be heard, that is, to explain its views and observations orally or to submit written statements and comments. Oral hearings take place usually when discussions on a proposal of conditions and obligations concerning the concentration are inevitable. In simple cases, the administrative process is basically written. Furthermore, the parties to the administrative proceedings have the right to inspect administrative files during the procedure and to file their replies to the Statement of Objections (in Slovak *Výzva pred vydaním rozhodnutia*) before the issue of the final decision (*see* Part III, Chapter 1, §3, IV).

§3. Clearance and Conditional Clearance

417. The AMO considers each concentration individually, taking into consideration the situation and the level of competition on the respective relevant market.

418. The reviewed concentration can be cleared by the decision of the AMO if it does not significantly distort effective competition in the relevant market, mainly due to the creation or strengthening of a dominant position[675] The main test while evaluating the effects of concentration on the market is still the dominance test. The AMO uses the same or similar criteria for the determination of dominance as for the assessment of dominance within the abuse cases. Furthermore, the creation of a full-functioned joint venture will be approved only if coordination of competitive behaviour is not prohibited as an agreement restricting competition.[676]

419. The Council of the AMO according to the CA valid until 30 June 2014 confirmed the decision of the first-degree department by which the concentration of *Südzucker and Saint-Luis Sucre* was prohibited.[677] In reviewing this decision, the Council had to establish whether the transaction would create a collective dominant position on the relevant market with a negative effect on economic competition. The Council stated that the transaction would lead to structural changes on both relevant markets of production and sale of sugar for manufacturers and final consumers. The

674. Section 10(14) of the CA.
675. Section 12(1) of the CA.
676. Section 12(2) of the CA.
677. Decision of the Council No. 2003/KH/R/2/121, 19 Jun. 2003; Decision of the AMO No. 2002/FH/3/1/272, 12 Dec. 2002; confirmed by Judgments of the Supreme Court of the Slovak Republic No. 4 Sž 122-123/03, 29 Apr. 2004 and No. Sž-o-NS 116/2004, 27 Apr. 2006, <http://www.antimon.gov.sk>.

Council further determined that due to the specificity of the relevant markets, the concentration would: (a) create conditions for coordination of behaviour which would influence the output of Südzucker AG on the market; (b) lead to an increased level of market concentration (only two independent companies would be present on the market); and (c) create a collective dominance.

420. The approval of a concentration issued by the AMO can be conditional. The conditions which the AMO imposes in its conditional clearance should insure that the concentration does not:

(1) significantly distort competition; or
(2) create a dominant position;
(3) strengthen a dominant position; or
(4) induce prohibited coordination of competitive behaviour.

The AMO may also impose other secondary conditions which should ensure fulfilment or control of fulfilment of imposed conditions or their achievement.[678]

421. In cases where a concentration significantly distorts competition, mainly by creation or strengthening a dominant position, or a joint venture leads to a prohibited coordination of competitive behaviour, and the negative effects of such a concentration cannot be eliminated by any conditions, the AMO issues a decision prohibiting this concentration.

I. Conditions and Undertakings

A. Content

422. The basic rules for the assessment of a proposal of conditions submitted by an undertaking are included in the CA.[679] Furthermore, the AMO assesses the proposal in line with the Commission's guidelines.[680]

423. If during the administrative proceedings, the AMO finds out that there are competition concerns related to the notified concentration, it informs the party to the administrative proceedings in writing on the identified problems and invites the notifying party to submit a proposal of conditions and obligations within the stipulated deadline.[681] The general rule is that conditions and obligations must be prepared and submitted by the respective undertaking on its own initiative. The AMO is not obliged to propose conditions which can lead to elimination of competitive constraints and its role is only to make the assessment of the submitted proposal. However, consultations with the AMO on the proposal are allowed and usually take place. Before the submission of the 'Final Proposal of Conditions and Obligations' the undertakings can request the

678. Section 12(3) of the CA.
679. Section 12(3)–(5) of the CA.
680. Commission Notice on remedies acceptable under the Council Regulation (EC) No 139/2004 and under Commission Regulation (EC) No 802/2004, Official Journal C 267, 22 Oct. 2008.
681. Section 12(4) of the CA.

AMO to carry out a consultation concerning the substance of the proposal as well as the procedural aspects of the submission.

424. The AMO is not bound by the submitted conditions and obligations. The notion of a 'condition' mainly means a commitment of an undertaking which primarily leads to elimination of identified competition problems. Whereas the 'obligation' represents a commitment of an undertaking which serves in securing: (a) the fulfilment of conditions, (b) the control of the fulfilment and (c) the achievement of the aim of a condition.

425. As already mentioned, during the assessment of the proposal, the AMO takes into consideration mainly:

(1) the character of conditions;
(2) the scope of conditions;
(3) the time frame for their implementation which means that the conditions must be fulfilled in a short time-period;
(4) the probability of the implementation;
(5) the completeness of the implementation.

426. The submitted conditions are assessed within the context of the relevant markets concerned. The ability to eliminate effectively and on a lasting basis the negative effects on competition is a substantial criterion for the approval of submitted conditions. Furthermore, the imposed conditions must be easily revisable. The AMO issues its conditional approval of the concentration only if the submitted conditions are sufficient to eliminate the identified problems.

427. The AMO imposes two basic types of conditions which are structural conditions and other conditions.

In structural conditions, the AMO intervenes directly into the structure of the respective relevant market in imposing obligations for undertakings to transfer certain 'market positions' to a buyer. These conditions include mainly the transfer of shares, the transfer of an independent company or a division, the transfer of assets based on which it is possible to achieve turnover, the transfer of or granting license for an indefinite period or until the patent expiration.

The structural conditions must be proposed so that the transferred business of an undertaking (transferred part) is an entity that is vital and able to compete, such as a subsidiary or a division which already is active on the market. Assets can also be transferred, provided that it is possible to achieve turnover via these assets and the buyer is able to incorporate them into its business effectively and rapidly. Further requirement for a condition to be approved is that the transferred business must have sufficient size and should not be dependent on the parties to the concentration, for example, in relation to supplies.

The structural conditions are primarily connected to the relevant market where competitive concerns arise, but in some situations, it may also be necessary to include activities connected to other relevant markets in the transferred business in order to guarantee the autonomy, viability and competitiveness of the transferred business.

Another requirement that must be fulfilled is the selection of a 'suitable acquirer' of the business. It is the responsibility of the undertaking to find a 'suitable acquirer'.

According to the AMO's approach, a 'suitable acquirer' is an acquirer which is competent and has an incentive to keep the transferred business as an active force in economic competition on the market on which the competition problem arose.

There are several factors which the AMO takes into consideration in assessing the 'suitable acquirer', such as economic relations to parties to the concentration, sufficiency of resources, experience and incentive to keep and develop the transferred business, position on the market and the possibility of gaining all relevant authorizations. Before the realization of the transfer, the undertaking must submit to the AMO not only its proposal of a 'suitable acquirer', but also a proposal of a contract. The contract is also subject to the AMO's approval. Furthermore, it must be observed that the transfer of business cannot be funded by parties to the concentration.

428. The AMO may also decide that the concentration can be realized only after the determined conditions are fulfilled,[682] mainly in cases where there is a risk of non-fulfilment of the imposed conditions[683] or where the execution of the condition is dependent on the identity of the buyer of the transferred business.

During the assessment of the proposal that company TESCO (a retail chain) submitted in relation to the concentration of *TESCO/Carrefour*, the AMO turned to several undertakings which TESCO indicated as potential buyers of the transferred business. The AMO reviewed real interests of these undertakings in buying hypermarkets in areas where negative effects on competition were identified (Cities of Bratislava, Žilina and Košice), and the time limit within which they would be able to acquire the transferred business and to run the business effectively without former experience. In evaluating the 'suitable acquirer', the AMO took into consideration the existence of undertakings which have sufficient resources and the experience and incentives to maintain and to develop the transferred business. After evaluation of the criteria concerning the 'suitable acquirer', the AMO came to the conclusion that realization of the transfer of the business represented a risk in relation to the identity of the proposed acquirer. The AMO found out that some of the proposed undertakings did not have a real interest in buying the business in the City of Košice, some of them would buy it only with the aim to transfer the business to other undertakings (the AMO concluded that this is in contradiction with the requirement to maintain the transferred business and develop it) and also some of potential buyers did not express any real interest in running the business. The AMO evaluated the Final Proposal of Conditions as insufficient and thus the concentration was prohibited.[684]

429. The AMO may use other conditions than those intervening into the structure of the market in cases related mainly to vertical and conglomerate mergers if specific circumstances such as, for example, the existence of exclusive contracts or the ownership of specific technology is present. These conditions thus represent mainly a commitment to provide key assets, technology, or license or a commitment to terminate exclusive contracts. The AMO does not necessarily need to define a time limit for the implementation

682. Section 12(6) of CA; for example, Decision of the AMO No. 2006/FH/3/1/146, 29 Dec. 2006, 27, <http://www.antimon.gov.sk>.
683. For example, Decision of the AMO No. 2006/FH/3/1/146, 29 Dec. 2006, 27, <http://www. antimon. gov.sk>.
684. Decision of the AMO No. 2006/FH/3/1/1/146, 29 Dec. 2006, part 8, 28–30, <http://www. antimon.gov.sk>.

of these conditions, so the undertaking is bound by the determined conditions until the decision is potentially changed.

430. The combination of structural and other conditions is also possible. The AMO does not treat conditions as appropriate if they consist of general declarations not to abuse a dominant position or commitments to regulate prices in a certain manner.

431. For the evaluation of the 'Final Proposal of Conditions and Obligations', the AMO can also conduct a public consultation.[685]

432. The proposal of conditions and obligations may include also the obligation to appoint the independent trustee at the expenses of a party to the proceedings. Trustee assists the AMO in supervision over the fulfilment of conditions and obligations or ensures the fulfilment on behalf and at the expenses of the party to the proceedings. Trustee should be independent from the undertakings concerned and undertakings belonging to the economic group of undertakings concerned.[686]

433. The decision on the conditional approval can be amended by the AMO if two situations arise. The first of them is the amendment of the decision where the fulfilment of the imposed conditions and/or obligations is not necessary because substantial changes of the state of competition on the market were identified.[687] In this case, the proposal for the amendment of the decision can also be submitted by the undertaking. The second situation is the amendment of the decision when the undertaking is not able to fulfil conditions and/or obligations within the time limit stipulated by the AMO's decision due to serious reasons.[688] The undertaking can ask the AMO for the extension of the time limit prior to its expiration. The assessment of the seriousness of the submitted reasons is subject to the AMO's discretion, but, for example, the impossibility of finding a 'suitable acquirer' will not be regarded as a serious reason.

434. The CA further stipulates what consequences arise in cases of non-fulfilment of conditions and/or obligations.[689] The non-fulfilment will lead to the revocation[690] of the decision on conditional clearance and to the prohibition of the concentration. It is not decisive whether the non-fulfilment is linked to all conditions or only a part of them. At the same time, the AMO is obliged to impose a fine of up to 10% of the total turnover achieved in the preceding accounting period.[691]

B. *Timing*

435. The AMO will ask the party to the administrative proceedings, in writing, to submit its proposal of conditions. In its written request, the AMO is obliged to explain all concerns which it has in relation to the concentration and its impact on the competition in the market. The party to the administrative proceedings has thirty working days from the delivery of the request to submit its proposal. After this deadline, the AMO will not take into consideration any other proposals. However, the time-

685. Section 12(7) of the CA.
686. Section 12(8) of the CA.
687. Section 13(3) letter a) of the CA.
688. Section 13(3) letter b) of the CA.
689. Section 13a of the CA.
690. Section 13a of the CA.
691. Section 38(2) of the CA.

period can be extended upon a justified request of the party to the procedure which needs to be submitted prior to its expiration. Based on reasoned request by the party to the proceedings in the cases worth special consideration, the AMO may accept the proposal also submitted after the expiration of deadline, provided that the time limit for issuing the decision still enables the AMO proper examination of the proposal.[692]

436. The time limit for issuing a decision on concentration[693] is not in effect during the time limit for the submission of the proposal. If the final proposal of the party to the procedure is submitted (it must be marked as 'Final Proposal of Conditions and Obligations') prior to the expiration of the deadline, the time limit for issuing a decision on concentration continues to run on the date of the delivery of this proposal.[694] If the proposal is submitted after the stipulated deadline or even if it is not submitted, the AMO issues the decision on prohibition of the concentration.

§4. Relations with Other Merger Control Authorities

I. Other Authorities Within the Local Jurisdiction

437. The AMO is the only administrative body within the jurisdiction of the Slovak Republic which can decide upon a concentration subject to merger control on its territory. Decisions issued by the AMO are subject to judicial review by competent courts (the Regional Court in Bratislava and the Supreme Court of the Slovak Republic, *see* Part III, Chapter 4).

II. International Coordination

438. The AMO's jurisdiction over the established concentration is dependent on the geographical scope of the concentration and the impact of the transaction on the Slovak market.

According to section 2(4) of the CA, the jurisdiction of the AMO also applies to activities and actions that took place abroad, provided they led or may lead to restrictions of competition in Slovak Republic. Nevertheless, the CA (section 2(5)) does not apply to restrictions of competition, the effects of which are apparent only on foreign markets, unless an international treaty published in the Collection of Laws of the Slovak Republic provides otherwise.

439. The AMO is bound by the EC Merger Regulation[695] and its jurisdiction over the concentration in Slovak Republic is dependent on the 'jurisdictional test' defined by this regulation and represented by the turnover-related criteria.[696] If the

692. Section 12(5) of the CA.
693. Section 11 of the CA.
694. Section 12(5) of the CA.
695. The Council Regulation (EC) No. 139/2004 of 20 Jan. 2004, OJ. 2004, L 24 (EC Merger Regulation).
696. Article 1 of the EC Merger Regulation.

concentration has a 'Community dimension', only the Commission will deal with the case and the AMO will not apply national law concerning the merger control.[697] As the notification of the concentration submitted to the AMO must also include information on the 'Community dimension' of the transaction,[698] the AMO can easily detect whether the notified transaction falls under its jurisdiction. The process of referral of the case with the 'Community dimension' is defined by the Merger Regulation and further specified by the Commission Notice on Case Referral in respect of concentrations[699] that are observed by the AMO. The AMO, for example, decided the case related to the concentration of *TESCO/Cerrefour*[700] which was referred (part of the case) to the AMO based on the Commission's decision according to the Article 9(3) of the EC Merger Regulation.

697. Article 21(3) of the EC Merger Regulation.
698. Article 11, Annex 1 of the Decree No. 170/2014 on Notification.
699. Commission Notice on Case Referral in respect of concentrations, OJ C 56, 5 Mar. 2005, 2–23.
700. Decision of the AMO No. 2006/FH/3/1/146, 29 Dec. 2006, <http://www.antimon.gov.sk>.

Chapter 4. Challenging of the Administrative Decisions

§1. Competent Courts

440. Decisions of the AMO are deemed to be individual administrative acts issued according to the procedural rules involved in the CA and the APC.[701] These decisions are subject to judicial review according to provisions contained in the Act No. 162/2015Coll. CPAC.[702] The AMO's decisions can be challenged by an administrative complaint[703] (in Slovak *správna žaloba vo veciach správneho trestania*) addressed to the Regional Court in Bratislava.[704] The procedure before the court is administered and the decision is adopted by a tribunal consisting of a presiding judge and two judges.[705] The administrative complaint can be filed against a decision.[706]

441. The judgment of the Regional Court in Bratislava can be appealed to the Supreme Court of the Slovak Republic. It represents the last instance of judicial review concerning the AMO's decisions, and its decisions cannot be further appealed.[707] Its seat is the City of Bratislava, and its decisions are adopted by a tribunal consisting of a presiding judge and two judges.[708]

442. The Constitutional Court[709] is entitled to decide on complaints of natural and legal persons if they claim a breach of their constitutional rights by a decision of an administrative body.[710] The Constitutional Court is composed of thirteen judges appointed by the President of the Slovak Republic for a twelve-year term.[711] The organization of the Constitutional Court as well as the process before the court is determined in detail by the Constitutional Court Organization Act.[712] The seat of the Constitutional Court is the City of Košice. The Constitutional Court reviews the AMO's decision only when the complainant has exhausted all remedies effectively provided by the law to protect his rights and/or freedoms.[713]

701. Act No. 71/1967 Coll. On APC (Administrative Code) as amended.
702. Section 194 of the CPAC.
703. Section 194 of the CPAC.
704. Section 15 of the CPAC.
705. Section 23 of the CPAC.
706. Section 177 of the CPAC.
707. Section 438 of the CPAC.
708. Section 21 of the CPAC.
709. Articles 124–140 of the Constitution of the Slovak Republic.
710. Act. No. 38/1993 Coll. on the Organization of the Constitutional Court of the Slovak Republic, on the Proceedings before the Constitutional Court and the Status of its Judges, Sixth section – Proceedings on Constitutional Complaints (the Constitutional Court Organization Act).
711. Article 134(1) and (2) of the Constitution of the Slovak Republic.
712. The Constitutional Court Organization Act.
713. Section 53(1) of the Constitutional Court Organization Act.

§2. Time Limits and Judicial Review

I. Judicial Review of Valid Decisions by Administrative Judiciary

443. Undertakings can challenge administrative decisions of the AMO by a complaint in re of administrative punishment submitted to the Regional Court in Bratislava (in Slovak *správna žaloba vo veciach administratívneho trestania*).[714]

444. Only the decision that became valid after exhaustion of all admissible regular remedies and also the decision against which a remedy is not admissible provided that it became valid, are subject to judicial review. This means that the applicant cannot file his administrative action against the AMO's decision if he has not appealed its first-degree decision.

445. Judicial review is initiated by an administrative complaint[715] submitted by the party to the administrative proceedings (a plaintiff) which claims that his rights were curtailed by the decision or the administrative proceedings. The action can also be filed by a natural or a legal person who was not treated as a party to the administrative proceedings even though this person should have been treated as a party to the administrative proceedings.[716] The joint complaint of several persons is also admissible.[717] The plaintiff must be represented by an attorney, unless the plaintiff or his employee acting on his behalf in the court has a degree in law.[718] The defendant is the administrative authority which decided the case in the last instance.[719]

446. The complaint against the AMO's decision has to be filed with the Regional Court in Bratislava within two months after the delivery of the decision to the plaintiff. Filing the action after this period has expired cannot be excused.[720] It must be borne in mind that the court will take into consideration only the argumentation, facts and grounds of the applicant that are submitted within the prescribed two-month period. The scope of the action can be extended only within the period stipulated for its submission; it can be reduced or withdrawn until the adoption of the judgment.[721]

447. The complaint does not have a suspensive effect on the enforcement of the decision, but upon the request of the plaintiff, the presiding judge may suspend its enforcement if the immediate execution of the decision can cause serious damage to the plaintiff.[722]

448. The court can also make a decision on the administrative complaint without a hearing provided that.[723] The hearing takes place only if: (i) one of the parties to the

714. Section 194(1) of the CPAC.
715. Section 194 of the CPAC.
716. Section 179 of the CPAC.
717. Section 34 of the CPAC.
718. Section 182(2) letter a) of the CPAC.
719. Section 180 of the CPAC.
720. Section 181(1) of the CPAC.
721. Section 183 of the CPAC.
722. Sections 184–189 of the CPAC.
723. Section 107(2) of the CPAC.

proceedings asks for it; (ii) it is necessary to exercise evidence; (iii) the public interest requires so; (iv) it is necessary for the case; (v) it is stipulated by the act.[724]

449. The court confirms the AMO's decision and dismisses the action as not justified if the decision and the administrative procedure were in compliance with the law.[725] The court revokes the AMO's final decision (the decision of the Council) and, if it is reasonable, also the first-degree decision, and refers the matter back to the AMO if one of the following circumstances occur:

(1) the AMO's decision is based on incorrect legal appraisal of the matter;[726]
(2) the findings of facts based on which the decision was issued is contrary to the content of administrative files;[727]
(3) the facts identified were insufficient to consider the matter;[728]
(4) the decision is not reviewable for its incomprehensibility or for insufficiency of reasons;[729]
(5) the issued decision is based on an invalid act of law;[730]
(6) the procedure involves defects which could influence legality of the challenged decision.[731]

450. The court also revokes the decision of the Council (if necessary also the first-degree decision) and refers the matter back to the AMO for further proceedings[732]

451. The court revokes the decision and at the same time stops the judicial proceedings if the decision is issued by the administrative body which was not authorized to issue such a decision.[733] The AMO is bound by the legal position adopted by the court in its judgment.[734]

452. The court is generally bound by the state of the facts which were determined by the administrative body at the time of issuing the challenged decision and may only hear evidence that is necessary for the review of the decision.[735] However, the court is not bound by this general rule and can also hear evidence itself also on the proposal of the parties to the proceedings.[736] If judicial review concerns the decision by which the AMO imposed a fine, the court may decide differently on the amount of the fine, especially if the AMO while imposing the fine exceeded the administrative discretion.[737] Consequently, in these situations, the court's judgment supplements the AMO's

724. Section 107(1) of the CPAC.
725. Section 190 of the CPAC.
726. Section 191(1) letter c) of the CPAC.
727. Section 191(1) letter f) of the CPAC.
728. Section 191(1) letter e) of the CPAC.
729. Section 191(1) letter d) of the CPAC.
730. Section 191(1) letter a) of the CPAC.
731. Section 191(1) letter g) of the CPAC.
732. Section 191(3) and (4) of the CPAC.
733. Section 191(1) letter a) of the CPAC.
734. Section 191(6) of the CPAC.
735. Section 197 of the CPAC.
736. Section 197 of the CPAC.
737. Section 198(1) of the CPAC.

decision.[738] This approach is only admissible if there are no circumstances which cause revocation of the AMO's decision.

The Regional Court is not bound by the reasons and argumentation submitted in the complaint for example if the AMO insufficiently established the facts of the case.[739]

453. The judgment of the Regional Court can by challenged by an appeal submitted to the Supreme Court of the Slovak Republic, provided that the appeal is admitted by the CPAC.[740] The appeal is not admissible, for example, if the appeal is directed only against the reasons of the Regional Court's Judgment. The appeal against the Regional Court's judgment, provided that it is admissible, needs to be submitted to the Regional Court in Bratislava within one month from the delivery of the judgment to the undertaking.[741] The Supreme Court reviews the Regional Court's judgment within the scope and on the grounds specified in the appeal (*kasačná sťažnosť*) unless the law stipulates otherwise.[742]

454. The Supreme Court decides on the appeal without a hearing, in general.[743] Hearing may take place, for example, if further evidence is needed. The Supreme Court upholds the Regional Court's judgment when it is correct.[744] It changes the Regional Court's judgment by which the administrative complaint was dismissed and revokes the AMO's decision and refers the matter back to the AMO for further proceedings if the AMO's decision is unlawful.[745]

455. The Regional Court as well the AMO are bound by the Supreme Court's legal opinion expressed in its revocation judgment. The decision of the Supreme Court cannot be further challenged as it is the final decision.

The proceedings concerning inactivity (*konanie o nečinnosti)*[746]

456. In the proceedings on inactivity, a natural or a legal person can require the Regional Court in Bratislava to issue a decision in which the court imposes on the AMO an obligation to act and to decide a case. At the same time, the court stipulates in its decision the adequate time limit not exceeding three months for issuing the AMO's decision. The defined time-period can be extended upon a justified request of the AMO. The court, upon a repeated action, may fine the AMO by a penalty for non-adherence to the obligation to issue a decision within the stipulated time limit. The proceedings on unlawful interference (*konanie vo veci nezákonného zásahu)*[747]

457. The CPAC also includes provisions concerning proceedings of the court against unlawful interference of the AMO. Any natural or legal person can file an action in the court claiming that they have been curtailed of their rights or protected interests by an unlawful interference, other than a decision, and at the same time, this

738. Section 198(4) of the CPAC.
739. Section 196 of the CPAC.
740. Sections 438–449 of the CPAC.
741. Section 443(1) of the CPAC.
742. Section 453 of the CPAC.
743. Section 455 of the CPAC.
744. Section 461 of the CPAC.
745. Section 462(1) of the CPAC.
746. Sections 242–251 of the CPAC.
747. Sections 252–263 of the CPAC.

interference was aimed directly against this person or it was eventually executed directly against this person. The applicant can seek protection before the court if this interference continues or a threat of its repetition exists.

458. The complainant may ask for the revision of already-terminated interference of the AMO, if the complaint cannot be filed at the time the alleged interference took place.

It is necessary to mention that undertakings under the investigation of the AMO, especially when the AMO conducts the down-raid, may challenge the approach of the AMO during the investigation by submitting complaint against unlawful interference (in Slovak: *žaloba proti inému zásahu orgánu verejnej správy*). As the prior approval of the court with the inspection in business premises conducted pursuant to section 22a of the CA is not required, undertakings can use such complaint against the unlawful interference as the only legal means of defence against the so-called fishing expedition of the AMO.

459. If the court comes to the conclusion that the action is justified, it issues a decision by which it imposes on the AMO the obligation to discontinue the violation of the applicant's rights and at the same time orders the AMO to restore the status quo existing prior to the interference, if possible. The court shall dismiss the action if it is not justified or admissible. The decision of the Regional Court can be appealed by submitting of so- called *kasačná sťažnosť*.

II. The Constitutional Court's Review

460. The Constitutional Court is entitled to review decisions of the AMO in the proceedings on constitutional complaints.[748] A constitutional complaint may be filed by a natural person or a legal person who claims a breach of their fundamental rights and freedoms by an unlawful decision, measure or by other encroachment. According to the principle of subsidiarity, the constitutional complaint is admissible only if the complainant has exhausted all effective remedies which are provided by the law to protect his fundamental rights.[749] The notion 'effective remedy' includes also extraordinary remedy – the appeal on points of law[750] (in Slovak *dovolanie*). On the other hand, the

748. Act No. 38/1993 Coll. On the Organization of the Constitutional Court of the Slovak Republic, on the Procedure before the Constitutional Court and the status of its Judges as amended (the Constitutional Court Organization Act), Section Six – Proceedings on Natural and Legal persons' Complaints.

749. The system of constitutionality protection is anchored in the Constitution in the principle of subordinateness. This principle also defines the range of competence of the Constitutional Court in granting protection to constitutional rights and freedoms in relation to the competence of general courts, and this in such a manner that the general courts are primarily responsible for the interpretation of law, but also for the observance of those rights and basic freedoms that are granted by the Constitution or an international treaty. On this principle is based the rule '… that granting protection to a specific right or freedom in proceedings before the Constitutional Court is basically not allowed if the person asking for it, has not used all effective means available in proceedings before general courts … ', Ruling of the Constitutional Court I.ÚS 48/2000, 6 Sep. 2000, CFR 2000, 430, translation by Mgr. Bc. Daniel Uherek, Ph.D.

750. Ruling of the Constitutional Court I.ÚS 24/02, 13 Mar. 2002, CFR 2002, 246.

extraordinary appeal on points of law (in Slovak *mimoriadne dovolanie*) is not deemed to be the effective remedy provided by the law.[751] Furthermore, the Constitutional Court stated that:

> From the principle of subordinateness of general courts to the Constitutional Court... also ensues that in case of proceedings before general courts the complainant has to ask for the protection of his rights and freedoms together with the argumentation supporting it in these proceedings and only after that in the proceedings before the Constitutional Court. If the complainant in defending his basic rights and freedoms in the proceedings before the Constitutional Court uses the argumentation that he might have addressed, but has not addressed to the general court in the proceedings before it, the competence of the Constitutional Court to review the new argumentation is not given.[752]

461. The constitutional complaint does not have a suspensive effect.[753] Upon the request of the complainant, the Constitutional Court may grant a temporary injunction that suspends the execution of the challenged decision, provided the execution of the contested decision might entail greater damage for the complainant.[754] The temporary injunction may be revoked by the Constitutional Court without any motion if the reasons for its issue lapsed.[755]

462. If the complainant decides to withdraw his complaint, this action does not necessarily lead to the dismissal of the proceedings, as the Constitutional Court may continue in the proceedings if the challenged decision seriously violates extremely, the complainant's fundamental rights or freedoms.[756] If the Constitutional Court upholds the complaint, it determines in its ruling which fundamental rights and freedoms were breached by the decision and it quashes the respective decision.[757]

463. The constitutional complaint has to be submitted within two months from the day the contested decision entered into force.[758] If the undertaking decides to challenge the AMO's decision before the Constitutional Court, it has to submit its constitutional complaint within two months from the last day of the court's decision by which all effective remedies were exhausted entered into force.

§3. Scope of Judicial Review

464. The scope of judicial review is limited by the CPAC. The valid and enforceable decision of the AMO can be challenged by the complaint addressed to the

751. Ruling of the Constitutional Court I.ÚS 67/02, 27 Jun. 2002, CFR 2002, 307.
752. Ruling of the Constitutional Court I.ÚS 149/04, 5 May 2004, CFR 2002, 633, translation by Mgr.Bc. Daniel Uherek, Ph.D.
753. Section 52(1) of the Constitutional Court Organization Act.
754. Section 52(2) of the Constitutional Court Organization Act.
755. Section 53(4) of the Constitutional Court Organization Act.
756. Section 54 of the Constitutional Court Organization Act.
757. Section 56(1) of the Constitutional Court Organization Act.
758. Section 53(3) of the Constitutional Court Organization Act.

Regional Court in Bratislava.[759] The complaint needs to be submitted within two months from the announcement of the decision to the respective party to the proceeding. Primarily, the court reviews the legality of the decision and proceeding which preceded the adoption (*see* Part III, Chapter 4, §2, I) of the decision based on the facts and the legal situation present at the time of issuing the challenged decision. Moreover, the court can find evidence necessary for the review of administrative decisions also based on the request of the parties to the proceeding.

The court is not bound by the argumentation and reasoning provided in the complaint in particular when: (i) the AMO insufficiently established the facts; (ii) the conclusions of the AMO are in contradiction with the evidences gathered in the administrative files; (iii) the AMO applied principles of criminal punishment during the administrative proceedings for the imposition of penalty; (iv) or the AMO ignored rules applicable to its administrative discretion when imposing the fine.[760]

The AMO's administrative discretion as such is not subject to judicial review, which means that the court reviews only whether such a decision is issued within the terms and boundaries specified by the law and whether the AMO does not exceed the scope of administrative discretion.

There is a possibility to file an appeal against the Region Court's decision (in Slovak so-called *kasačná sťažnosť*), if the specific condition for such appeal are met[761] (*see* Part III, Chapter 4, § 2, I). The Supreme Court will assess the appeal against the Regional Court's judgment within the argumentation submitted in the appeal.[762]

465. The Constitutional Court's decision is generally based on factual findings arising from previous proceedings, which means that it evaluates the situation relevant at the time of issuing the challenged decision.[763] The Constitutional Court is not authorized to appraise the arguments of the complainant that were not submitted before courts in preceding proceedings even though the complainant has eventually submitted them.[764]

759. Section 194 of the CPAC.
760. Section 195 of the APC.
761. Section 439 of the CPAC.
762. Section 453 of the CPAC.
763. Section 55 of the Constitutional Court Organization Act.
764. Ruling of the Constitutional Court I.ÚS 149/04, 5 May 2004, CFR 2002, 633.

Selected Bibliography

Bejček, Josef. *Kartelové právo*. Brno, Czech Republic: Masarykova univerzita, 1995.

Bellamy, Christopher & Graham D. Child. *European Community Law of Competition*. 5th edn. London, Great Britain: Sweet & Maxwell, 2001.

Drgonec, J. *Ústava Slovenskej republiky, Komentár*. 2nd edn. Šamorin, Slovak Republic: Heuréka, 2007.

Kalesná, Katarína. *Právo proti obmedzovaniu hospodárskej súť aže, Komparatívna analýza* (Bratislava, Slovak Republic: vydavatelské oddelenie Právnickej fakulty UK, 1995).

Kindl, Jiří. *Kartelové a distribuční dohody*. Prague: C.H. Beck, 2009.

Košičiarová, Soňa. *Správny poriadok, Komentár*. Šamorin, Slovak Republic: Heuréka, 2004.

Munková, Jindřiška & Jiří Kindl. *Zákon o ochraně hospodářské soutěže, Komentář* Prague, Czech Republic: C.H. Beck, 2007.

Munková, Jindřiška, Pavel Svoboda & Jiří Kindl. *Soutěžní právo, Beckovy mezioborové učebnice*. Prague, Czech Republic: C.H. Beck, 2006.

Procházka, Radoslav & Juraj Čorba. *Právo Európskej únie, Vybrané otázky pre právnu prax*. Žilina, Slovak Republic: Poradca podnikatel'a, 2006.

Raus, David & Robert Neruda. *Zákon o ochraně hospodářské soutěže, Komentář a související české i komunitární předpisy*. 2nd edn. Prague, Czech Republic: Linde Praha, 2006.

Raus, David. *Oršulová Andrea, Kartelové dohody*. Prague, Czech Republic: C.H. Beck, 2009.

Raus, David. *Oršulová Andrea, Zákon o ochraně hospodářské soutěže*. Prague, Czech Republic: Wolters Kluwer, 2014.

Selected Bibliography

Index

The numbers here refer to paragraph numbers.

Abuse of a dominant position, 49, 79–81
Administrative fines, 115–129
Agreement restricting competition, 38, 43, 57
Agreement restricting by effect, 39, 57, 78
Agreement restricting by object, 39, 57, 78
Amalgamation, 50, 286
Ancillary restraints, 24, 193, 391

Bid-rigging, 14, 39, 127, 130, 151, 188–191
Block exemption, 14, 21, 41

Cartel agreement, 11, 12, 44, 132, 143, 171, 176, 179, 186, 191
Client allocation, 173–180
Collective dominance, 72, 241,419
Cooperation agreements, 201–216
Concerted practices, 43,74
Concentration, 50–54,
Conglomerate merger, 307–308
Comparable fulfilment, 79, 256, 257
Criminal enforcement, 146–158

Damage, 132–141
Decision of association of undertakings, 43
De minimis, 37–42, 76, 78
Discrimination, 254-263
Distribution, 221–234
Dominant position, 70–73, 239
Dominant undertaking, 239–284

Economic Sense Test, 279
Economic value, 248, 300
Essential facility, 14, 240, 277–279
Ex-ante regulation, 34, 69, 107–109, 111, 351
Excessive prices, 113, 246–253
Ex lege exemption, 41, 47, 58, 388

Exclusive distribution, 225–226
Exclusive dealing, 227–228
Exclusionary practices, 264–284
Exploitative practices, 245–263
Equally Efficient Competitor Test, 283

Fidelity rebates, 272, 273

General clause
- Prohibition of cartel agreements, 46
- Prohibition of abuse, 79, 239, 260

General sector inquiries, 315–318
General investigation, 315–318
Group boycott, 183–184

Hard-core cartel, 13, 68, 97, 148, 151, 164, 173,181, 318, 321
Herfindahl-Hirschmann's index (HHI), 203, 298, 299
Horizontal agreements, 159–216
Horizontal merger, 296–300
Hypothetically Reasonable Efficient Competitor Test, 283

Information exchange, 195–200
Innovation limitation, 181–182
Investigating powers, 95–97
Imprisonment, 148, 152

Joint control, 86, 213, 288, 289, 299, 310, 405
Joint production, 212
Joint purchasing, 213–215
Joint selling, 216
Judicial review, 443–459
Joint venture, 85–86, 309–312

Know-how licensing, 238

Index

Leniency Programme, 14, 127, 149, 350
Legal privilege, 346

Market allocation, 173–180
Market extension merger, 305–306
Market power, 70–73
Maximum price, 217, 224
Meeting competition defence, 258
Merger, 285–286, 294–308, 391–439
Merger test, 60

Non-compete obligations, 192, 193, 225, 234
Notification, 82, 352, 387–390
Nullity, 143

Party to the administrative proceedings, 320, 322, 324, 352, 353, 360–363, 367, 406416, 435, 445
Patent licencing, 236
Precedent, 29–31
Per se prohibited, 161, 222, 224
Predatory pricing, 265, 266
Pre-notification, 82, 402, 403, 407
Price fixing agreements, 171, 172
Price recommendation, 217, 224
Price squeeze, 281–284
Product extension merger, 305–306
Production limitation, 181–182
Prohibition to exercise rights from concentration, 123, 321, 412
Public interest, 11, 17, 36, 37, 63, 126, 345, 448
Public Prosecutor, 154–155

Qualitative selective distribution system, 230
Quantitative selective distribution system, 233

Rebates, 272–274
Relevant market, 65–69
Resale price maintenance, 39, 43, 165, 217, 222- 224
Restriction of competition, 78
Refusal to deal, 275–280
R&D agreements, 204–207

Selective distribution, 229–233
Settlement Procedure, 14, 96, 97, 129, 130, 371
Sole control, 288, 294, 300
Specialization, 208–210
Standardization, 211

Technology licensing, 235–238
Trademark licensing, 237
Tying, 268–271

Undertaking, 48–49, 61–64, 239–284, 422–436
Unilateral conduct, 21, 387
Unfair competition, 17
Unfair pricing, 246–253
Unfair trade conditions, 246, 247, 251–253, 281
Unlawful restrictions of competition, 55

Vertical agreements, 217–238
Vertical merger, 301–304

Made in the USA
Monee, IL
14 March 2026

46153215R00116